David Lampe

MODERN SCIENCE FICTION

Its Meaning and Its Future

Modern Science Fiction

ITS MEANING AND ITS FUTURE

JOHN W. CAMPBELL, JR.

ANTHONY BOUCHER

DON FABUN

FLETCHER PRATT

ROSALIE MOORE

L. SPRAGUE DE CAMP

ISAAC ASIMOV

ARTHUR C. CLARKE

PHILIP WYLIE

GERALD HEARD

REGINALD BRETNOR

Edited by **REGINALD BRETNOR**

Coward-McCann, Inc. New York

TO HELEN, *my wife*

Contents

Preface

MODERN SCIENCE FICTION is a unique phenomenon. As a recognized and coherent form, it is scarcely a generation old. Since Hugo Gernsback fathered the first science-fiction magazine in 1926, it has developed independently, owing almost nothing to our main literary streams. It has attracted a wide, intelligent, and active readership without the benefit of high-pressure publicity or pathological sensationalism. Its presently increasing popularity is a result of its own special merit—its validity for the age in which we live.

Perhaps because of this independent evolution, the critical and interpretive literature of science fiction has not kept up with the development of the form itself. I do not mean, of course, that such a literature does not exist. Much thoughtful comment has been published in the editorial columns of the better science-fiction magazines, in their book-review sections, and in certain of the specialized "fan" magazines. More may be found in prefaces to some of the many anthologies issued during the past few years. Occasional rare essays have even appeared in such periodicals as *Harper's* and *The Saturday Review,* and in one or two of the academic quarterlies.[1]

This material, obviously, is too widely scattered to be generally available, and too unorganized to present a comprehensive picture. Besides, much of it now is either obsolete or obsolescent. Therefore,

[1] A notable example is Fletcher Pratt's "From the Fairy Tale of Science to the Science of Fairy Tale," published in the Spring, 1948 issue of *The Pacific Spectator,* then under the editorship of Edith R. Mirrielees.

in the planning of this book, it seemed better to me to start afresh, to outline a general framework of approach, and, within that framework, to give each author full freedom to present his viewpoint.

An editor, assembling a symposium, may strive either for conformity or for diversity of perspective and opinion—a choice which will be dictated partly by his own temperament and partly by the nature of his subject. If, for example, he wishes to elucidate a proven thesis or "prove" a dubious one, he may—risking infinite dullness—choose conformity. If, however, he honestly desires to explore a subject—and if it is his purpose to interest, rather than to anesthetize, his readers—he will choose diversity. In the present instance, I fortunately was spared the weighing of one choice against the other, for modern science fiction is much too young, much too dynamic, and much too vast in its potentialities to be interpreted adequately from any single standpoint. There could be one choice only: diversity, of talent, background, perspective, and opinion. On this basis, and on the basis of their individual competence, the authors of this book have been selected.

The result has not disappointed me. It is a book full of opinions with which I disagree—sometimes profoundly, as in the case of Philip Wylie's evaluation of the influence of science fiction. It also is a book full of ideas which I, for one, had not anticipated, challenging ideas which opened up fresh fields of speculation, ideas with which—envying their authors—I found myself completely in agreement. It is, I think, a book which does no violence to the spirit of modern science fiction—for modern science fiction, at its best, seeks to stimulate thought, not to eliminate the need for it.

This is not the first book to deal with science fiction.[2] It is, however, the first general survey of modern science fiction against the background of the world today. It is the first attempt to examine modern science fiction in its relation to contemporary science, con-

[2] Lloyd Arthur Eshbach's short symposium, *Of Worlds Beyond, The Science of Science Fiction Writing,* contains essays by several of the foremost writers of modern science fiction; within its scope, it is extremely good. J. O. Bailey's *Pilgrims Through Space and Time* is primarily a historical study which scarcely concerns itself with modern science fiction.

temporary literatures, contemporary human problems. Having taken the approach of the ecologist, rather than that of the anatomist, for its model, I have made no effort to confine its authors too rigidly to the defined limits of their subjects, or to inhibit their discussion of whatever matters they considered pertinent. Under these circumstances, naturally, I have allowed myself a similar degree of liberty in the writing of my own chapter.

I am convinced that this policy has produced a better and more interesting book than we might otherwise have written. And I sincerely trust that our readers, in this at least, will find that they agree with me.

There are a few topics which, in retrospect, I could have wished to see more fully treated: the importance of good science fiction as an agency for general education and orientation; the scientific possibilities of good science fiction in originating or (perhaps more frequently) in fertilizing novel hypotheses and new inventions; the influence, on science fiction, of cultural anthropology and of the life sciences. However, as it is not the purpose of this book to pretend omniscience, and as none of its authors believes that he has said the final word about his subject, I feel that we may be forgiven our errors of omission.

For my part, I hope that some of our readers will find here a better general picture of modern science fiction than they had before. I hope that others will be introduced to modern science fiction as a spontaneous, living literature. I hope that still others will be sufficiently encouraged (or annoyed) to attempt the criticism and the interpretation of modern science fiction. In such results will lie the measure of this book's success.

By way of explanation, the chapters in this volume, with one exception—or rather an exception and a fraction—have been written especially for it. The exception is Arthur C. Clarke's "Science Fiction: Preparation for the Age of Space," which is a revised and lengthened version of an article first printed in the *Journal of the British Interplanetary Society*. The fraction consists of several pages in the chapter by L. Sprague de Camp, adapted by him from a short article published in *Galaxy*.

I wish to thank the ten other authors of this book, and most especially Anthony Boucher, whose encouragement helped to make it possible. I also wish to thank Lloyd Eric Reeve for his assistance, and Ralph C. Hamilton for good suggestions generously given.

REGINALD BRETNOR

Berkeley, California
September 1, 1952

Science Fiction Today

The Place of Science Fiction

by JOHN W. CAMPBELL, JR.

JOHN W. CAMPBELL, JR., *has done more than any other man to develop modern science fiction as a mature literary form. Indeed, its history may quite accurately be said to date from his assumption of the editorship of* Astounding Science Fiction *in 1937. By background and by education, he was especially suited to this role. His father, an electrical engineer, aroused his interest in physical science at the age of three. His grandfather, a lawyer and a Congressman, interested him in philosophy at the age of six. His mother introduced him to science fiction, of the Jules Verne and H. G. Wells variety, when he was eight.*

Educated at Blair Academy, M.I.T., and Duke University, he started taking nuclear physics at M.I.T. in 1928, in the belief that atomic energy would be the major field of advance during his lifetime. But in 1932, when he graduated, there was not much of a demand for nuclear physicists. However, he had started writing science fiction as a freshman, and that still was in demand. In succeeding years, his reputation as a writer rivaled his editorial reputation.

Mr. Campbell is married. He and his wife live in Mountainside, N. J., with their four children. His hobbies are photography, radioelectronics (with the call letters w2zgu) *and philosophical-psychological research.*

CIVILIZATION as we know it is based on the existence of the art of writing—history begins, of course, when the ability to write began. A brief visit to any major library will, however, quickly demonstrate that not history, but fiction, constitutes and always has constituted the major use of the permanently recorded word.

That very fact is worth noting and considering; when man finally achieved a means of recording truths so that no failing of memory or change of viewpoint would becloud the issue, the means was used primarily for recording that which might have been, could possibly be, or might someday be. There is frequently a curious, but decidedly important, difference between what a man *says* he believes, and what his actions *show* he believes. Mankind, over the last four thousand years or so, has *said* it wanted to record facts imperishably; mankind, over the last four thousand years, has devoted practically all of its efforts in the recording line to setting down imperishable records of dreams, wishes, hopes, and fears.

The immense excess of fiction over factual material in libraries is not an accident; it is, instead, an absolutely valid expression of what man's true nature is—whatever he may say or even believe his nature is. Man is *not* a realist; he's an idealist first, and a realist second.

Actually in a library containing only modern works, the material will have a huge preponderance of fiction, plus a heavy mass of science books, and a small section on history. Idealism first, then science . . . and science should be recognized for what it is: mankind's rebellion against the world as it is. Science is an effort to make the world become what the idealist wishes it were. Finally, there is history—the recorded failure to make dreams come true. Its major importance is that, by studying it, we may find the factors that caused the original fine purpose to go astray, so the next time we can start out with that same fine purpose, and this time make it work.

Science fiction is the perfectly logical offspring of the basic nature of man. Once, man depended on magic. He tried it for a long, long time. Actually, he got some very definite results, which led him to keep at it. But it didn't develop, and eventually it was abandoned as a blind alley to the goal. Science took its place; the scientist replaced the mystic, the cyclotron replaced the magic wand —and this new kind of a magic wand is not built of moon dreams and bats' wings. It's built of mathematics and highly purified heavy hydrogen, extracted from ordinary water by elaborate processes. Also, this newer-age magic wand leads to enchantments which, when waved over a city, cause that city to vanish in a puff of flame.

In science, mankind found a means of making dreams come true in terms of steel and copper, magnetic forces and the quantum mechanics of atomic nuclei. But science, by its nature, is absolutely without ethics, volition, or moral judgment—it consists solely of facts. It is rooted on, and entirely bounded by the single dictum, "If it works, it's valid."

"Valid" in that sense does not mean "true." The scientist does not hold that his newest theory is true, or good, or beautiful; he holds only that it is valid—that it works in every case so far known, and might even, conceivably, actually be true. But "true" is a term outside the field of science; science is simply that which works.

Science is, as a result, so inhuman, so utterly unsuited to mankind, that no human being can *be* a scientist; he can only set apart a certain section of his mind to think like a scientist. A man can be an engineer; an engineer is a man who uses the sterile, harsh and uncompromising rigidity of science to act as his tool in serving a human need.

The whole function of science, the magic that works, is lost if it does *not* serve to fulfill mankind's needs and dreams and to ward off the fears. Yet the very nature of science is such that science, as science, cannot recognize hope or fear or good or evil. Sulfuric acid is a substance; it is not fear, even in the hands of an insanely jealous woman about to throw it in her rival's face. It is not hope, even when it is purifying a lifesaving drug. It is simply a structure of two hydrogen atoms, a sulfur atom, and four oxygen atoms—neither good nor evil nor possessed of any motive whatever.

Uranium is not evil, though it be in an atomic bomb, nor good when it's in a power plant delivering heat to a winter-chilled city. It is simply and solely uranium.

A magic freed of motive, science is capable of serving mankind—but something outside of science must determine what that service can be and should be and might be.

The Dark Ages broke up in the Renaissance; an era of almost totally static culture, in which what little learning there was was hidden behind the walls of monasteries, gave way to an era of tremendous growth and exuberance, a new freedom of thinking and action and learning. Living on the sunny side of that period of change, it seems a bright and happy thing.

It was all hell broken loose and rampaging through the continent. Institutions that had endured for nearly a thousand years were blowing up in bombshell violence all over Europe. A society that had been more stable than any western man had seen since ancient Egypt went to pot in a century.

Somebody had made an invention—the invention of the craftsman, the productive worker who was not merely a producer, but a respected artisan. Greece had honored artists; Rome had honored soldiers and statesmen. The Renaissance honored the productive creative worker for the first time in history.

For the first time in history, a civilization, a cultural pattern, acknowledged and recompensed the creative producer.

When you change a cultural pattern as violently as that, the result is inevitably bound to be misery, warfare, and heartache. That is, it will be, unless a great deal more of the nature of social forces is understood than has ever been understood so far!

The Renaissance settled down, however; the guilds arose, and a period of centuries of stable culture followed. A man didn't have to worry much; he could get along very comfortably by simply being an apprentice as a boy, a journeyman as a young man, and a master craftsman as an adult. The society was run along well-worn grooves, with very little bumping or trouble.

Until someone invented a machine that could turn out more high-quality goods in an hour than a master craftsman could produce in a month.

The explosion that followed has been fairly adequately studied; the Industrial Revolution, however, had settled down fairly smoothly by about 1890. Again, a man could understand his world. He could know how to select a means of making a living as a young man, and feel that that would be a good, solid, established and respected way of life. A man could enter the business of buggy-whip making and feel that he was starting on a sound, useful career that he could contribute to, and which would in turn contribute to him.

And in 1900, the world began to slip again. By 1910, the world had slipped so far that it was no longer possible to consider it just a passing phase of small meaning. The Industrial Revolution had ended by 1870, really; by 1910 the world had entered the age of permanent change. It became accepted, by 1920, that there were new ways of doing things that had not yet been discovered, but which would, of course, be found—that, however things were being done, a better method would be found. That buggy-whip manufacturing was gone forever, and that phonograph-motor manufacturing (remember the hand-cranked, spring-driven mechanical phonograph motors?) was a new occupation. But of course even that new occupation might not be a lifetime career.

During the 1930's, relief authorities found that it wasn't a *job* a man wanted, or even a job that paid; he wanted a job of the specific type he had selected as his life work. A carpenter might be offered higher pay or offered a steady job as a machinist—but that wouldn't do. It was misinterpreted generally as a false pride, or a mulish refusal to do anything but what he wanted.

7

After all the centuries of experience with how human beings behave, it seems we should have learned: when a man has chosen a set of ideas on how to live, he has a vast tendency to stick to that system of ideas. Actually, a human being displays the characteristic that he will die rather than change his ideas of how to live.

The amount of human misery which that has caused is quite remarkable. The Industrial Revolution was simply a battle over the need to change versus the refusal to change.

No true revolution is simply a process; naturally, the process is all that can be pointed to—named with dates of history, places and times. Actions can be described; motives are invisible, intangible and almost indescribable, yet actions and processes come only after a motive exists. Motives are causes, yet only the results, the actions, are tangible enough to be described accurately. The Industrial Revolution consisted largely in a series of actions and reactions following the introduction of a *single* new idea—the idea that *things* could be induced to *do* things. Up to that time, actually, manufactured articles were precisely that—*manus* meaning hand. A table is a thing that *is* something. A bowl *is* something. But a weaving machine is not in itself useful to man; instead of *being* something, it *does* something.

The Industrial Revolution produced the results of the new motive—to make things that would do things for man, instead of merely making things that *were* things for man.

True, there had been many basic tool-machines around before the Industrial Revolution—the potter's wheel being one of the most common and important examples. But the general concept, and the motive resulting from it, had not been developed. The Industrial Revolution was its fruit.

The research revolution went even deeper. Where the Industrial Revolution produced machines that did things instead of having men do them, the research revolution introduced and developed the idea of designing machines to do things men never had been able to do, and that no living thing had ever been able to do. Instead of seeking to do a known thing better, the research revolution introduced the idea of seeking to do unknown, but better things.

The typical motivation-idea of the Industrial Revolution was to devise a machine that would weave as fine a piece of linen as the best handweaver could achieve, to machine-produce as fine a piece of silk as the best silk processors could turn out. The research revolution motivation-idea would be quite different. The effort would be to determine what the linen was to be used for, and determine what would be the ideal characteristics of a material for that purpose. Then devise, somehow, a material that approximated that ultimate ideal. The result might be utterly alien, totally un-linen in nature.

As an example, where the Industrial Revolution sought to produce fine linen goods for curtains, the research revolution produces drapes made of fine glass fibers. They, unlike linen, are absolutely fireproof, and make far safer drapes; they are immune to sunlight and air, so that they do not fade or grow brittle.

The research approach is to analyze the need, and fill the need—to change at a far more fundamental level. Glass curtains aren't a synthetic substitute, an ersatz, for linen—they're a boldly new approach to the problem, designed specifically to solve the actual problem.

The witch-doctors of old sought to find herbs that would help the sick. The Industrial Revolution doctor sought to find better methods of processing and refining the roots, leaves, and minerals used in medicine.

But modern penicillin is produced by an unnatural breed of penicillium plants. The original life form was altered by blasting its germ cells with hard X-rays and ultraviolet radiation, radiations from atomic materials, and a dozen other methods. The very nature of the living tissues was altered until a strain was found that produced more of the desired compound.

The whole approach of the research revolution is that man can do better than selecting from that which already exists—he can change the nature of existence to suit him better, and it implies also

9

the next step; that he can also change himself to fit better with what does exist and what can be made to exist.

Once the concept of the possibility of changing the nature of existence is clearly in mind, a totally new kind of problem arises. What kind of existence do we want to bring into being? The old viewpoint, "there's nothing new under the sun," made for an easy assurance; people wouldn't be able to introduce anything new, they'd just select different factors that already existed.

But in all the planet Earth, no refinable quantity of plutonium existed before men synthesized it. I've seen a little nylon "camel's-hair" coat covered with moth's eggs, and tiny moth's larvae—all dead. Here was a "fur" that was new under the sun, and the ancient species of moth died on it.

Let man deny that there is anything new under the sun—and he, like the moth, will starve to death on the familiar-feeling, familiar-looking, and yet unalterably alien, nylon nap.

About 1900 the research revolution started; it didn't gather much momentum for the first two decades. But then, the Industrial Revolution took centuries to get going to its full power. By the time the 1920's arrived, the concept of research was a basic one in our whole civilization; where before inventors had been rather freakish men, and a new invention something to gawp at—suddenly, inventing became a profession, and antiques became of wide popular interest. Invention was more common than unchanged designs.

To a certain point, that's a fine way to do things. The man who has as his fixed and unchangeable concept of how to live, the proposition that one lives by changing, nevertheless *does* have a fixed concept of how to live!

Quite naturally, America led the parade in that direction. This nation is made up almost entirely of people who pulled up all their roots and changed—and the descendants of those people. European things didn't fit in America; they had to be changed. Ideas that served well to govern a people never more than two hundred miles from the center of government didn't seem quite sound when applied to a nation with its capital three-thousand miles from one of its greatest seaports. Individual European nations had no domestic use for four-hundred-mile-an-hour transportation.

Today, European products generally are built with a solidity and endurance compatible with the idea that a good unit is and always will be a good unit. American devices are built generally on the basis that a good unit is one which will serve faithfully until the better unit now in the research stage gets into production. The unit being built is made by men who, on their way out, talk to the men developing the better unit. Yet no unit is considered adequate or proper if it does not function well and dependably until replacement is wanted.

Never before in history did such a situation exist. When the old craftsman built something, he built for the centuries to come. The idea that such work is not ideal is one that has been hard in the learning; the lesson has been learned today, at a level a bit too deep for full conscious realization, perhaps.

When a culture is oriented toward the proposition that change and improvement are possible, and that change and improvement will come, it becomes necessary to define what "improvement" is. And that's the hardest concept imaginable! George Washington believed he was improving the governmental structure of the world; so did Adolf Hitler. George Washington arrived at his ideas by open discussion with other highly able men whom he himself respected. They dissected his ideas mercilessly, they injected new concepts and opposing viewpoints, and they helped him find a true balance between seemingly conflicting desires and wants.

Hitler formed his group by selecting those who agreed with him, and destroying those who did not.

Open discussion, speculation widely considered and argued, is the best way we know today to determine what constitutes improvement. Still we won't always get the right answers—but we will stand a far better chance.

Society changes with enormous reluctance; it abhors speculation, imagination, or suggestions of changes in its beliefs. In our cultural pattern today, speculation is considered rather . . . perhaps "mentally unstable" is the term best approximating the mild abhorrence. The abhorrence used to be far stronger. And the result is that in science today, a man may write papers on logically supported, braced, and mathematically expressed theory. He may discuss at length experiments which have been performed. Or he may discuss in detail the engineering specifications of something being produced.

But a scientist, the culture holds, must not speculate in public.

The combination of forces in the civilization leads quite naturally to the old, old answer—a form of fiction in which those powerful social forces can be expressed. Fiction is simply dreams written out; science fiction consists of the hopes and dreams and fears (for some dreams are nightmares) of a technically based society.

What is "an improvement"?

At first, science fiction discussed the purely technical improvement. The early science-fiction stories, about 1925 to 1935, were largely concentrated on technical devices per se. The development of means of releasing the vast energies known to be present in the atom. Methods of developing television, or space flights. Speculations as to what might be on the moon or Mars.

But beginning about 1935, the emphasis gradually shifted from technical to over-all cultural considerations. "Yes, we could release atomic energy . . . but what would its effect on the culture be? If we had a free source of energy, would it mean the end of the coal, oil, and electric power industries . . . and if so, would that be advantageous to the culture as a whole?"

Science fiction is, at the present time, only about twenty-five years old as a self-aware system of literature. *Gulliver's Travels* is science fiction, of course, but it wasn't knowingly written as such. True, Gulliver traveled in a wind-driven sailing ship instead of a rocket; the strange worlds he encountered were called "islands" instead of "planets"—but the root thesis of science fiction is there.

Heretofore, change has been something the world dreaded and fought; science fiction is the literature of speculation as to what changes may come, and which changes will be improvements, which destructive, which merely pointless. Because our culture has now accepted change as the normal, instead of the abnormal, state of things, science fiction has become a regular instead of a sporadic phenomenon.

In the sense that science fiction is the literature of speculation about changes to come, Plato's *Republic* is science fiction of the sociological level. But it misses being true science fiction because it is presented simply as a logical argument, a presentation of an explicitly stated thesis. It's speculation with an explicit moral.

Fiction, however, is something quite different; any and all fiction shares one highly important characteristic. If a man seeks to induce another to accept his ideas by stating them as logical arguments and propositions, the other can deny the premise, contravert the logic, quibble about the logical points made, argue exceptions, and variously distract, befuddle, and involve the argument. All of these are legitimate and standard techniques for refusing to consider the other fellow's postulates and ideas. This material I'm writing now falls in that class; you can deny the questions raised with "Harrumph! Unimportant. Doesn't mean anything. Doesn't affect me in any way. Nonsense." Or you can cite exceptions, and argue individual points.

But any man who reads a piece of fiction, and roars angrily "That's not true!" can expect the author to say, reasonably, "But I *said* it was fiction. Why does it upset you so?"

In mathematics, a number which is multiplied by the square root of minus one is said to be an imaginary. But if you multiply something by the square root of minus one *twice*, it becomes real again. The fiction story is imaginary; the angry man who belligerently insists that it is imaginary is belligerent and angry because he's made it real for himself by insisting on making it doubly imaginary!

The peculiar characteristic of fiction is that it cannot be argued with. It does not argue with you; it exists apart from the real world, it says, and cannot affect you except by your own choice. But if you choose to be affected by it, you cannot argue with the author; you are forced to consider *why* it affects you. It's useless to argue that *Hamlet* is a false argument because the story's key motivating factor is the appearance of the Ghost, and ghosts do not exist. Shakespeare has presented the tale of a typical noble character, a typical self-determined martyr, who spreads misery, death, and madness to quite innocent people all around him. But of course that's not true; this play is merely fiction.

It may well be argued that, in Biblical times, a Samaritan would not have taken the particular road, in going from town A to town B, because Samaritans always take a different route. This would, of course, make the parable of the Good Samaritan entirely improbable, and thus defeat any logical argument contained in the material. But Jesus said it was merely a little fiction story, and therefore the point of the story remains unarguable.

Aesop discussed foxes and donkeys and lions and bears. Being purely fictions, they could not, of course, be argued for truth or logical consistency.

This whole technique of discussion is based on the ancient philosophical paradox of the type: "Epaminondas, the Cretan, says that all Cretans always lie." The author of fiction says, in effect, "I am a liar, and everything I say is a lie."

That particular situation is the one situation in which a human being is absolutely forced to use his own considered judgment.

In ordinary fiction, the individual is still able to accept the common cultural background as being truth; in science fiction, we can discuss robots or Martians or fiftieth-century people. It's simply a method of ruling out the basic fixed judgments of modern cultural beliefs, scientific beliefs, and everything else.

What would happen if you had a man who was incapable of acting in selfish self-interest, and invariably acted only for the best interest of those around him, to the absolute best of his ability?

Try such a story, and the reader, taking his cultural evaluations with him, says internally, "Huh! No man is ever going to be that way! Human beings are too thoroughly stinkers!"

The fact that every one of us has been brought up in a paranoid culture that assumes that idea as a fact without real proof doesn't appear in his mind. But as a science-fiction reader, he can consider a robot that has been specifically built by the engineers to have precisely those characteristics. It has been so designed that it is physically incapable of acting in any manner save that dictated by a logical analysis of the best possible determination of the best interests of human beings.

Asimov, who has a chapter further on in this book, has long discussed robots. But the robots he discusses are actually human beings in fancy dress; their problems are human problems, stripped and clarified sufficiently to make the essence of the problem clear.

In science fiction, the reader can be freed of cultural fixations more than in any ordinary literature. Problems which can not be discussed in ordinary work can be brought forth in direct, clear consideration—as problems of the Martians and the Saggitarians.

It's just fiction, you understand. The author says, at the start, "I am a liar, and the culture I discuss is a lie, and you cannot believe anything I say of it."

As the editor of *Astounding Science Fiction*, I have had many a fine evening of discussion with a group of extremely accomplished professional liars. As a long-time professional liar myself, I know the stuff such fictions are made of. And I know that no man invents pure fiction—just as every one of us knows, very deeply, that no man can invent all of his material. He must borrow from many facts, and assemble them in new arrangements; the labor of inventing 100 per cent lies is too great.

But when a man says, "I am honest, and honest men always tell nothing but the truth," we know it is exceedingly improbable. In order to tell nothing but the truth, he would have to be omniscient as well as having the purest good intent.

The culture we live in today accepts the need and the inevitability of change. But only gradually is it beginning to recognize, too, the vital necessity of discussing the nature of the changes that are desirable before making them and trying them out. Science is the magic that works; it contains no moral or ethical judgments whatever.

For a long time, through all history, if men tried a new idea, and it proved to be an exceedingly sour one, the result was disastrous to a relatively small group. Unfortunately, a small group, today, may be able to try out some interesting idea that happens to involve the annihilation of the planet Earth. The old method of trial and error comes to a point where it is no longer usable—the point where one more error means no more trials.

There are some things that you can never practice. You can practice your golf stroke indefinitely—trial and error is fine in that area. But, as the parachutists say, you can't really practice parachute jumps. You do it the first time, or you don't need any practice, only an undertaker.

Mankind has reached fairly well into the areas of no practice. A few more advances and we're apt to find that a few advanced scientists have elucidated methods that make it possible for any teen-age kid to prove he's not "chicken" by blowing one hundred square miles off the Earth with a home-made contraption.

Of course, we can seek to pull back from the areas of no practice; we may feel that we are wise enough to do so. Certainly; many people are. Those are just exactly the people who can be trusted to handle such power safely, because they do have sense enough to pull back from the no-practice areas. All that means is that, in pulling back, they will allow the ones who do *not* have sense enough to reach the area first.

Consider this problem: suppose there is a way to make a mind-broadcaster, one that would make it possible for a single individual to broadcast a thought which all human beings would be forced to believe. In whose hands would you trust such a device?

Fine, then how do you *know* such a device cannot be made?

What protection could there be against such a thing?

Probably, the only way defense could be developed would be first to devise the equipment, and then, knowing how it worked, devise a counterdevice. Thus, only by knowing how radio is transmitted can you know enough about it to prevent its effects.

You may not know it, but any radio engineer can arrange a device that will silence your radio's reception from a distance of several hundred yards. Quite a few apartment dwellers who insisted on roaring radios at midnight in the neighborhood of a radio-electronics engineer have discovered that that can be done.

But only a man who knows precisely how radio works can devise such a defense.

The only defense against a mind-controlling broadcast would be to understand precisely how such a thing could be done, and arrange the suitable defense. That's a very ancient principle; the fact that science is the magic that works suggests the old rule—that a black magician can destroy the uninitiated, and that only a more powerful white magician can erect a defense and destroy the black magician. If knowledge is power, then only by having more knowledge in the hands of the wise and understanding can we protect ourselves against the fanatic and thoughtless.

Science fiction can provide for a science-based culture—which ours is, willy-nilly, and must be, since science is inherently available by the nature of the universe—a means of practicing out in the no-practice area. We can safely practice anything in imagination—suicide, murder, anything whatever.

If we fail to practice in imagination—practice with free, open discussion and suggestions—we'll be back to the days of trial and error. But for only a little time; we've already done so much work that a few more trials and we'll hit the permanent error.

Science fiction is rapidly gaining in popularity and in general recognition, because it is a perfectly natural outgrowth of the true nature of our culture. Naturally, there is a tendency in any changing culture—which ours is—for the citizens of that culture to deny the changes, or the importance of the changes.

The atomic bomb has had a great deal to do with the increased interest in science fiction—but only indirectly. Atomic bombs are explicitly a scientific device; they involve the most advanced and esoteric understanding of the basic nature of the universe—the sort of ideas that people have, for years, shrugged off with "What's that got to do with me, huh?"

Magic wands that make a city vanish in a microsecond of unimaginable fire very definitely and specifically have to do with me. There are a lot of nice, pat, comforting phrases in our culture that have, for a long time, defined our attitudes. They don't work any more. "We'll cross that bridge when we get to it." (But the bridge vanished in a flash of atomic flame.) "Never trouble trouble till trouble troubles you." (But even though you don't consider that the other fellow's troubles are troubles of yours, he may. And he can prove it to you, too.) "Take care of today, and tomorrow will take care of itself." (Provided someone else hasn't decided to take the trouble to take care of tomorrow the way *he* wants it.)

Back in 1935, "everybody knew" that atomic bombs and rocket ships were just imaginings of the science-fiction writers—nothing to think about actually.

Are you willing to bet that it is, and forever will be, impossible for one man to make you believe anything he wants you to?

Personally, I don't know whether it is or not. I don't know enough about how I do thinking—nor does anyone else in the world today—to have anyone able to say it's impossible. So far as my own individuality, my own being, is concerned, it would make surprisingly little difference whether I was physically annihilated by some teen-ager who wanted to prove he wasn't afraid to start an atomic bomb, home-made style, or mentally annihilated by some thought-controller.

I consider that speculation is as essential to the safety of a civilization as insurance policies are to the safety of a family.

In 1940, the science-fiction writers, just as the professional nuclear physicists, knew that the basic mechanism of unlocking nuclear energies had been discovered. Inasmuch as many science-fiction writers had been trained as nuclear physicists, that fact is not particularly surprising. But the professional physicist had as his job the exploration of technical mechanisms that would actually release that energy. The science-fiction writer had as his business an investigation of that area of no practice.

The atomic bomb represents one of the points at which physical science directly impinges on sociological science, in an area that comes dangerously close to being a no-practice zone. The sociologist has never had great respect for the physical scientist as a predictor of sociological events. The physical scientist has been trained to consider purely, solely, and exclusively physical facts. No matter how ardently a man may wish that A and B would react to produce C—in physical science, desires, ardent wishes, and great human need simply fail to produce the slightest effect on A and B. The two substances produce precisely, solely, and invariably what they are destined by their own nature to produce. In consequence, in his professional life, the physical scientist must *not* consider human wishes.

The science fictioneer, however, can and does combine the two. Therefore in May, 1941, Robert Heinlein had a story published called "Solution Unsatisfactory." Heinlein is an Annapolis graduate—he has adequate physical science training. He has also worked professionally in politics. The difference between a politician and a sociologist is somewhat like the difference, in the old days, between an ironmaster and an alchemist. The ironmaster didn't know *why* his methods worked, but he could make iron that worked, and make it fairly reliably. The alchemist had many theories, and tended to have rather low respect for the dirty-handed, horny-thumbed ironmaster who had none.

Heinlein made some predictions in his story; remember that these were written before the end of 1940—when the Manhattan Project was yet to be really started. There were several major predictions, which were, essentially:

1. That the United States Government would establish a project to study the possibility of developing a military weapon based on the nuclear energy of Uranium-235.
2. That the project would succeed, producing a weapon capable of annihilating a city.
3. That the then-current war would be ended by United States use of the atomic weapon to annihilate an enemy city.
4. That the use of the weapon would, of itself, provide enough

19

clues so that any other industrial nation could duplicate the weapon in a relatively short time.

5. That the world would then find itself in the position of having "all offense and no defense"—that offensive power would so exceed defensive power as to leave the world open to devastation.

6. That a world government would be a necessity, and that one would be organized.

7. But that there would be one holdout against that government: the U.S.S.R.

8. That the U.S.S.R. would launch a short, sharp, atomic war against the United States, and would lose that war.

9. That there would then be a sharp political tussle to determine whether the United States or the United World would control the world government.

The last two points, of course, remain in the unfulfilled prophecy class. He may conceivably be entirely wrong on those two. He was wrong in some details, too; the atomic weapon he discussed was the use of radioactive fission products as a death dust. In 1940 it was not certain that a nuclear explosive was possible, but the possibility of deadly fission dusts was quite certain. If you reread the Smyth Report published immediately after Hiroshima, you will find that Heinlein's position in the story was precisely that taken by the scientists of the Manhattan Project in 1941—although Heinlein could not, of course, have known that at the time. Also, Heinlein was wrong in having Berlin the city destroyed by the atomic weapon.

Such errors of detail in prophecy are inevitable; the important aspect of imaginative exploration of areas of no practice is that the basic outlines of the consequences of a particular course of action can be worked out.

Up to about 1945, science fiction concentrated largely on physical science; this, actually, is a far less dangerous field than the field of the humanic sciences, because the available forces in the physical field are less powerful. The atomic bomb seems powerful and impressive—but remember that it is merely an expression of human will and thought, that human beings control and direct it. Human thought, not atomic energy, is the most powerful force for either construction or destruction in the known universe. It is this aspect that science fiction is exploring today—the most dangerous and most magnificent of all *terra incognita* still lies a half inch back of your own forehead. Naturally, that is the next great area of exploration for science fiction!

There's one final point I'd like to consider. I've tried to show that science fiction has a natural place, and a necessary place, in our present society. The remaining question is, obviously, whether science-fiction magazines are actually doing anything having a detectable influence on society.

In the case of my own magazine, *Astounding Science Fiction,* the readership represents only about 0.2 per cent of the population of the United States. This minute fraction would appear to be completely unimportant, and the effect of such magazines, consequently, of small significance.

However, reader surveys show the following general data: that the readers are largely young men between twenty and thirty-five, with a scattering of younger college students, and older professional technical men; and that nearly all the readers are technically trained and employed.

The nature of the interest in the stories is not economic, not love, but technical-philosophical.

The reader, then, is a technically trained, philosophically inclined, imaginative man between twenty and thirty-five.

The circulation is of the order of 150,000; the readership apparently about double that; 300,000 represents a good one third of the young technical personnel of the nation.

Repeated studies by psychologists, economists and others have shown that nearly all the creative work of mankind has been done by young men between twenty and thirty-five; the older man specializes in executive management of the enterprise created during his younger years.

We can say, then, that the magazine is reaching about one third of the men in the most creative age levels who are interested in technical developments. And this culture we live in is based inescapably on technology.

Science-fiction magazines are not entirely without effect, despite their relatively small circulation. They have a very real place in our culture—and our culture of tomorrow is going to find its place in one of the science-fiction worlds of today.

The statement, "Something will happen in the future" seems one of those sure-thing comments, but one lacking any useful applicability. Of course something's going to happen—but what?

It does have applicability, however. Since something's going to happen, we might as well take a little trouble and see what "somethings" might happen, and select one that suits us. Since something's going to happen anyway—it might as well be a something we like!

The Publishing
of Science Fiction

by ANTHONY BOUCHER

ANTHONY BOUCHER *is especially well qualified to discuss the special problems of science-fiction publishing, for he has a unique and intimate knowledge of two highly specialized and, in some respects, highly similar publishing fields: science fiction on the one hand; mystery on the other.*

Mr. Boucher is co-editor, with J. Francis McComas, of The Magazine of Fantasy & Science Fiction *which, since its first appearance, has had the reputation of being one of the top three in the country. With Mr. McComas, again, he also edits a "true crime" magazine put out by the same publisher.*

Since 1937, he has had published seven novels and numerous short stories and novelettes in the mystery field. He is a former president of the Mystery Writers of America. As Anthony Boucher, he reviews "whodunits" for the New York Times Book Review; *as H. H. Holmes, he does the same thing for the* New York Herald Tribune. *He also edits a mystery reprint line.*

His interest in science fiction dates back to the nineteen-twenties, and he has been an active science fiction writer since 1941. He has published numerous short stories, both in the field and in such magazines as Esquire, *and many of these have been anthologized. He has edited three anthologies, two of crime, and one of fantasy and science fiction.*

Mr. Boucher resides in Berkeley, California.

PREFATORY APOLOGIA: the intention of this chapter is to be purely objective, historical, and statistical. Here you are supposed to find the sober facts about the publishing of science fiction, as opposed to the more colorfully individual commentaries thereupon in other essays. But subjective critical opinion will, I imagine, keep breaking through, no matter how resolutely I try to stem it. It will be impossible to disguise my very deep (and very different) admirations for such men who influenced that publishing history as Hugo Gernsback and John W. Campbell, Jr. It will be impossible to keep from intruding my own ideas as to the definition of science fiction. It will probably even be impossible to refrain from an occasional autobiographical footnote.

So it will be more precise to define this as a report, as nearly accurate as possible, by one who has been a casual reader of science fiction for thirty years, an intensive reader for thirteen, a writer for twelve, a reviewer for ten, and an editor for four. Those credentials guarantee, I hope, a certain knowledge. If some nonfactual opinions which wander in make you feel like ordering pistols for two and coffee for one, please take up your quarrel with me and not with Mr. Bretnor.

I

The publishing history of science fiction, as a specialized field, is just over a quarter of a century old in magazines, and less than five years old as far as general trade hard-cover publishers are concerned. To understand its present and its possible future, one needs first to survey the general field of specialized fiction, and in particular the history of the mystery story, which is probably the most nearly analogous phenomenon.

The Publishing of Science Fiction

The distinction between "popular" and "serious" fiction (or indeed any branch of entertainment) is strictly a twentieth-century phenomenon. From Euripides through Shakespeare to Dickens, the most "serious" writers of "classics" were also the most "popular" and even "commercial" of writers. It is something of a matter of chance that Sophocles' *Oedipus Rex* is technically and structurally a pure whodunit (and a brilliant one), but it is no accident that Dickens' deliberate attempt at a strict mystery novel, the infinitely provocative uncompleted *The Mystery of Edwin Drood,* was published precisely as all his other novels were—as "another Dickens," rather than as a work set apart, to be judged by a different set of values.

The Sherlock Holmes stories of Conan Doyle, the lost-race romances of Rider Haggard, the science-fiction novels of H. G. Wells, the westerns of Owen Wister—all appeared simply as *fiction,* and met the same reviewers, the same publishing promotion, the same market (and even often the very same readers) as the novels of George Meredith or Henry James.

Gradually, in the last thirty years, fiction has been split up, by critics and publishers alike, into a series of specialized categories: the serious novel, the mystery, the historical novel, the western, and many others, with the latest being the science-fiction story.

This ghettoization has at least four causes, all of which to some extent affect each other: a tendency of individual writers to specialize in turning out one single kind of fiction; a similar tendency on the part of individual readers to read only one kind; a new school of criticism, dominating our critical quarterlies and our Departments of English, which insists upon seeing a sharp distinction between commercial appeal and literary quality (a distinction which would have startled the wits out of any playwright of the greatest literary period of our language, the Elizabethan Age); and certain purely economic factors to be discussed a little later.

From Poe through Collins and Dickens and on to Doyle, a detective story was simply something which a novelist happened to write. J. S. Fletcher (for whom Woodrow Wilson entertained such inordinate enthusiasm) was probably the first man to be looked upon primarily as a writer of detective stories, rather than as a writer of fiction who produced detective stories.

After World War I, the mystery novel began to boom, both in sales and in the number annually published; and also began to be regarded as a specialized division of publishing, set apart from general fiction. The reasons were numerous: the "for-relaxation-I-read-mysteries" endorsements of Wilson and countless other prestigious names; the establishment of Doubleday's Crime Club, a publishing house within a publishing house devoted exclusively to whodunits; the growth of specialized magazines concentrating on this single branch of fiction, including such memorable pulps as *Black Mask* and *Flynn's* (later *Detective Fiction Weekly*); the development by literary periodicals of specialist mystery reviewers (of whom Dashiell Hammett was among the first!).

By the 1930's the publishing policy of segregation was absolute. Mysteries were labeled as such, sold as such, reviewed as such, and read as such. I do not add "bought as such," because until the advent of the twenty-five cent paperback book, mysteries were not, practically speaking, bought at all; they were only rented. They regularly out-rented the average $2.50 "straight" novel, and yet were always priced at $2.00—an economic mystery which no detective writer has ever solved.

This setting apart from the general fiction market has both its advantages and its disadvantages. Specialized reviewing, for instance, means that a justified rave notice on a superlatively well written mystery story will fail to reach the general fiction reader, who would enjoy that book at least as much as his usual fare; at the same time, it means that the reviewer's enthusiasm *will* communicate itself to a sizable body of intensive specialist readers who do not care to prowl through accounts of numberless straight novels to find their particular meat.

The economic situation is analogous. In the first days of this

26

ghetto treatment, a mystery published specifically as such could not possibly lose money: the number of rental libraries which took every whodunit published guaranteed a basement sale of around fifteen hundred copies, which covered the advance royalty and cost of manufacture. (This is no longer true; the average minimum sale of a mystery is not enough to cover those costs. But the majority of mysteries sell to a book club or a twenty-five cent reprint house or both; and on such deals the publisher takes 50 per cent of the proceeds—a good deal more than he has paid out to the author in royalties. So it is still largely true that it is impossible to lose money publishing a line of mysteries; on an average, the lightning of subsidiary rights will strike often enough to more than make up for the few which go into the red.)

But at the same time it was, and is, impossible to make really *big* money on a book labeled "mystery" (or "novel of suspense" or—God help us!—"psycho-thriller" or whatever label is in vogue). If the mystery novel has a basement of sales (which the unlabeled novel does not; a good book with strongly favorable reviews can still sell as few as four hundred copies), it also has a ceiling. In 1929, S. S. Van Dine's *The Bishop Murder Case* ran up an advance sale of seventy-five thousand copies; but such possibilities are as dead as the rest of that aureate year. Today five thousand is a good sale; ten thousand an excellent one; fifteen thousand or twenty thousand a miracle to be attained only by two or three top writers. Whereas there is absolutely no ceiling on the hard-cover sales of an unlabeled novel.

For writer and publisher alike, the question is one of gambling. Segregated publishing means a positive small profit. Unsegregated publishing may mean anything from fabulous success to crashing failure. After the strictly segregated 1930's, the '40's and '50's have seen more and more experimentation: pure detective stories published as straight novels (at $2.75 or $3.00), novels with no detective or mystery element published as whodunits (at $2.50). (The relative prices—which have, in view of the general

27

cost of living, risen astonishingly little since the '30's—are a clearer guide than the blurb copy or any other factor as to which category the publisher intends the book to be classed in.)

Meanwhile, as indicated above, the mystery writer's income is now derived relatively little from his hard-cover editions, and chiefly from his paperback reprints, with first and second serial rights and book club sales as occasional additions. Tired of paying out 50 per cent of their major income for the prestigeful privilege of appearing in hard covers, more and more writers are looking with warm favor upon original paperbacks, priced at twenty-five cents or thirty-five cents and paying all the royalties, unsplit, to the author. Some prophets even go so far as to forecast the eventual disappearance of hard-cover whodunits, with all mysteries labeled as such making their first appearance on the newsstands.

II

I have treated the publishing history of the mystery story at such length because it is, among specialized fields of fiction, the most analogous to science fiction. Both are, at their best, entertainment for the intelligent, "escape" literature which is stimulating rather than numbing. They help to fill the artificial gap between the "serious novel" and pure trash; they can amuse the discriminating reader without wearying his mind—but without insulting it.

(Arthur C. Clarke has suggested that the formalized detective story has become pure fantasy, while science fiction represents true realism. In any case, the best work in both fields is aimed at, if not precisely the same readers, much the same level of culture and intelligence.)

The history of the publication of science fiction already bears many resemblances to the developmental stages of the mystery novel, and perhaps analogies from the later stages may help us in extrapolating the future of future-fiction.

Like the detective story, science fiction was first written and published by people who (like M. Jourdain speaking prose) had no specific notion that they were producing science fiction. This essay has no desire to probe back into predawn history; see August Derleth's *Beyond Time & Space* (Pellegrini & Cudahy, 1950) for Plato and Lucian and Kepler. But within more recent memory and in America, Poe and Fitz-James O'Brien and such more neglected figures as Edward Everett Hale and the California lawyer W. H. Rhodes ("Caxton") found scientific concepts stimulating to their imaginations and wrote fiction with no thought of seeing it eventually classified as "science fiction."

Throughout this century, indeed, a few science-fiction novels have appeared each year—by Wells, by Stapledon, by Wylie, by Huxley, by Orwell—simply as novels; and, following the economic rules outlined above, have usually been either marked successes or painful failures.

Science fiction as a thing apart developed first in magazines rather than in books (as did the "hard-boiled" detective story, though its more formal brothers grew up as essentially hard-cover phenomena). And one man is primarily responsible: Hugo Gernsback.

In 1908 Gernsback, a stripling of twenty-four, founded *Modern Electrics,* the world's first radio magazine. "I do not recall," he now confesses, "just *what* prompted me"; but in 1911 he began to vary the magazine's factual content with a fiction serial called *Ralph 124C41+.*

Fletcher Pratt is hardly extreme in calling this "the first science-fiction story ever written." Far more scientifically accurate and plausible than the works of Verne or Wells, it is a masterful job, in Mr. Pratt's words, "of supplying the people of the future with technical inventions which are the logical outgrowths of those currently in use or logically developed from currently accepted principles"—a method which is perhaps the only decisive factor in separating science fiction from other imaginative literature (and which, it must be confessed, has become almost a lost art in 1953).

As fiction or even as English prose, *Ralph* is unreadable today; but its latest edition (Frederick Fell, 1950) deserves the attention of any serious student for its ingenuity of method and, after forty-odd years, the astonishing percentage of accurate scientific prophecies. The technicians reading *Modern Electrics* in 1911 did not worry about style; they merely realized with delight that here was fiction even more absorbing than the factual articles on the latest technological developments.

Reader reaction was so favorable that Gernsback continued to insert in such later fact-magazines as *Science and Invention* specimens from his own and other hands of what he liked to call *scientifiction*. (This neologism is in its way appealing; but it is guaranteed to baffle typesetters and proofreaders. It always comes out in print as *scientification*—which is why it has been almost entirely superseded by the simpler term *science fiction*, with or without a hyphen.)

Finally Gernsback took the daring step of devoting an entire magazine solely to this form of literature. Up until after the first world war, American pulps had been unspecialized fiction magazines, carrying cheek by jowl a detective story, a western, and a work of imagination, supernatural or scientific. In the '20's, as we've seen, the specialized detective magazine reached great heights, of circulation and of quality; and in 1923 appeared the first magazine devoted exclusively to imaginative fiction, *Weird Tales*, which often carried interplanetary or interspatial adventures along with its more usual eldritch horrors of unspeakable gibbering doom.

In 1926 Gernsback founded *Amazing Stories*. The first issue (April) was devoted largely to reprints (Verne, Poe, Wells); but within a year *Amazing* was publishing new fiction by such still familiar names as Murray Leinster, Curt Siodmak, and T. S. Stribling.

The editorial emphasis of this new publication was, of course, all 24Cable. (*That* will probably bother a typesetter, too; perhaps I should explain that Ralph's numerical title means—honest! —"one to foresee for one." The + is an honorific.) The stress was on the scientific gimmick, which was often brilliantly developed; the writing and story construction were such that it is all but impossible for any reader in 1953 to return to the stories of this period. Nevertheless, as many readers of my generation can testify (I was fourteen when *Amazing* hit the newsstands), this came as such a vividly stimulating new kind of fiction that one overlooked all defects and avidly fell to.

In 1929, Gernsback left *Amazing*, which continued under other editorship, and founded a trio of magazines: *Science Wonder Stories, Air Wonder Stories*, and *Scientific Detective Monthly*. The last unfortunately failed (one wonders if a corresponding project mightn't be a sound idea today); the first two were combined in 1930 to form *Wonder Stories*. In the year of merger, Gernsback met his first real competition when the Clayton pulp chain started *Astounding Stories of Super-Science*, edited by Harry Bates.

In 1936 Gernsback retired from active participation in science fiction when the Standard chain took over *Wonder*, rechristened it *Thrilling Wonder Stories*, and installed Leo Margulies as editor. Meanwhile he had seen a small boom in the competition, rising to a high in 1931 of nine pulps devoted in whole or in large part to science fiction, and a slump falling to a low of four in 1937—a nadir never to be reached again.

During the depression years magazine science fiction continued along the course on which Gernsback had set it—essentially bad writing of high ingenuity (though other editors were not so careful as Gernsback to see that the ingenuity bore some relation to plausibility). Here and there a striking individual talent would appear—in the powerfully conceived mood stories of Don A. Stuart, in the outrageous interplanetary farces of Stanley Weinbaum, shining like a naughty deed in a drably good world. But these had very little effect on the field as a whole.

It did begin to become evident, however, that *Astounding* (edited 1933-1937 by F. Orlin Tremaine) was the magazine to watch for a greater novelty and even depth of concept, an occasional higher peak of writing.

Then in 1937 occurred the most important editorial event since *Modern Electrics* ran a serial: John W. Campbell, Jr., took over the editing of *Astounding*, which was shortly rechristened *Astounding Science-Fiction*. (Today the hyphen has been dropped, and the word *Astounding* is printed in disappearing ink.)

In 1953 science fiction is really "science" *fiction*. Under Gernsback it was *science* "fiction." Campbell, who had shown what he could do as a writer under the "Don A. Stuart" pseudonym, now undertook as an editor to lay equal stress on both words, and to produce *science fiction*, which was well written, well constructed, valid as stories about people, and yet as scientifically provocative and accurate as *Ralph* 124C41+.

The names of the writers whom Campbell developed are a sufficient description of how well he succeeded: Robert A. Heinlein, Theodore Sturgeon, Lewis Padgett, L. Sprague de Camp, A. E. van Vogt, Alfred Bester, Malcolm Jameson, Eric Frank Russell, Cleve Cartmill, Isaac Asimov, Clifford Simak, Jack Williamson. . . . My apologies to many omitted colleagues, but the list would be too long. In fact, just about every top-ranking "name" in the field today (with the one major exception of Ray Bradbury) either was discovered by Campbell or began to hit his best stride in *Astounding's* stable in the early 1940's.

To be completely nonobjective, I still think that *Astounding* around, say, 1939-1945, represents the high point of the equal stress on both terms in science fiction. Almost any issue during that period contains more absolutely memorable stories, in concept and in treatment, than the average anthology today. There, my children, was the Golden Age. . . .

Resumption of statistical objectivity: from four magazines in 1937 and five in 1938, the pulp science-fiction field took an abrupt jump to thirteen in 1939. With the prosperity of that defense period, it increased to a high of twenty-two magazines in 1941. Wartime paper shortages killed off many of these, and postwar letdown did for most of the rest. The loss was small to any save the most avid fan. Most of them were purely opportunistic ventures, ineptly published and edited.

In 1945 the number was down to eight, and around there it stayed until the deluge started in 1949. Late that year appeared *The Magazine of Fantasy* (changed with its second issue to *The Magazine of Fantasy & Science Fiction*), edited by Anthony Boucher and J. Francis McComas. Several short-lived publications followed; then late in 1950 came *Galaxy*, edited by H. L. Gold.

Après nous . . . well, go look at a newsstand. If all currently promised publishing ventures materialize and no magazines fold after this is written (in mid-August, 1952), you should find over *thirty* science-fiction pulps.

This is obviously far too many . . . and yet perhaps not quite so much so as you think at first. Science fiction has become a much bigger cosmos than Gernsback ever envisioned; it appeals to readers on a number of different levels. (Does the reader of the defunct *Spicy Detective* now read *Ellery Queen's Mystery Magazine?*)

Critics more impartial than I can obviously be have often bracketed Campbell's *Astounding*, Gold's *Galaxy* and our *F&SF* as the three top quality magazines in the field. Even these three (and their respective readers) differ markedly as to the meaning of "quality"; and there exist a great many readers who quite legitimately don't want "quality" under any definition, who want nothing more than rousingly wild adventure stories with a faint patina of interplanetary patter. There may well be a practical market for ten or a dozen magazines. As to the other eighteen or twenty, you may put them on the list. . . .

Nor are the pulps any longer the only magazine market for science fiction. Around 1940 an editor of the *Saturday Evening Post* told me, "The *Post* has only three tabus: controversial politics, controversial religion, and," he added in one breath, "fantasy-except-by-Stephen-Vincent-Benét." And however other critics may interpret the term, "fantasy" to him included science fiction.

33

In 1947 the *Post* reversed itself by launching a notable series of science-fiction stories by Heinlein. Since then almost every major slick magazine has indulged occasionally, and a few (most eminently *Collier's*) have made science fiction a regular feature.

III

To the book-reading public, to whom presumably this book is addressed, the interesting phenomenon is the development of hard-cover science-fiction publication, particularly since, to that public, science fiction seemed to come suddenly out of nowhere about seven years ago. To be sure, as I've said earlier, there had always been occasional science fiction novels not labeled as such. There had even been unsuccessful efforts to introduce imaginative pulp literature to book readers (notably by E. P. Dutton & Co. with John Taine, and by Henry Holt & Co. with L. Sprague de Camp and Fletcher Pratt).

The reason always given for the acceptability, almost overnight, of hard-cover science fiction to the American public is the atom bomb, which proved that the imaginings of science-fiction writers may be immediate future fact. I'm not sure how much sense this makes. Science fiction has made other correct predictions, from submarines to television, with little impact. It has also made some howling false predictions; and in any case very little contemporary science fiction is devoted to detailed scientific prophecy. The true reason will, I'm sure, turn up in one of the other essays here collected; for the moment let's just accept the fact and look at its history.

Roughly science fiction stands today, in book publication, where the detective story did twenty years ago: it's a form that has always existed to some extent, but has now acquired enthusiastic specialist readers . . . which means specialist publishers, specialist reviewers and all the other phenomena we saw with the mystery.

In at least three respects, however, the picture is different.

Despite Ellery Queen's often repeated and perfectly valid assertion that the short story is the true detective form, the publishing norm is the full-length novel. Anthologies of short stories do not amount to more than 2 per cent of the mystery books published in each year—the annual *Queen's Awards,* the annual *Best* edited by David C. Cooke, usually an anthology from Mystery Writers of America, and perhaps one other. Collections of shorts and novelettes by individual authors may amount to as much as 3 per cent; the remaining 95 per cent is novels.

In science fiction since 1949, on the other hand, anthologies have represented 19 per cent of the total, individual volumes of shorts and novelettes 23 per cent. In the first eight months of 1952, very nearly *one third* of all science-fiction books published have been anthologies!

(Anyone else attempting this same survey will, I am sure, come up with different figures. No two critics can agree on: What is a mystery? What is science fiction? Where is the line between a novelette and a novel? And the statistics are not simplified by the practice, fortunately becoming rarer, whereby publishers call a book of short stories "a novel" simply by replacing the story titles with chapter headings—a vice which also prevailed in the early days of the detective story.)

The present science fiction "boom" began with anthologies . . . and we might as well begin by settling once and for all the question of "What was the first science-fiction anthology?"

In 1943 Donald A. Wollheim brought out *The Pocket Book of Science-Fiction* (but that was a paperback), in 1945 the Viking *Portable Novels of Science* (but that was only full-length novels).

In 1946 two enormous compendiums of shorts and novelettes appeared close together. Groff Conklin's *The Best of Science Fiction* (Crown Publishers) had an earlier publication date. *Adventures in Time and Space,* edited by Raymond J. Healy and J. Francis McComas (Random House), was conceived earlier and had obtained permission to skim much of the cream of the Golden Age before Conklin got under way.

Each of these four books has some legitimate claim to the title

35

of pioneer. All are still in print, and required reading. But actually these are all Johnny-come-latelies. The *first* science fiction anthology appeared as early as 1937! It was called *Adventures to Come*, was published by McLoughlin Bros., and was edited by one J. Berg Esenwein, M.A., Litt.D. (I am *not* making this up). It is not only the first but indisputably the worst (as of this writing) in its field—subliterate and unscientific trash by unknown writers, apparently aimed at a teen-age audience.

Moral: when intensive literary research establishes a long-disputed fact, it is often not worth knowing.

Further moral: an anthology is not necessarily a selection of the best work available—something that is going to become more painfully obvious season by season if the present trend goes on.

The pioneers mentioned and their immediate successors, especially the series by Conklin and Derleth, all but exhausted the stories in old magazines which deserved reprinting. Yet publishers (and presumably readers) keep wanting new anthologies. The anthologist has three desirable courses to follow:

He may (like Judith Merril) devote detailed research to finding the scarce nuggets overlooked by previous prospectors.

He may (like Everett F. Bleiler and T. E. Dikty) forget the past and concentrate on selecting the best from contemporary magazines.

He may (like Raymond J. Healy) commission and edit new stories which have never appeared in print before.

But all these methods combined will not provide the twenty or more anthologies promised by the end of 1952. Much more often the anthologist will compromise by selecting stories either often reprinted already, or hardly worth the effort of resurrecting.

It's doubtful if any specialized field can lay as much proportionate stress on the anthology as science fiction does today. Probably within a few years the output will simmer down, as with the mystery, to a few standard annuals and an occasional collection based on unusual research or a novel idea.

Another way in which science-fiction book publishing differs not only from the mystery but from any other field I know is the existence of a number of small semiprofessional houses which publish nothing else. The first of these was Arkham House, founded in 1939 by August Derleth and Donald Wandrei, originally with the single purpose of bringing together the writings of H. P. Lovecraft. Most Arkham publications fall definitely into the field of the supernatural, but the list has contained not a little science fiction, including such important items as the first book edition of A. E. van Vogt's *Slan*.

The story of Arkham's first publication is typical of the early days of these small houses. Lovecraft's *The Outsider and Others* was printed in an exceedingly limited edition of 1,268 copies at $5. Derleth solicited advance orders at $3.50; he got 150 orders. It took four years to sell the remaining 1,118; $5, readers protested, was too much (for a book of 553 pages and over 360,000 words!). And as soon as the edition was finally exhausted, it became the rarest of collector's items—a bargain at $20 and sometimes changing hands for as much as $100.

From 1946 on, a number of similar houses sprang up all over the country, concentrating, unlike Arkham, on science fiction and trying, each according to its lights, to lend hard-cover permanence to what it deemed the best of the pulp "classics." In most cases the editorial choices were wildly capricious; the distributing mechanism was nonexistent; the editions were minute; and the profit to author and publisher was invisible.

Yet these countless Presses and Houses, some of them dying in the birth throes of their first and only book, played a strong part in persuading commercial publishers to take up science fiction. They proved that a small but intensive book-buying public wanted it, that an edition of two or three thousand could sell out completely—and that sort of guaranteed minimum is, as with the mystery, something no publisher despises.

Of all these amateurs catapulted into the publishing world, those with shrewder editorial taste or sharper business acumen managed to survive. Aside from Arkham (which now only edits

its books, and releases them through a standard commercial house), four are still regularly active, and at least two of these have virtually reached full professional status.

The third marked difference from the mystery is indicated in this story of the specialized houses. The devotees of science fiction are willing, even eager to *buy* hard-cover books—not merely rent them, or wait till they appear at twenty-five cents. The result is well illustrated by the experience of Doubleday & Co.

This vast publishing house, among all its other activities, publishes specialized lines in both mysteries and science fiction. In fact, it publishes as many mysteries as any other three houses combined, and an almost proportionate amount of science fiction. Sales in both fields run about the same (somewhat higher than with most other houses): five thousand for a normally successful book; ten thousand for a smash hit. But a mystery is dead within six weeks after its publication (some even say it is dead on publication date); it will never sell another copy in its original edition. Whereas the science-fiction book runs up the same initial sales as the mystery, then continues to sell indefinitely in a steady slow trickle, *even after it has appeared in a paperback reprint.*

Simon and Schuster and other firms have had the same experience. A whodunit is, practically speaking, out of print before the reviews appear (a discouraging thought to a professional reviewer); a science-fiction novel is a permanent backlist item, sure of small but steady reorders.

It may be that it took a long time and some spectacular historical events to develop a public for hard-cover science fiction; it may be that it took the publishers a long time to realize that the public was there. In either case, it was about ten years after what we call "modern science fiction" came into being in the pulps that a commercial publisher launched a specialized science-fiction list.

That publisher was Frederick Fell in 1949. Simon and Schuster, Doubleday and others were hard on his heels. The first impulse of all of them was, like the amateur houses, to reprint, to exhume pulp novels and give them the dignity of hard covers.

Obviously there were dangers in this policy. The book audience is not the same as the magazine audience. Stories remembered, quite justly, as magnificent in their period may seem less attractive on re-examination. And very few publishers venturing on science-fiction lines had editors with the combined knowledge of the special field and of literature in general which had distinguished the great creative mystery editors.

Figures show the inevitable trend. In 1949, there were fifteen science-fiction novels reprinted from magazines to five without previous publication; in 1950, twenty-nine reprints to thirteen originals; in 1951, seventeen to fourteen. And in the first eight months of 1952, only eight reprints to fifteen brand-new novels! The trend is even more marked if one considers that many of the "reprints" in 1951 and 1952 were written with book publication in mind, but had the financial good fortune to sell first serial rights.

How much science fiction—novels, anthologies, and all—is being published? How big is this "boom"?

Again the statistics can be argued; the lines of classification are impossible to draw precisely. But by my count, forty-one books were published in 1949; sixty in 1950; fifty-seven in 1951; and forty-five in the first two thirds of 1952. To put it in another way, there is approximately one science-fiction book published for every four mystery novels; and the proportion seems, after the initial spurt, to have leveled off pretty evenly.

IV

What does this boomlet mean to the writer of science fiction? Have the creators of this "only lively spontaneous manifestation in the contemporary short story" (says the *Kenyon Review* yet!) come into their financial own?

Not quite, I'm afraid. Horace Gold once described the bad old days in the 1930's when the only science-fiction market was the pulps, there were very few of them, and their rates were "microscopic fractions of a cent payable upon lawsuit." Now a writer

39

can sell to the slicks, to the films, to radio, to television (if he will sign away rights to his typing finger and his wife's honor[1]); but book and magazine publication is still not creating any Croesuses. Mystery Writers of America have long complained that "Crime does not pay . . . enough!"; and the same appears to be true of Time and Space.

A very few magazine markets pay two or three cents a word— sometimes up to five for big names. Most of the thirty-odd periodicals you were earlier invited to investigate on your newsstand have a base rate of one cent, which is no better in today's inflation than the abominable half cent of the 1930's. For readers unaccustomed to studying writers' rates, two cents a word means $100 or less for the average short story, $1200 for the average novel. Hard-cover royalties on the reasonably successful book work out to about the same, anthology reprint of short stories to much less.

I know a man who has been turning out a steady 30,000 words a month and selling all of it—the equivalent of five or six book-length novels a year. His annual income from writing has been $3600. There must be some way of being just as poor with less effort.

I don't intend to imply that the blacksnake-wielding publishers are getting rich either. Many of these markets, even the lowest, are paying rates as high as their circulation justifies. For though every publisher holds his exact circulation figures in as deep secrecy as he would the report of a Wassermann positive, no science-fiction magazine has a circulation that any general periodical would consider impressive or even adequate.

The economics of science-fiction writing is not part of the proper topic of this essay; it belongs rather to the deliberations of the newly organized Science Fiction Writers of America. But these economic factors influence any possible picture of the future of science-fiction publishing; and I would be untrue to the tradi-

[1] A remark included in the hope that the Screen Writers Guild's strike will have made it ridiculously dated by the time this book appears. (It has. *Ed.*)

tions of the craft if I closed without some attempt at extrapolation and prophecy.

Forecasting trends in publishing is as tempting and just about as safe as developing a system for beating the bank at roulette and somewhat more perilous than interpreting the quatrains of Nostradamus; but here's the way the future looks to me at present:

Science fiction will remain a steady, unspectacular part of trade-book publishing, probably a little more profitable than mysteries or westerns—with, of course, an occasional book making a marked splash outside of the limited specialized pool.

The adverse effect of science fiction on the publication of mysteries, so often prophesied, has failed to develop in four years; as many mysteries are being published and sold as before the invasion. What competition there is between the fields may, at most, eliminate some of the substandard trash published on both sides.

There will soon be a sizable proportion of books impossible to classify specifically as science fiction or mystery, and appealing to both publics. Five of 1952's science-fiction novels have had dominant mystery-detective elements, and several whodunits have included a touch of science fiction. The problems involved in achieving the perfect blend would demand a long separate essay; but so many professional writers are interested in both fields, and the straddling of two markets is so obviously desirable commercially that the problems are certain to be solved.

Publishing emphasis will be more on the novel and far less on the anthology; and the novels published will be new works rather than resurrections.

Most hard-cover novels will appear later as paperback reprints —a trend already becoming apparent.

Original paperback novels will begin to appear, if such distribution can be developed that they will be more profitable to the writer than hard-cover royalties plus fifty per cent of reprint. (This will also probably mean a larger infusion of sex into a field which has throughout most of its life scrupulously avoided the subject.)

Possibly even before this book appears, some publisher will have realized the potential market for a science-fiction book club, along the lines of Detective Book Club, Mystery Guild, or Unicorn.

The number of magazines will settle down to at most a dozen; and the survivors will be forced, in competition with each other, to adopt minimum standards on word rates and purchase of rights. And in 1963 the editor of the year's seventeenth anthology (with an advance sale of 43,000), chosen from the thirty-eight extant magazines (each with a circulation of 250,000, but buying all rights for one cent a word), will reprint these remarks in his introduction as a prime specimen of the fallacies of extrapolation.

Science Fiction in Motion Pictures, Radio, and Television

by DON FABUN

Don Fabun *has reviewed science fiction for Joseph Henry Jackson and the* San Francisco Chronicle *for the past three years, and has been active in science-fiction fan circles for some time. He is editor and publisher of* The Rhodomagnetic Digest, *one of the best of the fan magazines, put out by that excellent organization,* The Elves', Gnomes', and Little Men's Science Fiction, Chowder, and Marching Society.

By profession Mr. Fabun is an advertising man and publicist. Recently, after five years as a copy writer for McCann-Erickson, he took over the editorship of a general interest magazine circulated to Kaiser Aluminum Corporation customers. Born in Illinois, he is a graduate of the University of California. Throughout the war, from '42 to '46, he served in the Merchant Marine, mostly in the South Pacific. He and his wife live in Berkeley, California.

WITHIN the last few years there has been a tremendous increase in the presentation of science-fiction themes on mass media, particularly radio, television and moving pictures. The movement has been observed with mixed emotions by those who are steady readers of science fiction. On the one hand, they are glad to see their special interest given such wide currency, and, on the other, they are disappointed in the final result, feeling that not only is the choice of science-fiction material badly made, but that its conversion to the new media is badly done.

Actually, there are so many obstacles to converting the more serious types of science fiction to radio, television and motion pictures, that it is a wonder it is attempted at all. It is even more of a wonder that, very rarely, one of these attempts succeeds, or at least partially succeeds.

An illustration of these difficulties may be gained from considering the following analogy. Suppose, for the moment, that the editors of *Life* magazine, desperately in need of fresh material, are asked to convert the articles and columns in *The Saturday Review* into an issue of *Life*. The analogy is not as inexact as it seems at first glance.

Basically, *The Saturday Review* is a class magazine; it is edited and published for a specialized audience whose common denominator is a liking for books. In order for a reader to understand and appreciate the reviews and columns of *The Saturday Review*, he must have had enough of a reading background to understand easily and sympathetically what a reviewer means when he says, "His style is a strange mixture, compounded of the disciplined precocity of an Oscar Wilde and the undisciplined turbulence of a Tom Wolfe. . . ." Without sufficient background, the greater part of the material appearing in *The Saturday Review* can only appear to be gibberish.

Now consider the plight of the editors of *Life*. Their magazine is not, primarily, a written one, but put together almost entirely of pictures. So there is the technical difficulty of making the meaning of written words come through as a form of photograph. But there is the far more troublesome problem that the editors of *Life* cannot take for granted a common understanding on the part of its audience. *Life* must appeal to an audience so diverse, culturally, geographically, socially and economically that its only common denominator is the ability to look at a two-dimensional picture and realize that it represents a three-dimensional scene.

The difference between *The Saturday Review's* audience and *Life's* audience is not primarily a matter of intelligence; it is a matter of cultural awareness and background. There is no connotation here that the *Saturday Review* audience is in some respect superior to that of *Life*. Or, if there is a superiority, it is only that the *Saturday Review* reader is also usually capable of enjoying *Life*, too, whereas you certainly can't take for granted that any *Life* reader, taken at random, is capable of enjoying *The Saturday Review*.

What would *Life's* hard-pressed editors do? First, they would discard all of those reviews that are obviously aimed at special, isolated interest groups. Out would go the reviews of little books of poems, experimental drama, the massive tomes on the lives of obscure men of letters, the scholarly dissertations on Shakespeare and the common daffodil. Thrown out too would be the "Double-Crostic" and the "Literary Crypt," the reviews of classical records, commentaries on foreign movies, and erudite guest editorials.

They would concentrate on reviews of books that are certain to have a large audience: lush historical novels, book-club selections, cartoon collections by artists who are already known in mass magazines, and the more presentable of the ubiquitous war novels. By selecting a proper medley of large-bosomed Southern belles, mud-slogging Marines, and the racier of the cartoons, *Life* could come up with an issue that would be quite readable, might even be a great success. But the regular *Saturday Review* readers (at first delighted that their special interest was finally going to be given a "break" and presented to a mass audience) would be appalled. This, they would say, is not what we meant at all.

The analogy, as far afield as it might appear to be, actually parallels quite closely what is happening today, and will happen tomorrow, when an attempt is made to convert serious science fiction into acceptable forms for a mass market.

Science fiction, as a literary form, got its start in the United States in pulp magazines whose total combined circulation would not keep a single large radio station on a paying basis, and which is an insignificant drop in the bucket compared to the enormous audiences that must be reached, and entertained, by a major network. The group that regularly buys and reads science-fiction magazines today is not one-tenth the audience reached by *Life* alone and an even smaller fraction of the audiences reached every day by the major radio and television networks.

This small, but homogenous, group of readers has, as its common denominator, a general reverence for a scientific (or pseudoscientific) approach to problems and a general dislike for nonscientific literature. Because it is a self-conscious group, with reasonably well formulated ideas of what "real" science fiction should be, it has guided the development of the more serious varieties of science fiction through active fan clubs, letters to science-fiction magazine editors, and the creation of a spontaneous body of amateur publications devoted to getting a certain sort of story accepted and printed. As a result of this effort, a well defined type of literature has arisen, in the same sense, but not in the same way, that westerns and detective stories became a type.

While this science fiction that has evolved from the relationship between magazine editors and the more articulate of the fans, ranges all the way from "space opera" to the sophisticated "socio-psychological" stories, as a type it conforms to the expression of a myth. This myth, not yet in wide acceptance among the population at large, is that the mind of man is capable of solving all problems directed to it by the exercise of rational thinking and through the logical disciplines of orthodox science.

Westerns are built on a myth, too, namely that the West, and the people who conquered it, were engaged in a great, romantic adventure. This is so widely accepted in our time that it may be taken for granted the public will respond to the literary or dramatic presentation of it. Detective stories are built around another commonly accepted myth; that murder will out and that the organized forces of society are capable of dealing with it.

But the myth on which science fiction is based—the common ground that is shared by *aficionados* and casual readers alike—is not so widely accepted. To a non-science-fiction audience this myth has to be sugar-coated, disguised, or fully explained.

The emphasis on rationality, the supremacy of the intellect, and the formal laws of logic and mathematics, not only distinguishes science fiction, but in the main disqualifies it as a popularly acceptable form of literature and as mass entertainment. This philosophy, acceptable unconsciously to the science-fiction audience, is one that has to be carefully disguised or explained away when presented to a mass audience.

The most practical (and practicing) social psychologists of our time are the advertising people. Furthermore, it is they who select the fare that is to appear before mass audiences on radio and television. Successful advertising does not make an appeal to the rational part of man, but to a limited range of emotional responses which can be triggered by the manipulation of certain stereotyped symbols. Show business, insofar as it must appeal to and entertain an audience which will react to advertising messages, must also be based on emotional appeals. Like advertising, shows directed to a mass audience must manipulate stereotyped symbols in such a fashion as to trigger an emotional response from the listeners. The soap opera does this most obviously, but its stock ingredients —the beautiful heroine, the unmistakable villain, the clean-cut, Nordic young man, the obvious story line whose end is foreseen

47

and predictable—all these are to be found in the other types of successful mass entertainment, too. The struggle between "good" and "evil" is always, in these media, an obvious one, and there is no doubt in the sponsor's mind, nor that of his audience, that whatever misfortunes and setbacks befall the hero or heroine, in the end "good" will triumph.

It is not surprising, therefore, that when the purveyors of mass entertainment began looking into science fiction as a possible source of new story material, they instinctively chose that form of science fiction which comes closest to the types of entertainment they were already familiar with, and which they knew, empirically, would be acceptable to a mass audience. In the science-fiction field this was, inevitably, the "space opera," which, in its most common form, is only a thinly disguised cowboy story. For "Old Paint" substitute rocket; for the Great Plains, substitute interplanetary space; for the villain, substitute pirates on an asteroid or a monster from Mars. The story line is clear and true; the nature of the conflict, and its ultimate outcome, is never seriously in doubt. Right triumphs, evil is banished (until the next episode) and everyone, including the sponsors, is happy.

As a result, the air today is littered with "space operas," particularly in the television field. We have *Captain Video, Space Patrol, Space Cadet* and their predecessors, successors and imitators. They are substitutes for westerns; directed to the same understanding audience, and produced with the same weary manipulation of cardboard characters and formula situations.

It could scarcely be otherwise. Any form of entertainment that is intended to reach a mass audience requires an enormous investment. The sponsors who put up the money in radio and television do so only on the basis that it is cheaper to reach customers through these media than by the use of penny post cards, billboards, or display ads in magazines and newspapers. "Cost per thousand" is the end-all and be-all of advertising; shows are picked primarily because they can command a large audience at a low per-thousand cost. No sponsor, no network, no advertising agency can afford very often, nor for very long, to take much of a chance with program material. Therefore, they choose—and pay the bills for—those forms of entertainment which have already proven certain to entertain a large audience.

It may be objected that this is true for the "juvenile" audience, but that the situation should be, must be, different for an adult audience. Unfortunately, this is not correct. As far as radio, television and motion pictures are concerned, there is only one audience, and its name is juvenile. The most common adjuration in the copy rooms of large advertising agencies (and only large agencies have the sponsors for network radio and television) is "Put the cookies on a lower shelf." Any theater manager who stands in the lobby of his theater and listens to the remarks of his departing patrons will agree that, no matter how juvenile his fare for the evening, many of the people going out apparently have failed to understand it.

In science fiction and mass entertainment there meet two forces whose philosophic, literary and moral bases are diametrically opposed. Is it any wonder that they are able to meet successfully only on the basis of their lowest common denominator?

A complicating factor, which presumably will pass with time, is that today the three mass-entertainment media, radio, television and motion pictures, are locked in a life and death struggle to capture, at the same hours each day, what is fundamentally the same audience. This struggle has both a favorable and an unfavorable effect on science fiction and its adaptation to mass-entertainment forms. It is good, in that the highly competitive nature of this struggle leads sponsors and producers to look feverishly for new types of entertainment that will capture a portion of the audience now being held by one of their competitors. It is bad in that, in a competitive situation of this type, and with the stakes so high, there is all the more reason to stick to traditional "proven" forms. The result: where science fiction is used hopefully as a new form of entertainment, it is used in an old way and in accordance with formulas that have proven successful in the past.

In the struggle of the titans, it appears that the moving picture industry is being the hardest hit. Since 1946, the gross income on films has been steadily dropping. Due to the peculiar distribution system used in the industry, a larger and larger percentage of the audience is within the control of a smaller and smaller number of theaters. Thus in 1951, 65 per cent of the theaters seating more than 400 people each were doing 91⅓ per cent of all the weekly business. There were 647 circuits of four or more theaters, offering more than 7,250,000 seats in 8,605 theaters, and there were 8,275 independents offering 4,052,375 seats. It is obvious that only the major releases, shown in the theaters that do 91⅓ per cent of the business, are likely to be huge box-office successes. There can only be a limited number of releases, due to the physical limitations of the circuit system, and these releases must, in the main, have a heavy percentage of the fare that has traditionally supported Hollywood. The percentage of straight gambles, like science fiction, must necessarily be very small. The gamble, at best, could only be sure to attract the "fantasy" audience, and that has never been a large one. Assuming that modern science-fiction adaptations by major studios began after the war, here is the sort of background they had to build on in trying to attract the "fantasy" audience as the nucleus for a science-fiction audience: of 442 films in 1944, one was a fantasy; of 390 films in 1945, five were fantasy; and of 425 films released in 1946, two were fantasy. It is not surprising then, that even in its extremity, Hollywood turned with reluctance to science fiction and even today handles it gingerly.

Even if they were in a position to disregard audience experience, the producers could take little refuge in the belief that perhaps science fiction represented an art form that would give the studio prestige, if not profit. Of the one hundred outstanding motion pictures of all time, listed in the *International Motion Picture Almanac* (1951-1952) only one could conceivably be considered science fiction, the Decla-Bishop production of *The Cabi-*

net of Dr. Caligari (UFA) which was released in 1919 and still creaks its way around the "art" circuits.

Two English productions, released in the early thirties, were "real" science fiction and reasonably successful: H. G. Wells' *The Man Who Could Work Miracles* and *Things to Come,* but they were only tantalizing. Hollywood could not be certain that American productions of science-fiction themes would have the same success with American audiences.

In this same period *Buck Rogers* and *Flash Gordon* were hits with kiddie matinee and popcorn circuits but there was no indication that their thinly disguised western-adventure stories would appeal to mature audiences. Paramount got mildly excited about science-fiction prospects in 1934 and bought *When Worlds Collide* as a possible De Mille epic and then gave it up as "too fantastic."

After the second world war, when television began to eat into the theater audiences, the major studios cast about for a new type of entertainment and rather cautiously began producing feature length science-fiction releases. Of these, it might be said that Lippert Productions' release of *Rocket Ship X-M* was the first successful one. The word successful is used in its Hollywood sense, and has little to do with the general disapprobation with which more experienced science-fiction fans greeted it. *Rocket Ship X-M* cost only $94,000 to produce, a drop in the king-sized Hollywood bucket, and by October, 1951, when it had run through its circuits, had picked up $700,000 in box-office receipts; a fairly respectable figure and one that made Hollywood take a second look at science fiction.

Almost simultaneously, George Pal (who already had a wide reputation as the successful producer of the "Puppetoons") released his first major science-fiction, Technicolor opus, *Destination Moon.* It hit the screens of the land backed by all the fanfare and hoopla accorded a major studio release, and went out over theater circuits which held a large share of the audience. It was an immediate success and on its first run-through, picked up $1,800,000 in United States and Canadian showings and an additional $1,000,000 in British theaters. Science fiction had come to Hollywood.

Practically everyone with a more than passing interest in science fiction is familiar with the story of the production; the special sets and gimmicks; the problems of lighting and space suits and all the rest. Technically, the picture was as accurate as Hollywood could make it, aided and abetted by a team of experts, and only the most carping purist could find very much to be unhappy about. In essence, the picture was a documentary. It lacked story—or rather, what story it had was based on the rather unreasonable assumption that the engineering that could build a successful moon rocket in the first place was inadequate to the task of figuring a high enough safety factor and sufficient return fuel. But it drew American audiences, millions of whom knew of science-fiction themes only through comic books and hypoed space operas. It drew them because it was novel, it was a tremendous spectacle, it was given a tremendous build-up in the press, and because it capitalized on a growing public awareness that modern technology and science fiction were running just about neck and neck.

Destination Moon was an artistic success as well as a box-office success. Bosley Crowther, astute movie critic for the *New York Times,* listed *Destination Moon* as one of the "Ten Best Pictures" of 1950, picking also a British release that bordered on science fiction, but was actually a suspense thriller, *Seven Days to Noon. Destination Moon* was the first science-fiction picture to win an award by the Academy of Motion Picture Arts and Sciences, presented to George Pal Productions and Eagle-Lion Classics in 1950 for "Special Effects." It wasn't exactly an Oscar, but it helped. Box-office and critical recognition and artistic success, all rolled up in one picture, is a combination that opens the doors of Hollywood.

Perhaps one might ask for a little more box office. That $1,800,-

ooo, while a nice piece of change, didn't really rate. It was not until *The Thing* crept out of the RKO studios that Hollywood realized it had laid a golden monster. Even before its initial run through was completed, *The Thing* had rung up over $2,000,000 and it had a big future ahead of it. It had been helped a great deal by the simultaneous appearance of a sort of song called "The Thing" on jukeboxes all over the country, but even without this purely coincidental help, *The Thing* would probably have waddled to success.

The Thing is worth looking at more closely, because it illustrates much that is good and much that is bad about Hollywood's treatment of science fiction. What is good about it, of course, is that it made money and thus helped influence other producers and studios to experiment with science fiction. What was bad about it was that it took one of the finest science-fiction stories ever written and made a complete and inexcusable mess out of it. *The Thing,* according to the screen credits, was based on "Who Goes There?" by John W. Campbell, Jr. A pilot who missed his base as far as this one did would be grounded for life.

"Who Goes There?" is a science-fiction classic. The entire plot centered around the problem of how to identify, isolate and eventually destroy an alien entity which can assume the physical appearance, personality and mentality of any living thing with which it comes in contact. The sled dogs (this was in the Antarctic), the men of the party—any living thing became, itself, a monster on contact and each of these was unaware of it. How can such a monster be trapped? Even the scientists performing the tests might themselves be monsters; there was no way to tell. Except one. The ingenious solution was scientifically accurate, philosophically satisfying, and a triumph of logic.

That was the story. In the hands of the Hollywood scenarists, it became something else altogether. The monster arrived in a "flying saucer," although there seemed to be no reason why it should. The saucer itself was destroyed by a series of cumulative stupidities that should have made the United States Air Force sue RKO for libel. The "Thing" which somehow escaped from the completely irrelevant saucer turned out to be a giant vegetable. For reasons that are completely shrouded in darkness, the vegetable looked remotely like a man, walked like a man and seemed to have a voracious appetite for men, although obviously this characteristic must have been rather hastily acquired. To complicate things, a scientist was introduced who was about as silly as you can get outside of the comic books, and he tried to communicate with the monster in a manner reminiscent of the tourist in the Orient who discovered he could talk Chinese if he just shouted English loud enough.

Strangely enough, the wave of nausea that should have swept the audience as soon as it had grasped what Hollywood had done to "Who Goes There?" simply failed to develop. Even the *New Yorker*, whose movie critics have never lavished any great affection on Hollywood, managed to squeeze out a few mildly favorable words about *The Thing*. Very few science-fiction people were capable of the effort.

The Thing has been singled out for more detailed treatment because it was not an adaptation of a conventional space opera, but was the Hollywood version of a highly successful science-fiction story. It illustrates much of what has been said earlier. "Good" science fiction depends on intellectual stimulation and the logical development of a premise granted by the audience in advance. But mass movie audiences do not go to a theater for intellectual stimulation, they go to be "entertained." Mass movie audiences are willing to grant any premise, including the one on the marquee that says "Movies Are Better Than Ever," but it doesn't give a hoot in a popcorn bag whether that premise is carried to its logical conclusion.

But to the man who must produce money-making movies, the illustration is a clear one. *Destination Moon* was a tour de force, and successful in its own way. But *The Thing* was, in *Variety's* words, a "Socko." Give a science-fiction story the horror elements that have kept poor Frankenstein touring the circuits year after year, throw in a little space and fancy words, and the public will take to it in a big way. The subsequent development of science-fiction motion pictures, following *Destination Moon* and *The Thing,* is illustrative of the way Hollywood learned its lesson.

United Artists released *The Man from Planet X,* of which the *New York Times* said, "*The Man from Planet X* landed at the Mayfair on Saturday and he and the picture make up one of the most excruciating bores ever to emerge from that pinpoint on this planet known as Hollywood."

Twentieth Century-Fox released *The Day the Earth Stood Still* in September, 1951, and one reviewer, perhaps a little tired from sitting in too many hard loges, said, "We've seen better monsters in theater audiences on Forty-second Street." There is little doubt that this was true, for *The Day the Earth Stood Still* was a wan mish-mash of several science-fiction themes, carried out in a weary manner which made one think that the producers must have had a captive audience in mind. Nevertheless, it was highly successful.

Motion Picture Herald runs a weekly film buyers' report which is made up of ratings by a selected cross-section of the people who buy films to be shown in theaters. On this scale, pictures are rated "excellent," "above average," "average," "below average" and "poor." In the period October—December 1951, five major science-fiction pictures were playing, and the comparison between them, from a movie buyer's point of view, is illustrative.

On this scale, *The Thing* pulled twenty-six "excellent," forty-eight "above average," sixteen "average" and fourteen "below average." By comparison, *The Day the Earth Stood Still* drew one "excellent," thirty-three "above average," and thirty-three "average." *When Worlds Collide* managed to get a thin four "excellent," seven "above average," five "average," nine "below average" and seventeen "poor." *Five,* which was just beginning to hit the screens, got no "excellent" ratings, pulled three "above average" and six "average." Even the poor *Man From Planet X* managed four "above average" and fourteen "average"—but in all fairness it must be said that it pulled twenty-five "poor" ratings, too. The remaining science-fiction picture appearing at that time was *Flight to Mars* which had just begun and dragged down two "excellent" ratings, two "above average," and one "average."

The important thing about these ratings, insofar as they affect the use of science fiction in films, is that the men who made the ratings are hard-headed business men and their chief interest is in those very pictures which represent the poorest use of science fiction.

Two pictures on that rating deserve special mention. *When Worlds Collide* was George Pal's second big-time entry in the science-fiction field. *Destination Moon* had been a winner, all the way around, but there was a general feeling that it lacked "story." In essence, it was a fine, topical documentary. But it was a tour de force; you can't go on filling the loges with documentaries, no matter how good. *When Worlds Collide* was intended to remedy this deficiency. It was a true Hollywood spectacle, with all the charm that word has had for movie audiences since the days of *Ben Hur*, and it had "romantic interest."

The story, a well-worn science-fiction classic by Philip Wylie and Edwin Balmer, was in the tradition of the catastrophic type of science fiction in which the world is about to be destroyed and science comes to the rescue. The story line is a simple one; it tells of the near approach of another star and its planet, the disruption their gravitational fields cause on earth, and the construction and launching of a rocket that enables a group of humans to escape earth before the star crashes into it. A reasonably strong romantic story could be developed within this setting, and George Pal made the most of it. Spectacular scenes of earthly cataclysm, staged and filmed partly in miniature and with considerable ingenuity, provided sufficient come-on for those members of the audience who hadn't realized there were other planets until now.

When Worlds Collide—entered as a maiden in a field that included such strong starters as *David and Bathsheba, Show Boat, American in Paris, The Great Caruso,* and *Streetcar Named De-*

sire—managed to finish well behind the ten top box-office hits, but within the 131 films that grossed a million or more in 1951.

An interesting sidelight is that *When Worlds Collide* illustrates the manner in which the exigencies of Hollywood presentation modify the basic science-fiction story. A time lapse of seventeen days between the disasters (the effect of the approaching gravitational forces and the final catastrophe when the runaway star smashes into earth) was necessary for story purposes, although, as the producers said, "It is altogether too great for astronomical good sense, since the velocity of the arriving star and planet would be tremendous as they approach the sun." And the incoming sun, shown one-eighth the diameter of earth's sun, was made that size so that there would be a scientific excuse for its dull red luminosity, necessary for the purposes of Technicolor.

From a science-fiction point of view, perhaps the greatest deficiency of the picture was that it was based on an old and outworn theme. Purists pointed out the power source for the escape rocket was insufficiently explained. Others, with photographic background, maintained that the cataclysmic scenes were obviously miniatures (although, as a matter of fact, some of them were not) and that they, and the Chesley Bonestell backgrounds, were dubbed in was obvious to anyone who knew anything about photography. What can you do with such people?

At least, Hollywood and the angels who put up the money for productions were not too disheartened. They knew what happened when you went too "arty."

An excellent illustration of "artiness" is Arch Oboler's *Five* which was shot independently in the hills of Santa Monica but released through the regular channels of Columbia. *Five* is perhaps the purest example of the "socio-economic" or "socio-psychologic" science-fiction story. It was magnificently photographed, and incredibly well cast. It dealt with conflict between the last five persons on earth after an atomic cataclysm. Despite all the factors that should have made it the greatest picture of its type and time, *Five* had only mediocre success, and there were many science-fiction people who did not think it sufficiently exciting nor sufficiently scientific to classify as "true" science fiction.

The experience of Hollywood, in short, has been that neither spectacle nor accuracy is enough; nor is an emotional story line. What is needed is a formula story with a fancy science fictional background, a high adventure element, and lots of "schmalz." But, in a time when popcorn sales in the lobby mean the difference for many theaters between going out of business or staying in it, Hollywood is ready to smile on anything that has even mild "b.o.," as *Variety* puts it. Science fiction promises to have mild "b.o."

A large number of science-fiction motion pictures have been scheduled, along with the revival of such creaking vehicles as *King Kong*, which, bolstered by adequate television and radio promotion, is dragging its mangy and aged body through the summer circuits. Among American films scheduled at the time this is written, are *Miracle from Mars*, adapted—the word strikes horror to a science-fiction fan's heart—from "Red Planet"; *Voyage to Venus*, a sequel to *Flight from Mars*; *Atom Men*, the first motion picture story based on cybernetics; *The Gamma People*, starring Peter Lorre; *Twonky* by Lewis Padgett, being filmed by Arch Oboler; Albert De Pina's *I Captured the Sun*; *War of the Worlds*, directed by George Pal; *Project No. 7*; *Run for the Hills*; *City Beneath the Sea*; *Spaceship to Saturn*; *Invasion USA*; *Hard Luck Diggin's*; *Atlantis*; *The Woman Hater*; *Morning Star*; *Los Alamos*; *Destination Unknown*; and the Stapledon classic, *Odd John*. British studios have in mind making *Private Planet*, *Thunder from the Stars*, and *Lethal Dosage* 100.

It is an impressive list. It indicates that, whatever science-fiction readers may think of what happens to their favorite stories when Hollywood gets through with them, the movie producers themselves have found science fiction a mildly profitable field to explore. Occasional "good" science-fiction pictures will appear among each year's studio releases, just as today there are a few good westerns and a few good adventure stories. If this happens, if Hollywood becomes adept at handling science fiction, and if every year will furnish several evenings of excellent entertainment, science-fiction fans will be more than pleased. Sociological forces and the rapid increase of our awareness of science will have a tendency, too, to increase the size of the potential science-fiction audience. All in all, despite the fact that it has had to start, through sheer economics, with the least satisfactory type of science-fiction story, the motion picture industry would seem to be a hopeful place for the production of enjoyable science-fiction entertainment in the years to come.

Hollywood is not the only entertainment industry that has been hard hit by television. Radio is fighting desperately to hold its mass audience, too. And that's not easy. Even with its greater experience in show business, and the listening habits built up in large segments of the population, radio is having a hard time battling the one-eyed monster in the living room.

Radio has never had any really conspicuous success with science fiction, but, from time to time, has made do with it. Like the moving pictures, science fiction entered radio through the space opera. *Buck Rogers* began in 1932 and was sufficiently successful with the juvenile audience to command a number of "blue-chip" sponsors, including Kellogg, Cocomalt, Cream of Wheat, and General Foods. It reached its peak between 1933 and 1935, gradually lost its hold and finally went off the air altogether during the second world war. Peter Paul candy attempted to revive it for television on ABC in 1949, but poor Buck was dead.

Allen Ducovny, producer of the highly successful *Captain Video* television show, to be discussed later, told a reporter from the *New Yorker* why he thought Buck passed away. "One of the big troubles that kind of program finds itself facing is that in the last few years youngsters have become pretty aware of what science can do and what it can't do, so they're fairly critical on technical grounds . . . Buck Rogers went in heavily for disintegrator-ray guns and mad scientists. Kids will only accept so much of that today."

Buck Rogers actually had begun to pass away in 1938 when *Superman* came on the air. *Superman* tossed the *Buck Rogers* pseudo-science into the scrap heap and substituted what was little more than fantasy, but at least acceptable fantasy. All of the electro-mechanical wizardry of *Buck Rogers*, no longer in key with an advancing awareness of science, could be summed up in the attributes of *Superman* without affronting recently developed juvenile sophistication in scientific matters. The fantastic attributes of *Superman* are well known to just about everyone who is neither deaf nor blind, but one of his greatest physical feats is not so well known. *Superman* stood alone on Mutual at 5:15 P.M., and held his own against a solid Blue Network of kiddie-slanted adventures that was practically guaranteed to leave Mutual talking to itself. *Superman* won out and stole heavily from the Blue Network audience.

If the trouble with *Buck Rogers* was that his fictional science wasn't good enough to keep up with real science, the trouble with *Superman* was that he was too good, altogether. A hero who can not possibly be beaten by any enemy soon is no longer a hero but only a bore. Frantic efforts were made to invent a chemical that would get through Superman's thick hide and render him helpless in the hands of his enemies, but the attempt came too late. Superman (whose X-ray vision earned him a 4-F draft rating during the war because during his eye test he mistakenly saw right through the wall and read the letters from a chart hanging in an adjoining room) was his own worst enemy and he went off the air in 1949, hoist by his own regard.

Buck Rogers, Flash Gordon, and *Superman* represented, in radio, the same sort of beginning that science fiction had made in movies, but by the late thirties, when *Lights Out* was putting on occasional science-fiction thrillers, things were looking up. Again paralleling the route science fiction had traveled in its trip up the ladder in movies, science fiction came in on the tail of fantasy programs, and was directed toward fantasy audiences.

The mass-entertainment feature that marked the entrance of

science fiction into the big-time entertainment world was the famed Orson Welles radio adaptation of H. G. Wells' *The War of the Worlds*. Presented with all the apparent authenticity of a radio newscast, this Mercury Theater presentation occasioned one of the biggest hubbubs in radio and furnished social-psychologists with an array of social phenomena that is still debated in classrooms.

To anyone who has read the script of the Orson Welles broadcast, which is available in full in a recent science-fiction anthology, it is obvious why *War of the Worlds* was such a tremendous success. The impact it had on the people of New Jersey and elsewhere in the country that night can only partially be ascribed to the broadcast itself; there were certain elements of timing and coincidence that magnified the normal effect of the show itself. But even without its attendant phenomena, the show was a magnificent production. And here, perhaps, lies the key to the successful adaptation of science-fiction themes to adult entertainment which will attract mass audiences and still hold the interest of science-fiction fans. If the story is sound to begin with, if the adaptors can change it into a colloquial idiom acceptable to the mass audience, and if the flavor and basic idea of the story are preserved throughout, then science fiction can become an important mass-entertainment form. This adaptation is somewhat easier on the radio than in either motion pictures or television for the simple reason that the elaborate sets and costuming and the costly special effects needed in the visual media are not needed on radio. More time and expense can be put into successful story adaptation. Radio, as a matter of fact, is probably the most promising of the mass media for science fiction at the present time, if only because the listener supplies in his own imagination the monsters and scenes that have to be so painfully, and usually inadequately, furnished on the screen.

There was no immediate follow-up to the success scored by the Orson Welles show. Not many studio programs have the talent to draw from that Welles had at the Mercury Theater, and, in any case, it was hard to tell whether it was the science fiction that made such a smash hit, or a peculiar combination of circumstances that had little to do with the program itself. (This is a problem that may be partially resolved when George Pal produces *The War of the Worlds* in Technicolor on the screen. It will be the soundest story he has had to work with, and his successes with *Destination Moon* and *When Worlds Collide* show that he is in sympathy with the general aims of science fiction.)

By the time radio was ready to ease itself out of both the space opera and fantasy categories of science fiction, and Welles had pointed the way, television appeared on the national stage and stole the show. The history of science fiction in radio is that of an ailing sister following her big brother around, and such shows as *Dimension X* and *2000 Plus* have done little to redeem it. Like the motion pictures and radio before it, television is entering science fiction through the space-opera route. The same factors that influenced this entry in radio and motion pictures also influence television. Space opera comes closest to the format and presentation of formula adventure and Western entertainment. It is therefore the surest of any of the forms of science fiction to strike a responsive chord in any large-scale audience. As in radio, television's science-fiction offerings are primarily aimed at the less sophisticated of the juvenile audience, and, like *Buck Rogers* and *Flash Gordon* before them, the offering has propitiated the Nielsen ratings.

The cereal serials in science fiction are not the only science fiction that television is broadcasting, but they are the most important, from the standpoint of the audiences they command and the amount of time they have been on the air.

Captain Video, which first went on in June 1949, is the oldest and most successful of the big-time shows on the "snap, crackle, pop" circuit. For half an hour every day, five days per week, it telecasts live and filmed presentations over twenty-four network (Dumont) stations to an estimated 3,500,000 youngsters. Appearing at 7 P.M., *Captain Video* is dished up with dessert for the kiddies and has (presently, anyway) nothing more redoubtable in the way of television competition than *Space Cadet,* which will be discussed later.

Captain Video is no mean package, as shows go. It is reputed (*Collier's,* January 5, 1952) to be signed for by General Foods on a five year, $10,000,000 contract for Post Cereals. This is enough money to produce ten *Destination Moons,* Technicolor and all, and it shows why, when you lay it on the line in television, you're playing for big stakes. And the 3,500,000 audience would fill half the seats, five nights a week, in all the major circuit theaters in the United States! If science-fiction themes and ideas can make the grade on television, they can make it anywhere.

Television is a voracious medium; it eats up stories and talent and money like nothing else on earth. The *Captain Video* show is reputed to be one of the most strenuous in the field, requiring that the cast rehearse four and a half hours per performance, five days per week, in addition to the time required for memorizing lines.

To a certain extent, *Captain Video* has dominated the approaches used for juvenile science-fiction shows on television. "No bloodshed" and "no violence" are among the taboos it has set up. These are rigidly adhered to in *Space Cadet* and *Space Patrol,* both of which are, in a sense, derived from *Captain Video.* The general philosophy underlying the show is that good people work for peace, and for the peaceful subjugation of the enemies of peace, and this philosophy also carries through the other shows.

Adventure and nonviolence are difficult to achieve in the same format, but science fiction comes to the rescue. *Captain Video* and his Video Rangers are armed with superweapons, including a cosmic ray vibrator that shakes their victim into submission, an atomic rifle that pelts him with atomic energy, a thermoid ejector which heats him up, a nucleamatic pistol which acts as a paralyzing ray gun, an electronic strait jacket which encases the prisoner in invisible restrainers, and an electronic prison cell with invisible walls of force that do the same job.

63

Captain Video has his secret base hidden on earth, from which he ventures forth in the space ship *X-9* to undertake various missions in the interests of peace. He is, himself, a completely independent agent, but accepts special missions from friendly governments and planets if they contribute toward universal peace. His conflict, then, is with people or things who might disturb the peace maintained by the "Interplanetary Alliance," a sort of multiglobal United Nations.

In order to keep up with his busy schedule, Captain Video uses a number of science fictional inventions, including a remote carrier beam that enables him to tune in on events in the past; the opticon scillometer, which permits him to see through any object; the discotron, a portable television unit that enables him to watch anything that is taking place anywhere; and the radio scillograph, which enables him to hear anything that is going on anywhere.

Of these extraordinary instruments, all of which, we are to believe, have been invented and perfected in the twenty-first century, A.D., the most useful, at least from General Foods' point of view, is the "remote carrier beam." Since Captain Video numbers among his Rangers some from the days of the Old West, he is able to "tune in" on what is going on there. Halfway through the program, he or one of the Video Rangers dials in the Old West, and there follow seven action-packed minutes of western movies. This neat gimmick assures that the little tykes who haven't quite been sold on science fiction, but who are still hot on westerns, will hang around on the living-room floor. In television, with smart programming, it is possible to eat your cake and have it, too.

So that's *Captain Video,* the venerable three year old that set the pace for science-fiction serials on television, the one that holds the largest juvenile audience, and the one people think of when they say, "Science fiction? Oh, yes. On television."

Its nearest rival, with an audience of an estimated 3,000,000—the two programs actually run nip and tuck in the Nielsen ratings—is *Tom Corbett: Space Cadet,* which began broadcasting in

October 1950 on Columbia Broadcasting System, but switched over to the American Broadcasting Company on January 1, 1951.

Broadcast three times each week, on a fifteen minute time spot, *Space Cadet* comes on the air at the same time as *Captain Video*, but doesn't manage to stay on as long. It is sent out over about forty television stations affiliated with the American Broadcasting Company. Because of its success, the sponsors, in January 1952, added a twice-weekly radio broadcast of the same show on a coast-to-coast American Broadcasting Company hookup.

Although the small fry may have trouble telling one from the other, *Space Cadet* does differ from *Captain Video*, if only in detail. For one thing, *Space Cadet* does not battle against living enemies so much as against the vicissitudes of space itself. Asteroids, runaway meteors, strange interplanetary diseases, and the like are the villains; again, there can be no violence, bloodshed, or death. The scene is an interplanetary West Point known as "The Space Academy"; the time, a good two and a half centuries ahead of *Captain Video*, is 2353 A.D., or thereabouts.

Each of the Space Cadets takes an oath which reads, "I solemnly swear to uphold the Constitution of the Solar Alliance, to defend the Liberties of the Planets, to safeguard the Freedom of Space, and to uphold the Cause of Peace throughout the Universe."

This sentiment is voiced by the Cadets before they go on their instructional and practice flights into space via the training rocket ship *Polaris*. Keeping tabs on them are Captain Strong, Commander Arkwright, and a beautiful girl named Dr. Joan Dale, who is supposed to be an instructress at the Academy, and who provides "romantic" interest. The Cadets meet and solve problems of space under the three pairs of adult eyes, and apparently acquit themselves well, since they somehow always win out.

Perhaps the chief charm of the program, for its audience, is that the Space Cadets live and act very much like teen-agers of 1952, and thereby establish a complete rapport with their audience.

Special effects developed by its technicians constitute another of the outstanding features of *Space Cadet*. One script called for the Cadets to land on another planet, which was going through the Silurian Age, or its equivalent. The story demanded living dinosaurs and Age of Reptile monsters, none of which are easily available to a hard-pressed prop man, and none of which could be squeezed into the usual television studio.

The *Space Cadet* technicians, employing considerably more ingenuity than the Cadets themselves are likely to show, got hold of a baby alligator and glued on fins and spiny ridges to make him look more like a monster, and gave the same treatment to a newt. Then, in an ecstasy of inspiration, they took a twenty-five-cent pet shop turtle and turned *it* into a very respectable looking monster. These jury-rigged beasts were shot on film and, through electronic superposition, made to appear about twenty-five times larger than the Cadets.

This whole problem of constructing "other world" scenery and monsters is a difficult one for television, because there is neither money enough nor time to construct the elaborate settings that might be justified in a motion picture on the same subject. Space suits, although required logically by the context, are frequently left out altogether, because it becomes difficult for children viewing the show to distinguish one character from another.

The West Coast equivalent of *Captain Video* and *Space Cadet* is still another adventure-serial known as *Space Patrol*, starring "Buzz Corry" and appearing fifteen minutes daily. It also goes out once each week on a nation-wide hook-up. Again, it is sponsored by a cereal company; in this case, the Ralston-Purina Company.

Space Patrol does duty against real live enemies (unlike *Space Cadet* but much like *Captain Video*) and the Patrol is working for the United Planets of the Universe in the interest of interplanetary peace and order.

Again, in this West Coast version of video science fiction, there is no violence, bloodshed, or death. Commander Corry's chief weapon is the "paralyzor ray gun," similar to the paralo-ray gun of the Space Cadets and the nucleamatic pistol of Captain Video.

On romantic interest, *Space Patrol* goes *Space Cadet* one better. In addition to a reformed villainess named Tonga, who runs about in tights as special assistant to Major Robertson, security chief of the United Planets, there is a winsome wench named Carol, also dressed in tights, who provides what the producers are pleased to call "extremely subtle and kissless love interest."

Coming in the same classification as the kiddy-science-fiction-space-opera show is one by Gene Autry called *Phantom Empire,* which appears for one half hour over National Broadcasting Company-TV. Gene Autry remains his old cowboy self, but right next to his ranch is the entry to "Murania," which is a futuristic civilization existing under the surface of the earth. It features such supermodern improvements as robots who do all the work, radium reviving rooms (which came in handy in one episode when Autry turned up dead), and radium generators. In a sense, *Phantom Empire* is a neat switch on the gimmick used by Captain Video. Captain Video rang in seven minutes of cowboy film to grab the western audience, and Autry's show, a western, rings in the lost civilization of Murania to grab off the science-fiction audience. Television is a strange but absorbing world.

The largest science-fiction programs appearing on television are beamed at the kiddies, but not all television science-fiction shows are. Columbia Broadcasting System has *Out There* as its entry, and American Broadcasting Company is showing *Tales of Tomorrow,* all beamed for the adult science-fiction audience.

Tales of Tomorrow, which reaches audiences on Friday evening, is produced by Foley and Gordon, producers of television "package" shows, and they can produce a performance of *Tales of Tomorrow* for a neat $12,000. (In a world where sixty-second commercials can run as high as $6,000 each, this $12,000 figure is quite reasonable.)

Unlike *Captain Video, Space Cadet* and *Space Patrol*—and not counting Gene Autry one way or the other—*Tales of Tomorrow* is not a serial, but produces a complete story on each of its half-hour broadcasts. Says George F. Foley, Jr., one of the producers, "The technique of our show is plain, old suspense melodrama. Basically, the story concerns both people and emotions in conflict. Our major problem is staging the scientific elements so they don't interfere with the basic human elements of the story. The science-fiction part is the gimmick which makes it interesting to the audience."

One of the adult science-fiction shows presented on *Tales of Tomorrow* was the television adaptation of Robert Heinlein's classic, "Green Hills of Earth." Unusual in the science-fiction field, Heinlein's story combines a great deal of sentimentality with a revival of a romantic folklore idea (the wandering minstrel) and manages to make it come off in an acceptable space-opera setting.

As it appeared on *Tales of Tomorrow*, "Green Hills of Earth" was followed in story line with reasonable fidelity, but it lacked—what Heinlein had in his original story—the ring of sincerity that made it acceptable. The television version became tawdry, despite its obvious advantage of being able to present a good ballad singer, high visual elements, and a pretty girl. The pressure that is on every production of a major television show had squeezed the story dry of its most essential element, and left the viewer wishing he had been content just to read the story.

Nevertheless, *Tales of Tomorrow* had tried; it had picked a good story, cast it well, and managed to present it within the confines of today's television, and one can't help but feel that, in time, this show or others like it will begin turning up, just as we may hope the motion pictures and radio will turn up, with really good science fiction.

Science-fiction writers, and those who are hopeful ultimately of writing science fiction, cannot help but feel that the extension of science fiction into the realm of mass entertainment opens new vistas to them. Certainly if one can sell a story to a magazine, and then resell it for radio, television and motion picture reproduction, one will make more money than was possible even a year or two ago.

Today, there is no easy way to write science fiction directly for radio, television or motion pictures, unless one already has established a name for himself in the science-fiction magazine or book field. There are good reasons for this, most of them stemming from the high costs of producing any kind of show in these media. The producers simply are in no position to take a chance on an unknown quantity.

For instance, one of the producers of *Captain Video* discovers likely prospects among the present crop of writers by reading the science-fiction magazines slanted for juvenile audiences. From the point of view of this producer, two things are absolutely necessary. The writer must have written, and sold, enough material to these magazines to establish him as a successful writer of their sort of material. Then the writer must demonstrate in his stories that he has a capacity for writing dramatically. There has to be a story—a real story—that can be translated into the medium of television. If the writer has established himself in the field, and his stories show promise of a feeling for dramatic action, then he might help to satisfy the needs of this five-day-a-week show.

On *Tales of Tomorrow* most of the material is derived from story rights obtained by Foley and Gordon, the producers, from authors of published stories. These are adapted by the authors or by professional television writers who are familiar with the limitations and requirements of the medium. Says Foley, "The important thing about adaptors is that they write good drama. . . . We can work the scientific stuff in on the stage."

By and large, nearly all television productions are written by television writers. The medium requires a thorough craftsmanship and a sound background. What they are primarily interested in is story material which can be reworked by skilled writing technicians.

The manner in which television science fiction is produced is exemplified by the routine for *Tom Corbett, Space Cadet,* an excellent account of which appeared in the *New Yorker* magazine for March 1, 1952.

The original story is written by a New York doctor whose hobby is science fiction, in collaboration with a former vaudeville actor. They turn the story outline and ideas over to the producer and a script supervisor. Willy Ley, the technical advisor for the program, is then called in to suggest a location in space that will fit the story idea. After he has suggested one, the television writers go to work on the script itself, turning it out a week after receiving the story, and hand it over to the show's director one week ahead of the actual telecast. Under the pressures and with the speed that television shows have to be produced, there is little room for experimentation or amateurism.

Although this is the procedure as it stands today, the time may come when science fiction may be written primarily for visual presentation on television or motion picture screens. It may be written by craftsmen who are skilled at writing with real actors and live broadcasts in mind, just as today's better writers are skilled in turning out really fine stories for the printed page. Even within the limitations of the visual media, there is still a great plasticity and a great chance for improvisation—but very few writers today are capable of exploiting it.

In time we may see the modern literary form called science fiction legitimately married to novel and exciting techniques of presentation, a combination which should bring us fresh and exciting entertainment superior to what we see and hear today.

Let us hope so.

Science Fiction as Literature

A Critique of Science Fiction

by FLETCHER PRATT

FLETCHER PRATT *is the author of thirty-nine books on a wide variety of subjects: naval and military history; the Civil War (Ordeal by Fire); Napoleon; a cook book (with Robeson Bailey); cryptography (Secret and Urgent); biography; four fantasy novels in a fine, humorous vein:* The Incomplete Enchanter, Land of Unreason, the Carnelian Cube, *and* The Castle of Iron; *and many science-fiction novels.*

He has edited an anthology of science fiction, World of Wonder. *He has translated books from the German and the French. He has written hundreds of stories, articles, and book reviews that have appeared in national magazines. His contributions to the critical literature of science fiction have been singularly perceptive and well-informed. He is also well known as a lecturer.*

During the war, Mr. Pratt was a correspondent covering naval activities. He is married, and divides his time between his apartment in New York and a large "Charles Addams" house in Highlands, New Jersey.

IN THIS COMPILATION there has fallen to me the somewhat uncongenial task of applying the whip; and at the beginning I find myself confronted with a capital difficulty—that of deciding which backs should feel the lash. If I say, for instance, that science fiction suffers badly from overwriting and adjectivitis, citing H. P. Lovecraft as an example (and there could be no better one for this particular literary sin), will not defenders of the art reply: "But that's not science fiction?" There has been some debate recently on where to draw the line between science fiction and fantasy, including a correspondence between Mr. John W. Campbell and Mr. L. Sprague de Camp, in which the former said anything the author considered possible was science fiction, and anything he didn't was fantasy; whereupon the latter retorted that in such a case "all stories of time travel, space travel faster than light, parallel worlds, telepathy, Atlantis, matter transmission" were fantasy for him.

With that debate I am not concerned except to note its existence. I merely want to get on record the fact that for the purposes of this discussion, anything that claims to have a scientific background will be considered science fiction. This gets in George Orwell's *1984*, but it leaves out Patrick Bair's *Faster! Faster!* which has closely similar thematic material. It keeps out H. Beam Piper's "He Walked Around the Horses," where the scientific rationalization came tied up neatly, but it admits Jack Williamson's *Darker Than You Think*, where the explanation was pretty wobbly in a scientific sense, but included in the story.

So it is not a very satisfactory definition. But this is less my fault than that of the writers (and readers) of science fiction, who generally seem to have made the definition their own. Indeed, one of the specific criticisms of science fiction today is that it includes

74

too many unscientific elements. When one encounters van Vogt's Gilbert Gosseyn, with his two brains and his capacity for instantly transferring his consciousness from a body on earth to one on Venus, a question instantly arises about the mechanism of the performance. The answer is that there isn't any; van Vogt makes a few mystifying passes with words, and the reader must take the essential facts on faith. The same van Vogt, in *The House That Stood Still*, presents us with a race of immortals, without the slightest indication of how the processes of mortality, which affect all other flesh, are disposed of. Raymond F. Jones in *Renaissance* places heavenly bodies in an absolutely impossible astronomical relation to each other, and we have to take it. And so on. A betting man with a good reference library could pick up quite an income on the proposition that at least one scientific impossibility could be found in any issue of any science-fiction magazine.

Not that there is any objection to scientific impossibilities per se, for today's impossibilities are tomorrow's facts, and it was once a fact that no smaller object than an atom could exist, just as we now know for a fact that nothing can move faster than the speed of light. But it seems to me that if the author is going to use speed greater than light or matter transmission, he at least owes us a reasonably plausible explanation of how these things work. Still more strongly does it seem to me that writers of science fiction should ascertain something about scientific facts bordering on, if not directly connected with, their stories. Anything else gets us that "pseudo-science" label we all hate so much, and is bad for the reader besides; it makes him pull up to hunt for the missing clue and risks losing him altogether. And science fiction cannot risk losing readers at the present juncture. It is either going to join the general stream of literature and become an important part of it, or it is going to be the affair of a clique, like the detective story or cross-word puzzles.

A good example of what I mean is Theodore Sturgeon's *Dreaming Jewels*. The basic assumption of the story (if one leaves out that old and corny mad scientist) is that of a basically crystalline form of life with remarkable powers of mimicry and regeneration. It is acceptable—barely—in spite of the fact that the reader who for a moment escapes the sway of Mr. Sturgeon's limpid prose begins to wonder about such things as reactions to food and what the mild solution of acetic acid in a salad dressing would do to those crystals. But Mr. Sturgeon is not satisfied with winning a qualified assent to his original assumption; he has to pile Pelion on Ossa by telling us that after a certain period these crystal-generated, basically crystalline forms of life become "finished," and fully human. Even a sucker for science fiction finds that one hard to take.

Why this happened is perfectly obvious. Mr. Sturgeon, like most science-fiction writers, was in a hurry to get his check, and thought the readers would not mind too much if he indulged in what cryptographers call forcing a solution, instead of taking the time to work out his story within the terms he set himself in the beginning. But it is rather more important to the purpose of criticism to investigate precisely *what* has happened, because it is happening frequently enough to make the occurrence a rather general accusation. It can be taken as a general rule of fiction, not science fiction alone, that the author is allowed only one basic assumption, within the confines of which the story must be worked out. This assumption may be very narrow, as in the case of H. G. Wells' "The New Accelerator," where a good story is worked out of an absolute minimum of material, an art at which Wells was a master. Or the assumption may be broad enough to include a world, as in E. R. Eddison's *The Worm Ouroboros*. Nor does the single assumption preclude surprise; Conan Doyle's "Red-Headed League" and "Speckled Band" are clear examples from outside the science-fiction field, and Cyril Judd's *Gunner Cade* is a fairly good one within it. It is only required that when new details are pulled out of the hat as a surprise for the reader they be wholly consistent with what he has already been told, and that they do not contradict anything he has been told.

In any form of imaginative writing, where the reader is asked to accept some very startling assumptions, this is most particularly important. The writers of pure fantasy, John Collier, for example, are well aware of this fact, and they are careful to take it into account. There is not a single inconsistency within the framework of "Evening Primrose," or "The Devil, George and Rosie," or "Thus I Refute Beelzy." Neither is there in Josephine Pinckney's *Great Mischief* or M. F. K. Fisher's *Not Now, But Now.* But the writers of science fiction, who ought to be more careful still, because the readers are asked to believe in a possible world instead of one frankly impossible, are notoriously careless in this regard.

They constantly give us impossibilities, not only within the general terms of science, which is bad enough, but within the special terms they have set for themselves. Pat Frank's *Mr. Adam* is a very jolly story, but it is an example. Also very close to this failure to stick to the pattern laid down are those stories in which the hero, confronted with an absolutely insurmountable obstacle, invents a new and potent weapon which dissolves all his difficulties. George O. Smith's gang on *Venus Equilateral* produces as many inventions as Edison; the scientific ingenuity displayed by the characters in Edmond Hamilton's *The Star Kings* and Murray Leinster's *Last Space Ship* is limitless—and incredible. Also, it ends by being boring; after the first two or three times round, the reader becomes aware that no matter what happens, the hero will affix the polarity of the reversed solenoid to the sub-binding sprocket and the enemy will disappear in a flash of lightning. There are never any production difficulties with the new gadgets thus invented, and they never have any bugs in them.

While we are on the subject of detail, there is another criticism that can be leveled at science fiction in general, and that is the lack of minor detail. The characters seem to float in space and live on air. It is almost impossible to find a science-fiction story—de Camp's *Rogue Queen* is an honorable exception and so is Campbell's "Who Goes There?"—in which any of the people involved eat a meal or go to bed or get a hair cut or relax with the space-time equivalent of a book.

Why is this important? Well, it is important for a very important reason. The reader knows his own life is made up of these minor actions. He has been transferred by the writer, with his own temporary consent, to an area of space or time where all the surroundings are so unfamiliar as to have little relation to the life he normally lives. If the writer is at all skillful, if the story is worth reading at all, there is a certain amount of reader-identification with one of the characters. Now if this self-identification is to form a real bond, if the reader is to get something out of the story emotionally or intellectually, that identification must be tied down with a few answers to such questions as: "When do we eat?" This need not necessarily interfere with the rapidity of action of the story, or dampen its effect. In both *Rogue Queen* and "Who Goes There?" the questions of eating and clothing are vital to the whole structure of the tale.

There is another reason why science-fiction writers could benefit by a good deal more concentration on detail. However frequently Mr. Campbell tells us that it is possible, we all know that the events in science fiction have not happened yet and probably will not. The reader is skeptical enough of the events in ordinary fiction, which has no future or faraway element; he requires constant reassurance from the writer in the form of recognizable details, such as the way John wiggles his eyebrows when he hears something astonishing, or the way Beatrice takes off a dress. In science fiction, where the whole framework of the story verges on the incredible, this is more necessary than ever. But science fiction is precisely the area in which we get the least of such reassurances, and I think this is one of the reasons for the low esteem in which it is held by the readers of other fictions, and for the difficulty we have in converting our friends.

Closely allied to this is a quite general failure to furnish enough details about the characters in a story or to distinguish them as individuals. What I mean can perhaps best be illustrated by citing the two Smiths, George O. and E², as particular offenders. Their people think alike, act alike, and talk so much alike that if in any given chapter of *Venus Equilateral* or the Lensman stories all the quotes were given to some other character, the difference would be imperceptible and the story would not be interfered with. Now quite aside from the fact that comparatively few science-fiction writers—or writers of any other kind, for that matter—have mastered the difficult art of writing dialogue that simultaneously reveals character and advances the story, this is a disease that seems peculiarly endemic in science fiction. It does not happen in the detective story, where three-hundred-pound Nero Wolfe takes a drink of beer and closes his eyes in thought. It does not happen in the western story, where Hopalong Cassidy speaks a dialect so peculiarly individual that it may be described as Sixth-Avenue Texan. It does not happen in any other type of adventure story whatsoever. Why does it happen in science fiction?

I think it is because almost any set of characters will do in the average science-fiction story. They merely have to be on stage, watching something happen or assisting it to happen, and the events tend to control the characters rather than the reverse. Edith Mirrielees has commented that in science fiction "the individual mind is seldom the center of importance. He is the object, not subject."

This is not always true, any more than any other generalization; there is quite a bit of subject in *Odd John,* for instance. But it is true enough so that a large proportion of science-fiction characters are not individuals at all, in the sense that they react to certain stimuli in a manner different from the immense majority of their fellow humans. The people tend to become types of the average man, set into the unusual circumstances which are the background of the story—with the exception of the "superman" tales, such as van Vogt's *Slan,* James Blish's *Jack of Eagles,* and the above-mentioned *Odd John.*

This is perhaps inevitable to a certain extent. As a matter of that convincing minor detail mentioned above, it is certainly true that the more ordinary the characters are, the more they move and talk like people on the street today, the more ready the reader's acceptance of their basically incredible surroundings. If one of the Kinnisons spoke in the incredibly advanced and philosophical language a Kinnison would speak under the terms of Mr. Smith's setting, it would not only give the story an extremely dubious air, but the reader probably could not understand what was being said. And the whole story of Williamson's *Dragon's Island* depends on the fact that *homo superior* is able to conceal the fact that he is *homo superior,* and to behave like anyone you might meet on the street.

Once again at this point fantasy has the edge on science fiction. It has a lower level of tolerance; both events and surrroundings are admittedly impossible from the beginning, and the writer is required to surround them with clearly recognizable and accurate detail in order to make the story palatable at all. Few readers have any difficulty in accepting Ray Bradbury's "Homecoming," but a great many have more difficulty with some of the same author's *Martian Chronicles,* because they affect to deal with what is real and familiar, yet include details that strain credulity—like the climate and air conditions on Mars, for example. That is, it is contended here that it is the business of science fiction to achieve more self-discipline—which is another way of expressing the desire for it to be more scientific.

It is also true that if a story is to examine the reactions of an individual to a really solipsist universe, not much is gained by making him a disciple of Fichte, and if he is going to be transferred two hundred years into the future, you cannot very well give him the genius and grasp of an Einstein. That is, by the nature of the material handled, science fiction is required to deal with rather ordinary people. But being ordinary doesn't mean being identical, any more than with the people you meet on the street. The complaint here is that the process of averaging has been carried altogether too far, that science-fiction characters are ordinary to the point of being boring, that if science fiction is to get the most out of its enormous resources, it must learn to present character with greater realism.

This lack of realism in character has led Bernard De Voto, probably the best literary critic in America, to describe it as "a form of literature which has succeeded in almost completely doing away with emotion." The criticism is a valid one, and human beings do have a good many more emotions than thoughts, and frequently a large part of what they take for thought is really emotion. And it is true that science fiction fails here; even when the plot calls for boy to meet girl aboard a space cruiser, they seldom do more than swoon into each other's arms in the last chapter.

This is all the more serious because it represents a neglect of resources. Science fiction offers unrivaled resources for the investigation of emotions that are dormant, rare or minor in most of us. Example: Isaac Asimov's "Nightfall" in which fear of the dark, which disappears with childhood in most of us, becomes a major issue. There need to be a good many more stories along this line—not specifically about fear of the dark, but about other little corners of the human emotional makeup, which is the fundamental building material of all true fiction. People in life show constant apparent contradictions—a man who has no objections to poisoning old ladies is particularly kind to cats, for instance—yet it is excessively rare to find any trace of this in science fiction.

Let it be hastily noted that the better female writers—Merril, MacLean, St. Clair, C. L. Moore—are more or less exempt from this criticism. But the general statement stands; and I do not think there is a single feature of modern science fiction more important, or where the art stands in more danger, than this area of character. It is easy enough to see how this characterlessness came about. A piece of science fiction by its very nature has two foci of interest—what is happening to the people in the story, and the idea being set forth, the philosophical, technical or other theory being developed. Mr. Stanton A. Coblentz has even gone so far as to say that the idea is everything and the people are not important at all. I am afraid that this one will not stand up in court, and there is certainly a clearly discernible tendency in the most recent science fiction to pay more attention to characters.

But the pressure remains. It exists at the writing level, where the author is frequently confronted with a brilliantly original concept which he simply cannot fit into a story. Being a writer and the rent being due, he probably puts it into what passes for a story and hopes for the best. This is what evidently happened in Karel Capek's *Absolute at Large,* for one.

The editor is under the same pressures, for much the same reasons; and at the consumer end, the fan reader can usually be seduced into finishing the story to find out what is going on. But the result is not literature and the reader, fan or not, becomes uncomfortably, if vaguely, aware of it. He will not read the story a second time, and if he mentions it to anyone else, he will attach an "if" to his recommendation. Examples of what I mean are T. S. Sherred's "E for Effort" (in spite of the fact that the idea is so good that the story has been twice anthologized), and Philip Latham's "The Xi Effect." There is really no story at all in either one; the science is dandy, but there is no fiction.

Sometimes, to be sure, the author fails in this respect because he has bitten off more than he can chew. The first third of both Karel Capek's *Absolute at Large* and Walter Karig's *Zotz!* are among the most delightful and hilarious science fiction ever written, but both books trail off and end lamely, because in neither case can the author work out a satisfying solution for the situation he himself has created.

Mention of "E for Effort" brings up the point that the reason many fine ideas fail to jell out into stories equally good, the reason characterization is often lost to sight, is that the author has been unable to handle his material without being too, too cosmic. It is like the history of pinball machines; when they first came out, you made points in 1's, 2's and 5's, but anyone who scores less than 300,000 points on a modern pinball machine is a ninnyhammer. E. E. Smith provides an example; the last time anyone looked he had whole galaxies at war with each other, and catastrophes that involved a couple of million suns were too unimportant to make the front pages.

Now this gigantism is bad in two directions. It runs to the

point of comic-strip absurdity for one thing, and for another, involves the writer in long "historical" explanations that make hard reading. Isaac Asimov's otherwise excellent *Foundation* series is a case where the story gradually became so overloaded with background material that it was almost impossible to carry on, and the series petered out rather than came to an end. And when L. Sprague de Camp discovered that the necessity for providing new sequences for Johnny Black had carried his intelligent bear from doing a favor for a family to saving the world, he thought it was time to quit. Johnny Black wouldn't look good in a space ship.

This is, of course, partly the editors' fault for insisting on sequels to a successful story. It has led to such examples as the dreary series that grew out of Wilmar B. Shiras' "In Hiding," and the confused and confusing book that developed from Jack Williamson's "With Folded Hands," a story which really had something to say, and whose whole point was lost in the longer version. The tendency to sequelize is something that needs to be watched, because it is something almost inherent in science fiction. Reader acceptance of a set of circumstances has already been established, the imaginary world has been built, and it is far easier to use it than to imagine a wholly new cosmos. But it tends to make science fiction sink into repeated formula, like the adventures of Perry Mason or the house of Jalna.

Before we turn completely away from questions of characterization, detail and dialogue, most science-fiction writers have another irritating habit that does nothing to win friends for the art: the habit of being extremely slipshod about language. The BEMs come charging in from far Arcturus and land at Washington airport speaking a brand of English a professor might envy; the intrepid explorers reach a planet of Messier 321 and are able to get into communication with the inhabitants at once; or the time travelers hop three thousand years into the future and find people still speaking idiomatic New York English. (How many people today speak any language that was used in 1000 B.C.?) I do not mean this happens every time, but it takes place often enough

83

to constitute a rather general criticism, and it is one of the reasons why non-science-fiction readers tend to regard the art as the property of a cult.

Moreover, this language matter is used here as a concrete example for another, and far wider, criticism. That criticism is that science-fiction writers generally do not take enough care in making their details consistent with each other. Robert Heinlein's "Roads Must Roll" is a well-written and fascinating story, but he has not asked himself whether a civilization with all the power sources depicted in his future history would need rolling roads. In *The Martian Chronicles,* Ray Bradbury sends a single-family unit by rocket to Mars without taking the slightest account of such problems as navigation and the handling of the machine, which would be quite a job for one man plus a woman. (I am deliberately, throughout this critique, choosing examples from the best, rather than the worst of science fiction, and from stories that have some rank as literature.)

Well, what of it? say you. Even the movies make slips like this and movie-goers love to catch them at it. This of it: when such an inconsistency takes place, the reader's attention is diverted from the story to the inconsistency, and once more the reality of the imaginary events has been lost. It is a good deal worse in a story than in a movie, because the latter, in a sense, deals with a captive audience; the film runs right on past the soft spot and even has a chance to re-establish the lost sense of reality. The reader of a book who catches his writer in a blunder often comes to a dead halt, and at least to a temporary one every time. Every piece of science fiction takes its readers to a world which is not this world, and the readers have a perfect right to demand from the gods who create these worlds that they do a complete job.

There is also the accusation that science fiction is often written as though it really were for a cult, an accusation outlined by the fact that Martin Greenberg found it necessary to publish a glossary of special terms in his anthology *Travellers of Space.* Terms like "robot" and "space suit" are so widespread or self-explanatory that no glossary is necessary for the inexperienced reader, to be sure. But it seems to me that writers should be very cautious about "disintegrator," "seetee," "space-warp," using credits for money, and similar items. Admittedly, they are quite all right with the fans, who understand what is meant, but if science fiction is ever to realize its full possibilities, the meaning must be instantly accessible to every reader, not just a few. Moreover, it is not hard to do; a few words of explanation before plunging into the consistent use of such terms is quite sufficient, and there is no objection to Will Stewart's writing a whole book about contra-terrene matter, providing only that he begins by telling us what he is talking about.

Another form of cultism is the intricate mystification indulged in by van Vogt and his imitators, and at least in *The Fairy Chessmen* by Henry Kuttner, under his alter ego of Lewis Padgett. Consider a sentence like this, from *The World of Null-A:* "If two energies can be attuned to a 20-decimal approximation of similarity, the greater will bridge the gap of space between them just as if there were no gap, although the juncture is accomplished at finite speeds." What does it mean? What kind of energies is the man talking about? Under what system are energies "attuned"? What instruments are used for the attuning? How can a gap be bridged as though it were not there, "although at finite speeds"?

Now I am perfectly well aware that the hardened science-fiction reader can absorb a number of such shocks, and Mr. van Vogt will reward him by keeping his fast-moving story going right through the road block. But we are not talking about members of the cult alone. We are talking about literature, and as literature it's nonsense and it's lousy.

Bear in mind that this is not the same thing as when George O. Smith tells us: "We can probably use our audio modulator to modulate a radio frequency, and then modulate the drive with the RF. Then we hang a receiver onto the detector gadget here, and collect RF, modulated, just like a standard radio transmission, and amplify it at RF, convert it to IF, and detect it to AF." In

85

reality this is technical double talk that makes little more sense than the van Vogt passage, but there is an important difference —the language is technical and Smith has carefully worked out a series of details which would be consistent with each other if certain hypotheses were true. Van Vogt uses language the meaning of which, if it has any technical meaning, must be very different from the one ordinarily attached to these words. As readers we do not so much mind being baffled; but we resent very highly being told we do not understand the English language. At least I do.

The superman story is also a cult—a cult within a cult. There are reasons for it, of course. It represents the mythology of science fiction, the age-old desire for gods to walk the earth and control the whirlwinds, and a certain amount of reader identification with those gods, the noblest and most powerful of human beings. But in science fiction the representation is usually on a very low level, a childish level, and it does not get science fiction much farther than the comic strips that carry the real Superman.

A very real difficulty in all types of superman stories, including those that only approach the classification, like E. E. Smith's Lensmen, lies in making the men really super. The whole procedure of science fiction in this regard is reminiscent of what happened at the production of Lord Dunsany's *Gods of the Mountain,* a play which reads very well, and which on the stage succeeded in building up an atmosphere of terror and brooding doom until the moment when the gods came stumbling on the stage, each with one arm uplifted. Invariably there were titters in the audience; these were not great and terrible gods at all, but a row of actors, about the size of anyone in the audience. I will allow an exception to the lack of super-quality in the case of Nelson Bond's "Conqueror's Isle," and another for the super-beings of S. Fowler Wright's *World Below,* but this is about as far as it goes. Even Stapledon's *Odd John* was less a superman than a badly integrated post-adolescent, who belonged on a psychiatrist's couch. Besides, if a superman really does go super on you, you can't tie him down at all. He has no bounds or limitations.

In fact, one of the main problems of the science-fiction writer, once he has imagined a character with some unusual ability such as telepathy or immunity to poison, may be stated as that of keeping things under control, of examining with minutest care the disadvantages that go with the unusual accomplishment. Otherwise the whole thing sinks to the Superman class. This problem exists even more seriously in pure fantasy—why don't the witches take over the world if they're so hot?—and has been brilliantly met by John Collier, among others. In science fiction it is usually not met—Heinlein's *Sixth Column* for example.

There is also another cult, or habit, that seems to be developing throughout science fiction at a fairly alarming rate, and that is the cult of the surprise ending. Murray Leinster's "If You Was a Moklin" makes a good example. For the benefit of those who have not read the story, it concerns a form of humanoid life on a distant planet. They love humans, and can imitate them to identity. The only trouble is that the moklin rate of reproduction is so fantastically rapid that if they escape their closed planet, they will populate the system with moklins to the exclusion of humans. It is finally decided to close the trading stations on the planet as too dangerous. In the last paragraph it turns out that the story is being told by a moklin who looks just like a human and is getting out on the last space ship to turn his race loose on the system.

Now with this story, as story, I have no quarrel. It is well and sympathetically told, there are none of the defects of characterization, false science, lack of supporting minor detail, poor handling of language and inconsistency that I have been yelling my head off about. But it is mentioned here as the example of a trend, a trend so prevalent that over half the stories in H. L. Gold's *Galaxy Reader of Science Fiction* definitely have the switch surprise ending, and some of the others are questionable. Not that Mr. Gold is specially addicted to the type, either; but the record is indicative and his magazine is a success.

87

That is, the trend is as insidious as that toward sequelizing, at least in the science-fiction short story. The resources of science fiction are so enormous and it is so easily possible to change the whole aspect of a story in a single sentence, that there is a temptation to do it every time, to pull out of the hat a surprise for which the reader has been prepared, but not completely prepared. This type makes bright, fresh reading, the reader slaps his knee afterward and wonders why he didn't catch the point in the first place —and when it happens often enough, it leaves him thoroughly dissatisfied.

Because it really isn't a story, it's a trick. It is as amusing as the magician taking a duck out of his pocket. But the second time you begin hearing him go through a certain line of patter, you are tempted to say to the person in the next seat: "Now there's a duck coming out of his pocket." You may even be proud of catching him at it. But detecting a duck coming out of a pocket is not the purpose of literature. The purpose of literature, if it has any beyond mere amusement, is the illumination of life through a segment of experience; and if the reader is only amused, you are nearly back to the level of the Superman comic strip. It is perfectly all right to play tricks on the reader once in a while, but when the whole repertory of a school of writing consists of such tricks, it is on the way downhill.

The switch trick ending is almost fatally easy to produce in science fiction, for when the writer is setting up a world that is wholly imaginary, nothing is simpler than to imagine into it details that will automatically trip the switch. But it is quite clearly not making the best use of the freedoms conferred by science fiction—the freedom to use any type of thematic material whatever, even abstruse philosophy or politics (1984 for example, and Albert Camus' The Plague, which is very good science fiction). It is like giving a man an invincible sword and having him use it for nothing but roasting weenies. In other words, I am asking science-fiction writers to take themselves a little more seriously.

At the same time, I would like to see them take themselves more humorously. Not that humor is altogether lacking from science fiction—Fredric Brown's *What Mad Universe* has persuaded more people to try science fiction than most other books—but the chances are that the reader on picking up a given science-fiction magazine knows that he is going to be entertained, perhaps excited, made to think or treated to information, but if he is going to do any smiling it will be with one corner of his mouth, and wryly. There is nothing at all wrong with introducing humorous elements into stories with a more serious purpose. Science-fiction writers just don't do it as a rule.

Of course, the shortage of humor may partly stem from the fact that the art as a whole is so very young. As an organized, thought-out type of writing it dates only from 1926, in spite of such precursor examples as Jules Verne and H. G. Wells, who were seeking a form in which to cast certain ideas, rather than looking for ideas which would fit into an established form. It is a matter of literary history that humor always enters any form rather late.

It is probably also true that time will take care of the beautiful babes in bathing suits who show a tendency to spill over from the covers into the text. (Time had better; boy-meets-girl has already pretty well cooked the goose of the normal short story, and even the variations of the formula are getting hackneyed.) But there is one tendency in science fiction that is so deeply bred into the structure of the art that it perhaps can never be altogether avoided and only partly avoided with the greatest difficulty and skill on the part of the writer.

It dates.

Writing of any kind is subject to dating through the improvement of techniques, or if you prefer it, the change in readers' tastes. No one today would accept the Victorian story in which the young lady faints on the lawn at the sight of her long-lost lover, and very few modern readers do accept the slow-paced narrative and abundant descriptions of Sir Walter Scott. Also there is the fact that speech-patterns change. "Fie! Horrid creature!" was a perfectly good reproduction of what a girl of Scott's day might have said, but today it is only burlesque.

Science fiction has already suffered a good deal from this type of dating, and from the fact that the early writers in the field did not know how to use their tools. Stories from the first months of *Amazing* seldom read well today (unless they are by Murray Leinster) and recent reprints of works like *The Blind Spot* and the stories of John Taine are of interest chiefly to collectors and antiquarians.

But science fiction dates in another way and for a far more fundamental reason. H. G. Wells' *When the Sleeper Wakes* is one of the best efforts of controlled imagination in the field, and his pictures of television and the socialized state are phenomenally and wonderfully accurate predictions. But the huge, slow-moving, flopping winged airplane which has to land on a platform and possesses no inherent stability has become ridiculous. *1984* will be obsolete in 1984, in spite of the fact that Big Brother is watching. Stories predicting the atomic age already have a faintly archaic atmosphere, even Cleve Cartmill's "Deadline," which sent the FBI men to put the arm on John Campbell.

I do not know that there is any cure for this, and perhaps we should be proud of science fiction's ability to prophesy rather than the reverse. But it certainly does hurt the status of science fiction as an art form. And that status as an art form is what science fiction must maintain and extend, or it will lose the "fiction" from its name and get back into pseudo-science.

ADDENDUM: I like science fiction, I read it and write it, and nothing said here should be taken to indicate the contrary.

Science Fiction and the Main Stream

by ROSALIE MOORE

ROSALIE MOORE, *though she has published short stories and essays in criticism, is primarily a poet—and, as a poet, she is interested in every form of imaginative literature. She is especially interested in science fiction, as a reader, and because there is science fiction in her family—she is married to science-fiction writer Bill Brown, whose memorable story, "The Star Ducks," will be familiar to many readers of this volume.*

Miss Moore's The Grasshopper's Man & Other Poems *was published in the Yale Younger Poets' Series for 1949. She has been the recipient of two Guggenheim Awards (1950-1951 and 1951-1952) to further the writing of a book-length treatment, in verse, of the Children's Crusade. Her poetry, her criticism, and her short stories have appeared in such magazines as the* New Yorker, Yale Review, Poetry, The Quarterly Review of Literature, The Pacific Spectator, *and in many others. She brings an unusual and fresh perspective to her comparative study of science fiction and the mainstream of contemporary literature.*

Rosalie Moore lives with her husband and their two children in Fairfax, California.

ROVING AMONG the clocked suns and dreamed deserts of science fiction—the scenery, of course, depending upon whose story you are in—I have thought, along with hundreds of other readers, that the imaginative literature of our time, in its various forms, is more often fun to read than the kind doggedly referred to as "mainstream."

The phrase "more fun to read" is not a disparaging one, since fun is the best possible reason for reading anything and usually merely the symptom of a deep and reasonable interest. At any rate it is one of the main stimuli for any "serious" art, so that if it is really fun: pricking, not dulling; stimulating, not sedative; time-*fulfilling, not merely time-filling—fun like the paintings of Paul Klee, the poetry of E. E. Cummings when he is at his best, the *Paris, France,* of Gertrude Stein, or the cartoons of William Steig, you had better take it seriously.

The productions of these people are not all fun in the same way or on the same level. I simply wish to suggest that I should like to make this chapter more of a binge and less of an investigation. The effort will be condoned by those who prefer a bannister to a stair, or a wake to an obituary.

Various as the values of science fiction are, I feel impelled to begin with the infectious one. What is the challenge one finds, whether in a titillation of the intellect ("Mathematics by Voodoo," H. Nearing, Jr.), or in the veteran laughter of the belly ("The Gnurrs Come From the Voodvork Out," R. Bretnor)? Is it a specious or merely a random value? To what will it lead us in the way of literary quality? Shall we let it go with a metaphor? Shall we say it is the enlarging of the halo on the incendiary bee which walks in the open across a breviary—in a rectory in Sussex on Sunday, in a bad light?

92

Science Fiction and the Main Stream

Since a metaphor is too apt to lead us, like the form we are discussing, out of this time and place and into some other, it is time to get down to cases.

A science-fiction story from *Fantasy & Science Fiction* begins: "A strange and beautiful instrument, the Gualcophone. You didn't play on it; *it* played on you. . . ." ("The Gualcophone," Alan Nelson.)

A mainstream story by Cecilia Bartholomew from *The American Magazine* begins: "The stories at first were just something imagined by Ellen Simpson. Later she began to wonder if she, herself, was just something imagined by the stories. Had she made them up? Or had they made her up?" ("The Paper Dream.")

The openings of these stories are similar. They are intriguing. They are imaginative openings. But the first story requires of you, the reader, a real orientation. You give your belief at the start, and do not withdraw it so long as the author writes well enough to support it, step by step. (He does.) Because you have picked it up in a science-fiction magazine, you begin to read this story with a qualm of pleasure (i.e., semi-uncomfortable, but delightful) for you know it might lead you anywhere.

With the Bartholomew story you can settle back knowing no radical orientation is demanded, that the "unreality" will pass. Its presence was alluring, but it would be uncomfortable to have it stay. It was a way of drawing you into the story, but will soon fade in the light of a logical explanation, leaving you with a story which is much the same as other "slick" romances you are used to.

(Actually, the imaginative element in "The Paper Dream" is more than a device; it is functional. The action of the heroine's stories upon her, and hers on the stories, *is* the plot—until toward the end when everything dissolves into a conventional denouement. This might have been a first-rate fantasy had the author so wished.)

But many a story of the "slick" type makes use of an illusion

93

of fantasy as a kind of trick, only, giving an interesting facet to an otherwise banal story. A fantasy opening arouses in the reader an immediate rush of interest, a feeling "this might lead anywhere." Nine chances out of ten, he can also have the assurance that it will not lead anywhere unusual, if he picks it up in a large-circulation magazine. (The exceptions are becoming more frequent all the time: "The Punishing of Eddie Jungle-Spit," Garrett Oppenheim, in *Liberty*, etc., but the chances are still against them.)

Many a story in a "quality" magazine, also, will make use of the suspense and illusion of fantasy, without giving you fantasy actually. These magazines do use truly imaginative stories (R. Bretnor's "Maybe Just a Little One," published in *Harper's*, is science fiction), but one feels that the imaginative story which is fitted within a realistic frame is usually the more welcome. There is a way by which the story can be explained on a logical level, or it can be interpreted as both fantasy and realism at the same time.

An example is "The Swiss Watch" by John Leimert in the April, 1952, issue of *The Atlantic*. Although it is introduced by the editors as a fantasy, it seems to this writer that it is, rather, a very charming familiar essay which is given an imaginative exposition. The illusion of fantasy is exploited, and then deflated. Since we shall discuss this story later, I shall not give further details at this time.

The point is that while there is a widespread infiltration of imaginative stories, and the fiction techniques concomitant to them, into all types of magazines as well as important anthologies —there is, for example, conceded to be a science-fiction "boom"— we find, at the same time, a large element of reservation about it. It is true that imaginative fiction is appreciated and demanded as never before. It is also true, I feel, that many readers and many editors hesitate when faced with an imaginative fiction story, per se.

"The Swiss Watch," which is considered a fantasy by the editors of *Atlantic,* is so prefaced: "Each year the *Atlantic* receives several thousand short stories in the form of fantasies, but it is a rare one indeed which kindles the imagination, much less the belief, of our readers; yet this is what John Leimert has done on three occasions."

The feeling seems to be that here, in spite of the disadvantages involved, is an imaginative story which made the grade—and which is going to be published alongside *Atlantic's* mainstream stories. Perhaps this note of apology should be examined, before we can get a clear look at the positive values and techniques of contemporary imaginative fiction.

For the purposes of discussion we shall define mainstream fiction as any fiction which is *not* fantasy or science fiction, an arbitrary distinction made in the interests of clarity.

Science fiction to me is any fiction based on an exploration of or application of any existing *or imaginable* science, or extrapolation from the same.

For fantasy I shall use the definition of the editor of this volume, who defines it as "imaginative fiction in which no logical attempt is made, or needed, to justify the 'impossible' content of the story."

Up to this point I have repeatedly referred to fantasy, although this is a book about science fiction. There are two reasons for this. One is that, in the initial phase of the discussion, it seems necessary to cover the whole field of imaginative literature, to which fantasy is in some respects basic. A second is that I believe a part of the resistance to *all* imaginative literature whatever is involved in the word, "fantasy."

Anthony Boucher in one of his many guises—as co-editor, this time, of *Fantasy & Science Fiction*—has said, "Our readers do not prefer science fiction to fantasy, but they think they do." (I.e., they like the latter if it is not so labeled.) He further mentioned that the magazine sold many more copies when it carried a science-fiction cover (a rocket ship landing on the moon, for instance) than when it carried a fantasy cover (a pale blue man sitting at a desk writing and holding the pen with his elegantly elongated nose, while a minute servingmaid climbs a ladder to his desk top, carrying a tray with coffee).

Where there is any choice, an anthology of imaginative stories will usually carry a science-fiction title (*Best Science Fiction Stories of* 1951, *Adventures in Time and Space,* etc.) although the science element in some of the stories is almost nil. Even among writers of imaginative fiction I think I have detected a sense of relief when an editor, or a colleague, diagnoses a story as science fiction, rather than as fantasy. The word is not popular.

The difficulty, I think, is largely semantic. In many people's minds "fantasy" is identified with "fancy" and all of its unfortunate associations. (That fancy is a large factor in much bad fantasy is partly the cause of this identification.)

"Fancy" in everyday language suggests the ornamental, the pretty, the pink: not mere decoration, but cute or precious decoration.

And "fancy" to the cognizant reader, who is just as frequently guilty of this false identification, often means fancy as opposed to imagination: the invented, the vapid fabrication, as contrasted with the imaginative vision which, however wild, is somehow parallel to, and rooted in, experience. The distinction was classically made by Coleridge: "Finally, good sense is the body of poetic genius, fancy its drapery . . . and imagination the soul that is everywhere . . ." (*Biographia Literaria.*)

When I was a child I had a book called *A Year With the Fairies.* It gave a whimsical account of the life of the average, well-to-do fairy. As I remember, they used morning glory blooms for phonograph horns, bathed their babies in tulip tubs, and used spider webs for telephone lines, with little acorns attached for the ear pieces.

This was fancy. For several decades there has been a strong reaction against this. People (especially editors) have been dashing into empty phone booths, dropping in at bars, or swinging onto the backs of moving trains—anything to avoid a certain type of author. He (or more probably she) writes fancy, frequently with her own illustrations.

All of this is understandable. But to close their magazines and book lists, as many editors do, to all fantasy (in children's literature, say) is wickedly arbitrary. Some of them substitute blanket prohibitions such as "no fairy tales," "no talking animals," to do their screening for them mechanically, whereas they of all people should be able to use their own good judgment as to what is, and what is not, true imaginative literature. Compare Puck, for instance, to the usual frost-on-the-window elf of Grandma's delight. Compare the leprechaun in James Stephen's *Crock of Gold,* a character if there ever was one. There are elves and elves, just as there are degrees of characterization in mainstream delineations. Some horses do fine talking, I always think, while others sound as silly as some of the people you meet in a strictly practical story.

Fancy in the adult imaginative field gives us the little men sitting on no stair—the whole army of ghosts, weres, and witches, which are conscripted only to scare you. You can distinguish them by the fact that they fail. Where they command your respect you can be sure they have tapped some basic fear or psychological conflict: that they are, that is, not merely creations of fancy. Fancy gives us the gadgets and trappings of science fiction, where these are used without further function. It gives us at once the mere scare story, the one which fails to come off, and the meaningless space opera.

Fancy in literature is not restricted to the realms of imaginative writing—to fantasy, children's or adults', or to poetry. (Fancy in poetry gives us the conceit: her lips are "rosebuds filled with snow.") A shallow mainstream story, based not on an understanding interpretation of experience but merely on wishful thinking, is as much akin to fancy as any other type of story, though it never has truck with a leprechaun or a rosebud.

The editor of this volume has sagaciously suggested that fancy is simply synonymous with psychologically untrue writing, with which I agree, and has offered the interesting observation that what might seem fancy to one reader, might be satisfactory "experience" to another.

But the point to be made here is not where fantasy and fancy mingle or diverge, but simply that they are so often regarded as one and the same, to fantasy's eternal detriment.

I have a feeling that you would have a harder time, today, publishing a fanciful story (or a *merely* fanciful story) in a fantasy or science-fiction magazine than in some other. Because in literary circles, and however you combat it, there is still an occasional sneaking feeling that you have to put up with a certain amount of preciousness in order to arrive at the gems of imagination which are nested in their midst like dewdrops in a musty old last-year's oriole nest. While science-fiction and fantasy editors are increasingly wary about publishing anything which is not, as you might say, an extrapolation of psychological truth or possibility.

Perhaps the greatest stronghold against fancy, in our time, is the *New Yorker,* whose late editor, one feels, could smell fancy in a manuscript without ever opening the envelope. James Thurber, for instance, is not a fanciful writer, in the sense of being merely fey. Mickey Spillane is a much more fanciful one.

And having brushed fancy's gauze wings from our eyes, perhaps we can continue now to the positive values and possibilities of imaginative contemporary fiction.

As a poet I am often called upon to interpret or defend values in another field of imaginative writing: a field, also, in which the scene is not necessarily realistic, the structure not necessarily logical. (Or perhaps I should say, not logical according to the kind of logic which we would expect in a legal brief, although it may have a parallel logic of its own.)

As for science fiction, my first point is this: that every type of fiction requires certain adjustments of the reader, and that those required by imaginative fiction, though they are somewhat more radical, are often more rewarding.

Even a "realistic" story requires a certain orientation. The reader must know what to expect. He has to accept certain conventions. Every story sacrifices one sort of verisimilitude for the sake of some other; the question is how much, and of what kind. The more sophisticated reader does not complain because a story makes its effects with whatever tools the writer chooses to use; he reserves his judgment for the amount of skill involved, and the net results.

A mainstream story in a naturalistic setting may tell you certain things about the situation involved, but not others. It is never realistically complete, but you accept the selection. It may, for instance, give details which emphasize only the sunny brightness of the scene, or only its desolation: "Like all stations, it was prosaic in its bareness—empty where the wind swept in eddies under the arches, stirring bits of paper and gum wrappers and commuter stubs, hollow-feeling and tinged gray with smoke and soot." ("It's a Nice Day—Sunday," R. E. Thompson, from *Prize Stories of* 1951 edited by Herschel Brickell.)

This opening scene from a mainstream story is realistic, yes; but the term doesn't mean much. It is a projection of somebody's feeling about the scene, if you want to see it that way—some character's, or the author's own. An imaginative story simply goes a little farther in that direction, and the first thing you know you are into the scenery of a writer like Kafka.

Although it uses no non-naturalistic elements, a mainstream story may be so thin as to seem "unreal"; it may, for instance, feature a heroine unbelievably irresistible and unbelievably ambitious. That is, she is a semi-abstraction, however tangible the counter over which she serves the hero coffee and donuts.

A story by Ray Bradbury may violate your expectation completely in its initial premise, but mirror your own experience exactly in the warmth and sympathy with which he handles the human predicament involved. (The best of the stories in *The Martian Chronicles, The Illustrated Man.*)

It is not the "realism" of the medium which convinces the reader in any case. It is the degree of conviction the writer

99

61194

is able to command. The famous statement that imaginative literature demands of the reader "a willing suspension of disbelief"
always seemed to me to be a negative statement of the case. The
modern reader, especially the reader of science fiction because he
is apt to be an alert and well-informed reader, is not willing at
any time to suspend disbelief. That would make him, heaven prevent, wide open to the corroding action of fancy. No, the most
you can say for the typical science-fiction reader is that he can be
had: he is there to accept anything the author has skill enough
to make him accept, and he stays only so long as the premise is
supported, step by step, illusion by illusion. But the attitude is a
fighting one, and always entails judgment.

Although he is a more skeptical reader, he is also a more co-
operative one. The science-fiction reader is willing to consider a
story with equal alacrity, whether it is told in terms of this world
or in terms of some other—not because he is tired of it all and out
to whet his jaded appetite by conquering space, but because he
has learned, God bless him, that the meaning of a story is always
metaphorical anyhow, that a good one bursts the bounds of its
time and place and goes on and on in the memory until
one knows it might have been told from one of a thousand different frames of reference.

This is the convention which the reader of imaginative fiction
learns to accept. The reader who has not learned to do this criti-
cizes science fiction for the wrong things: "It's OK for youngsters
and professors"; balances this by praising it for the wrong things:
"But it might be educational."

Modern poetry requires more in the way of initial adjustment
from the reader than any other contemporary literature, but in
the case of the best of the poetry, offers the greatest rewards.
(This is a personal opinion, perhaps!) But I do know that a
reader must be reminded often that the first time he sat down to
a sonnet, or a psalm, or especially a play by Shakespeare, he may
have been equally at sea. He has forgotten; he was conditioned
since.

Science Fiction and the Main Stream

Turning more specifically to the role of science fiction in contrast to mainstream fiction, let us look at Melvin Korshak's introduction to *The Best Science Fiction Stories of 1949,* edited by Everett F. Bleiler and T. E. Dikty. Mr. Korshak writes:

> Outstanding books using imaginative science were written and published when authors realized that fantasy of any sort gave them a freedom lacking in other types of stories. . . . Such books have the advantage of not only following the best trends of modern thought with their inquiry into metaphysical problems of modern man and the place of the human spirit in our complex and confused world, but also by the use of science fiction as a vehicle the writer has gained for his researches and inquiries freedom not so readily available in other literary forms.

The "freedom" which science fiction offers a writer, then, in Mr. Korshak's interpretation, is mainly a freedom for "his researches and inquiries"—that is, it offers complete freedom as to idea content. This is what people usually mean when they speak of the greater freedom of science fiction. It is a very important point, but for the present, it seems to me, has been somewhat overemphasized. The emphasis on subject matter, in discussing science fiction, has been detrimental to its appreciation as literature—has, in fact, constituted a block to its being considered seriously as literature at all. The fact that Jules Verne described the submarine before it was invented, or that Murray Leinster predicted the atom bomb with such accuracy that he was called upon by the F.B.I., is—for the purposes of this chapter at least—a splendid but secondary by-product of their stories.

A second point, and one less frequently made, has to do with the technical opportunities offered the science-fiction writer—the fact that he has great scope and freedom in the means of presenting his material. He may, if he wishes, experiment eclectically with every type of fiction technique. His editors are open to anything, so long as he produces a good story. This may be one reason why science-fiction writers, as a whole, look happier than other fiction writers—a statement, obviously, which I do not expect you to take too seriously.

At any rate, the freedom which imaginative fiction enjoys *as fiction,* its right to go anywhere in time, scene, or combinations thereof, to utilize any idea or facet of experience—this freedom brings with it important possibilities. It can mean the development of fiction techniques which have greater scope, accuracy, and satisfaction from the point of view of the modern reader.

Let it be said here also that this freedom brings with it greater organizational (and other) difficulties. Greater skill is demanded, and is not always forthcoming. Science-fiction writers are coping with their media valiantly, humorously, lyrically, doggedly, or sometimes just with a hollering bravado. As in any other field, they work with varying degrees of success. The possibility which one sees for science fiction as a medium for *great* literature (and the possibility is definitely there) is for the most part potential. It is my purpose in the remainder of this chapter to discuss these possibilities, with particular reference to certain limitations which I feel in contemporary mainstream fiction, or at least in a large percentage of that fiction.

Let us begin with a point already touched on: science fiction's greater freedom in the use of scene.

In the process of learning to understand and write poetry, I learned long ago (from Lawrence Hart) that a poem is not necessarily either bad nor good because it "describes," or rather comes to a focus in, a particular realistic scene. But it may easily be a more *restricted* poem because of this; the limitations of a particular time and place may limit not only the "setting" of the poem but what the writer can say and do with his material as well.

This is not to deny that many great poems have been written in this way. For one thing, the use of a simple, familiar scene is the easiest and most direct way to focus a poem, or a story. "The Elegy Written in a Country Churchyard" became a classic without ever leaving the churchyard, technically speaking. Many thoughts and facets of feeling are brought within this framework —the lyrical flights, the philosophy—but always with reference to a tombstone, a rose, something you can look at right there. Everything is easy to place, is linked to the framework.

Without this natural scene to tie it together, a writer must have some other frame of reference—something specially created within the tensions and patterns of the story or poem itself.

In fiction as well as in poetry, a writer has an easier job if he hews to the realistic line, tying everything to familiar, realistic scenes or to normal sequences of these as they occur in point of time. But there is always the possibility that he may account for the world better as he knows it and feels it, not merely as it is reputed to be, by shuttling among scenes and times variously, or by creating a completely imaginary scenery of his own.

In some of his poems, Baudelaire makes for you a scenery; you recognize it, although there is nothing quite like it. Poe does the same thing more obviously in "Ulalume," where he creates a scenery of ashen skies, dim lakes, and leaves that are withering and sere. You recognize it not as scenery so much as mood. A state of mind, and of feeling, are implicit in such a scenery. It is what you might call an objective parallel of the writer's emotion, and it most adequately tells his story, without his having to say, "I felt *this* way, or *that* way."

The same applies to fiction. The "country" of a story may be completely invented, as in the fantastic short stories of Dylan Thomas, or less radically in parts of that little known French classic, *The Wanderer,* a novel by Alain Fournier. But you can go there without feeling the foreigner, so perfectly is the invented country the mirror of a sharable experience. The imaginary place may be a meeting ground for you and the author, the place of identification.

Or a story may be told in a homely, naturalistic setting, into which the fantastic element is gradually introduced, as in Bill Brown's "Star Ducks." Part of the horror of Truman Capote's much anthologized "Miriam" stems from the fact that it begins in the parlor of a studiously innocuous elderly lady, into which one marches as happily as the proverbial fly.

These combinations, and they are endless, of the naturalistic and the fantastic produce some of the most effective fiction of all. Among these one finds certain of Shirley Jackson's stories: "The Lottery," "The Summer People." Reversing the action of the mainstream story which begins with an illusion of fantasy, only to resolve it, these remarkable stories begin in the accustomed world; end, you feel, in another.

"The Summer People," for instance, begins like a typical, competent mainstream story; it concerns an older couple who have a summer home on a country lake, seven miles from a small village. As summer people they have been courteously served by the village tradesmen, but when they decide to stay on at the lake, into the late fall, they begin to be treated as interlopers. Finally their rejection is complete, not only by the village, but by the world, and they end with their telephone wires cut, their car mysteriously tampered with and not working, the mail cut off, as they huddle near a radio whose batteries are "already beginning to fade," a storm brewing outside. ("The Summer People," *Best American Short Stories, 1951,* edited by Martha Foley. Originally published in *Charm.*)

You can, if you wish, consider this ending a realistic one because it can be interpreted completely in terms of natural causes. In my own mind, I feel certain that the impact of this and others of Miss Jackson's stories comes from her ability to add, gradually and remorselessly, a level of fantasy to the initial realistic one. Where the tale begins in what might be anybody's summer cottage, in any typical resort, it seems to end in a country created specially to reflect the old people's rejection and desolation: an objective projection of nightmare in terms of scene and mysterious, motiveless events. (*Why* the townspeople treat them thus is never dealt with.)

This is accomplished by the following means: first the friendly human element is abstracted from the tone of the story (i.e., the tradesmen first delivered their needs pleasantly, then refused politely, then refused morosely, and finally refused to communicate with them at all). Secondly, the human element is abstracted from the scene completely: it becomes a ghost story before your eyes: "Even the (radio) announcer, speaking glowingly of the virtues of razor blades, was no more than an inhuman voice sounding out from the Allisons' cottage and echoing back, as though the lake and the hills and the trees were returning it unwanted."

This is a reversal of a fictional technique I mentioned at the opening of this chapter: that in which a mainstream story will use the illusion of fantasy to enlist your interest, then discontinue it. I considered this initial use of fantasy for suspense as a trick, except in the rare case, as in Mrs. Bartholomew's story, where it is a functional device involving the whole plot. As a trick this use of fantasy promises more than the story fulfills; suspense and illusion are held out to the reader, only to be deflated. What about Miss Jackson's endings? Are they "trick" also?

This, I believe, is an entirely different matter. Any feeling of "trick" which you may feel in Miss Jackson's stories (and personally, I feel none in "The Summer People") comes, I believe, from an almost stark alignment of forces—from melodrama. It does not come from the fact that the story becomes, suddenly, an "imaginary" story.

In other words, a writer may combine any sort of fantasy with realism, or even substitute an imaginative line for his so-far realistic story line—just so long as he sustains it from the point at which he introduces it, all the way to the end.

This brings me to the crux of the matter, to the restriction which seems to be inherent in so many mainstream stories.

Most mainstream stories, whatever their literary quality or lack of it, force us to look at the world in a way which seems to me to be a gross oversimplification. They say, in effect, that there are two entities involved: the real, and the unreal. Everything is the one or the other. It is all right to write stories about unreality (i.e., that which is not fact), but it must, in the mainstream story, always be so labeled.

The trouble is, from the point of view of one's experience, life isn't *like* this. There seem to be kinds of reality, and degrees of reality. (See T. S. Eliot's *The Cocktail Party* for a dramatic presentation of this approach, and a brilliant one, using aspects of fantasy.)

This world of infinite possibility and infinite probability is the one in which science fiction operates, as do the other forms of imaginative writing. It is also the world of one's complete experience, where ideas occur, change—old meanings fade, and turn up in new forms. In most, at least in much mainstream fiction, the whole thing is shaken down, condensed, oversimplified, falsely crystallized. You either see a thing, or you dream it, and no real interaction occurs between the two. They are carefully partitioned.

What I want to point out, with reference to the Shirley Jackson story, for example, is that imaginative techniques allow a writer to say, with more accuracy and subtlety, the thing which she feels. Using strictly mainstream techniques, not only the tone of the story, but its very content would be blunted. Eliminating the imaginative element which seems to "take on a life of its own" —which seems to become fantasy—"The Summer People" would have had to rely, for its effect, simply upon the facts: the grocer would not deliver their supplies, the telephone wires were cut, etc. This is not to say that a good mainstream writer could not have brought all sorts of subtle implications to bear on the situation, while still treating it "realistically." But it would have been quite different in effect; and it would not have had the same meaning.

Only in the ending of the story, as it is handled by Miss Jackson, could you get the particular *kind* of threat one feels. It is not that "reality" turns into "unreality"; rather you feel a shift in the nature of "reality." This is the essential, shaking quality of such an experience as the one involving the old couple in the story; it is also the quality which mainstream techniques are apt to deal with inadequately, or put into incompatible terms. From any naturalistic scene in which the old couple might have been abandoned, you could have imagined a possible escape. From the nonhuman scene specially created by Miss Jackson to show them their fate, from every tree, every rock—a scene evolved specifically to *hold* them—there is no possible escape. What Thomas Hardy needed to make his particular ironic determinism convincing was an element of fantasy in the method of presentation. As it is, it breaks down for most contemporary readers, many of whom are nevertheless intrigued by a similar philosophy as it is handled by Franz Kafka through fantasy in "The Trial" or "The Castle."

Of course "The Summer People" is far from being a typical fantasy story. Many readers would deny that it is fantasy in any way. I particularly chose a story which was very close to a mainstream type of story in an effort to show what the addition of an imaginative level to the realistic one can do in bringing in another dimension of aesthetic effect, and of actual meaning.

Take, by way of contrast, "The Swiss Watch," the John Leimert story which is introduced as a fantasy but which does not make use of the advantages of an imaginative technique, except in the most limited way. Actually, it does not make use of an imaginative *fiction* technique, but what you might call a fanciful essay technique.

The story tells of a man who is given a Swiss watch. With it comes a guarantee which, according to the printed directions, will be voided if the back of the watch is removed. The owner is obsessed with curiosity; finally decides that there can be only one reason for such a prohibition: a colony of small flying ants is running the watch which, if they were not confined, would certainly fly away. So far, so wonderful. The whole length of the story is taken up with an ingenious but (to me) rather dull description of the ants, their labor organization, their sociological and psychological set-up, the problems of their foreman, assumed by the owner of the watch to be an exceptional ant named Andy, in keeping them working and thus keeping the timepiece going.

The reader comes to the end of the story, and suspense—which has almost been absent until now—mounts rapidly. The year is up. The life expectancy of the ants, the owner of the watch is certain, is a few weeks more than a year, which was the fact that determined the length of the watchmakers' guarantee. "The watch ran well and strongly as though all were activity, and warmth, and purpose, and then stopped as though all were nothing. Their time was up, and I felt there was no use winding, no use shaking. . . ."

After a brief interlude, the man removes the back of the watch and finds only wheels and springs.

I said a few pages back that a good story is always "metaphorical." By that I meant that it may be told in one of a number of different ways, or within one of several frames of reference. But once a writer has chosen a certain structure for his story, he must continue on in terms of that structure, or the reader is vastly disappointed. He may go from a relatively narrow perception of his problem to a more complex one—from realism to fantasy; but he cannot go from the more complex perception to a narrower one— from fantasy to the merely logical level. If he does the latter, he cuts the roots of belief away; instead of giving a sounder basis for his story by means of a logical explanation, as he thinks he is doing, he destroys the initial premise of his story—destroying its aesthetic "logic," and leaving the imaginative element therein dangling in air after the manner of fancy.

It seems to me that "The Swiss Watch" is a case (no pun intended) in which the verisimilitude of the story is sacrificed to the arbitrary, two-way value system of much contemporary fiction. For the owner of the watch to have found ants in the works, would have been, from this point of view, to have denied the "real" world—the empirical world which, in this way of looking at things, is the only world. (It does not even take into consideration that there might be a hundred different empirical worlds, depending upon your size, or depending upon how much you know, or upon a dozen other factors.) From *my* point of view, however, it would be just as bad, or worse, to have the man take the back off the watch and find that it was run by a colony of fly-ing ants. The story has not prepared for any such thing, and to find them would somehow be to deny the *real* world; it still would be based on the arbitrary two-way value system. What the story is really saying, to me—and I realize that nothing seems more fac-ile than rewriting the stories of a capable author like John Lei-mert—is that flying ants really do operate a one-year guaranteed watch, so long as it is closed, but that wheels and gears operate it the minute you remove the covering.

At least, this last would catch the feeling which a man *does have* about a watch, or this particular watch anyway, which nei-ther of the other two endings is able to catch. There is a gesture in this direction made by the author as a kind of afterthought. The protagonist leaves the watch open on the table, and later comes back to see "several large black ants . . . hurrying over the end of the table and down the leg. The last of them . . . seemed to be waving his feelers at me in farewell." This senti-mentality does not restore that dimension of the story which has been smashed and rejected. You have taken away my cake, and handed me back a bread crumb. In the first place, "large black ants" are not the kind which used to run the watch. It is like tell-ing me that although the nice ants, the ones I had become fond of, were only a joke, there are some real ants in another part of the country which, I will be glad to know, are going to go to heaven when they die.

Another story by the same author, published in the same maga-zine, *The Atlantic*, precisely achieves the effect and subtlety of meaning which "The Swiss Watch" just misses: it is "John Thomas's Cube" (in the August 1945 issue). This story, having set up the machinery for telling a story in an imaginative way, allows it to carry on in the same vein all the way through. It is consistent. This story concerns a hard metal cube which suddenly turns up in the back yard of a small boy (John Thomas) and which cannot be lifted, pried, nor moved in any direction. It stays fast as long as the boy wants it there, disappears when he is tired of it—all this much to the consternation of the adults involved. The story is meant to illustrate the reaction of a great many average people to a set of circumstances which contradicts their picture of reality. But having chosen an imaginative, and completely appropriate, way of expressing this point fictionally, Mr. Leimert neither destroys the illusion of the science-fiction element nor leaves it in doubt. The results are thoroughly satisfying.

Since beginning this examination of imaginative fiction techniques with their greater freedom in the use of *scene*, we have come rather far afield. What it amounts to, really, is that the imaginative writer is less tied to the literal level in developing his story; he therefore not only can spread out more and have a better time for himself, but he may actually deal with more complex, varied, or subtle material. For example, he is not required at all times to end his story with a flat "yes" or a flat "no"—to say bluntly, *it is real,* or *it is unreal.* He may, if he so desires, end it with a synthesis of the two, or with an equation, or merely a gasp. If he is a science-fiction writer, he can be assured his readers will be able to sustain such a mature ending without collapsing in a heap. This maturity the science-fiction fan does have, although he may have a somewhat childish preference for space ships and ray guns.

This sort of ending further eliminates all that tiresome explanation about the butler, or where Aunt Marian *really* went on Wednesday, all of that factual "tying up of loose ends" which never throws any real light on the story itself.

The struggle of fiction to free itself from plain empirical fact, and from practical logic, has been a long hard one, and one which concerns every writer and reader of imaginative literature. In some periods writers have been condemned for "not telling the truth." Any imaginative presentation of truth was considered immoral, for example, in a strict puritanical society, so that the only fantasy allowed was the moral allegory (e.g., *Pilgrim's Progress*). In contrast to the present tendency to present facts in a fictional way (in the manner of *True Magazine*), writers in the past often enhanced the prestige of their work by presenting fiction as fact, as witness the work of Daniel Defoe.

Without having to go to the lengths of disguising their fictions as "explorations" or "histories," most writers have been careful to rationalize their fantasies, presenting them to the reader carefully labeled as "dream," or "daydream." Chaucer took off for visits to a series of famous characters, historical or mythological, via the dream (*The House of Fame*)—a method at the height of its popularity during his time. (He could also use elements of straight-out fantasy magnificently as in "The Pardoner's Tale.")

And the dream continues, the creaky old technique, and is right there handy to pull *Seven Keys to Baldpate* out of the fire, or *Uncle Harry* in the movie version, or for that matter to "explain" Wonderland, as if it could explain anything about that fabulous place. It is interesting to observe how thoroughly the various screen versions of *Alice* cherish this logical frame. Or to see it slip in, so skilfully that you never even notice, into the conclusion of a modern mainstream classic like "The Snows of Kilimanjaro" (Hemingway). The story, of necessity, becomes fantasy to achieve its ending, although in the ending which comes after the ending we know that this was a dream.

We have discussed that technical (and psychological) freedom which imaginative fiction enjoys: the one which begins by leaving merely the realistic scene, and ends in divorcing the literal level completely.

There is another approach to the freedom which imaginative writing is able to employ, and one which pertains more specifically to science fiction.

Put it this way. At one time people, or many of them, thought they lived in a flat world. It so happened, also, that they painted pictures in two dimensions. Perhaps there was a connection.

Later artists discovered perspective and had a technique for expessing a more complex experience. You might say they were not a part of that world, or at least not fully aware of it, until they had a technique for expressing it.

Taking a further step: we are living in a dynamic world which seems to be moving constantly. Our knowledge of it is also moving constantly. There are no constant dimensions. You might say the term "dimension" has been replaced by something like "dimension-for-the-time-being." There is no single, settled view of the universe or of any separate part of it. And what are artists doing? Sometimes they try to present a subject in motion ("Nude Descending the Stairs," Marcel Duchamp), or a face as seen from several directions at once (the cubists, etc.).

Something comparable is happening in fiction. It seems to me that science fiction today offers us not only greater "freedom for our researches and inquiries," but better techniques for exploring and expressing adequately the kind of dimensions we now have, the kind of world of which we are aware. Although the following analysis is bound to be a gross oversimplification, I believe this technique may have evolved in some such way as this. It involves science fiction's special predilection for a fluid and functional use of time.

To begin with, a story which begins at the beginning with some simple, natural event, and follows it step by step in sequence until its conclusion, is not in any way a poor story (as we said about the poem limited to a simple, natural scene) but we might think of it as a fairly primitive type of story. Such a story might have been told by a Maori warrior around a campfire, recounting the day's events—or by a Norseman or an early Greek. The tale was more or less of an anecdote—a recounting of the actual sequence of events, and probably was not thought of at all as being different from the facts (i.e., "made up") but as a re-enactment

of them. It also would follow a simple, straightforward time sequence. In *Beowulf*, if I am right, there are no flash-backs.

In fact a flash-back would have been as difficult, perhaps, for
the audience of our primitive narrator to accord, as James Joyce
is to some readers today. The flash-back at one point must have
been downright confusing, for as soon as you have it, you have a
second period of time interpolated into the first, and the two must
be juggled in the mind and related. You also have a technique for
handling certain ideas which you could not handle with the simpler narrative technique.

Perhaps in a later culture your storyteller is telling of a battle,
when he suddenly interpolates a memory of a previous battle he
was in. Perhaps in the first one he was young and green and
afraid, but in the present one he was seasoned, and not afraid.
Perhaps the whole meaning of the tale comes from being able to
merge the two sequences, and compare them. A tool for more
extensive storytelling has been found, and a new dimension for
meaning.

Such a story, on a more sophisticated level, is "An Act of Faith"
by Irwin Shaw. The whole point revolves around the comparison
of a present sequence of events, in which the hero finds himself
involved, and another—in this case—almost contemporaneous
sequence, which involves the hero's family. This time, the latter
sequence is revealed not through a flash-back, but through a letter: a time-honored though rusty device for interrupting one set
of happenings to relate another. Because the Irwin Shaw story is
very well done, the formalism of the technique does not matter.

No need to go into the plot of "An Act of Faith" further. The
hero has come to a point of crisis and must make an important
choice; shall he choose on the basis of the kind of friendly world
he seems at that moment to be in, the present—or shall he choose
on the basis of his father's world, revealed in the letter: another
country, another time? Though he makes himself completely
vulnerable in doing so, he chooses the former.

Most mainstream fiction does not go much farther than this

in experimenting with time sequences, employing by and large straightforward narrative with the judicious use of flash-backs, or an occasional mild prediction based on data provided by the main narrative sequence.

What would a further development in these directions mean to fiction—a fluid technique for moving backwards from the present to the past and back again, and also into the future? To say that this would add nothing but confusion is to disregard the value of narrative development so far, as well as of similar developments in the other arts—painting, poetry, and music.

The ability to regard and use time in a flexible manner is one of the science-fiction writer's special interests. And now I am not referring to the content of the story (i.e., the hero "enters" the past, or "enters" the future) but to the method of storytelling. One of the most obvious examples is the Henry Kuttner story, "Happy Ending," which starts at the end, and ends at the beginning of the time sequence of the story. It is an exceptionally satisfying story from the point of view of plot, and by the time you are finished you are convinced its difficult footwork is justified by the results. With this complete reversal of the time sequence, incidentally, there is also a juggling of present time and future time throughout the story.

It is true that the most important work in this field has been contributed by the great experimenters of our time or just preceding us—notably James Joyce. It is also true that many mainstream writers are adapting these techniques to their own uses, or developing other valuable techniques of their own. (Margaret Shedd's "Return to the Beach," for instance, is told through blocks of material which go forward or backward in time interchangeably.)

But only in science fiction have a great many experimental techniques come through on a popular level; everybody is trying to find forms and techniques which are not prefabricated, but suited to the needs of his material. And the word "popular" is not a disparagement. I do not mean that the net results obtained in science fiction are poor, or are "watered down"—although in many cases they are. By popular I mean that there is a great gathering of momentum in imaginative literature of all sorts just now, due to the fact that it is breaking through all at once on a great variety of tastes and levels.

Coming at last to a look at the content involved in mainstream, as opposed to science-fiction stories, I have felt all too often that the effect of the mainstream story—over and over—was one of dejection and defeat. Obviously we live in a very perilous time; it is also a sharply challenging time, in fiction, as in other things. To put it in the crudest possible terms, the mainstream writer too frequently is concerned with saying, in the most sensitive possible terms, of course: "Isn't it terribly sad?" Whereas the science-fiction writer is concerned with saying, sometimes crudely, sometimes jocosely, sometimes with consummate wit and technical skill: "Precisely what are we going to do next?"

A number of the stories in the *Best American Short Stories* anthology for 1951, edited by Martha Foley, have this feeling of futility about them. "Her Breath Upon the Windowpane" by William Goyen is a portrait of a simple and good Negro woman, left in her old age sick and abandoned and asking, "Why?": "Been a Christian all my life. Why, after all this, should I be twisted with a twisted face and no one in the whole wide world to call to me Hattie Hattie . . . This is my reward." Of course this story and the one I shall mention next are very, very well done. But one keeps thinking, ". . . well done, as far as they go."

Roger Angell's "Flight Through the Dark" portrays the fear we all feel in the kind of world we find ourselves in, with the kind of wars and weapons which are turned loose in it: "Agnes is right, he thought. . . . Optimism is insane. . . . I must admit that I have been in the wrong camp. The hardy little army of optimists, still making plans, still raising families, still playing games, is about to lose one member. . . . I am joining the sleepwalkers, the insomniacs, the tremblers, the window-ledge boys, and the movers-to-the-country. It's just a matter of time now, and I might as well be on the right side."

Martha Foley, in her introduction to the volume, makes the point correctly that many of the stories, including this one, are "solved" by a turning again to the simple and wholesome values of everyday life, the immemorial values. Halleck, the protagonist in Mr. Angell's story, returns to his suburban life after his "flight through the dark" from Washington, D.C., to his wife, his family, their inconsequential little plans and preparations, and in these finds temporary stability and a measure of rest. I find this ending more disquieting than heartening.

In the first place, the "accord" of the story, which is no more than a resignation to familiar routine, carries nowhere nearly the conviction or the intensity of the "discord"—the fear, the flight. I believe in the immemorial values as much as anyone, and in the goodness of human life—but it needs to be brilliantly rediscovered, not glanced at nostalgically or desperately clutched.

Too much mainstream fiction is, I feel, a literature of reconciliation, and nothing more. The infatuation with "things as they are," a sort of fact-hypnosis, destroys us (if we let it) as people and as writers. Our only chance is to look at things as they are in the light of more possibilities: from more angles, from more viewpoints: a Martian's, a Magyar's, a magpie's. It doesn't matter whose, so long as we get around a little. From science fiction one gets the feeling that there is so much of interest going on (factual or fictional) that there isn't much time for nostalgia.

Once upon a time there was a kind of story known as "the typical New Yorker story." Anyone who has read the varied fiction in the New Yorker anthologies knows that there is no such thing, really, but a few years ago there was a legend to that effect. This was the frustration story par excellence, in which frustration was not only necessary, but fashionable. In contrast to the "slick" story (which was reputed to uphold the basic beliefs of the majority) and also the "quality" story (which was reputed to overturn them)—this story refrained from either action. Its whole art and criterion of taste was to refrain. In fact one had the feeling that the tensions and characters were set up for a story, which might occur if the reader wished (in the mind only)—or might not occur, because the writer refrained from completing it, as if to complete a story were vulgar. (Plot at that time was a horrid word, and in many quarters still is.) A hypothetical story of this kind is one in which a nice fellow, hopelessly unhappy in his marriage, arrives at a week-end houseparty, meets a good-looking girl (in a wan sort of way) who is nevertheless obviously incapable of love, thinks fleetingly of romance, looks out over the terrace to the swimming pool at the other guests sunning themselves or splashing listlessly, tamps out his cigarette. . . . It was a very well written story, but there it was.

Sometimes I think the despair one feels in mainstream stories is really the frustration of the author—not because he is in such a bad world, but because—as a writer—he is not coping satisfactorily with his medium. He may be trying, perhaps unconsciously, to make his stories turn out like somebody else's stories which he has seen published, a process which often results in his saying a cliché thing, where his original perception was fresh and interesting. Or he may be trying to make his perception of reality fit the arbitrary, black-and-white value system, which oversimplifies and changes his content.

Or in his effort to be responsible—a great weight, which often defeats itself—he may be trying too desperately to deal with "real" problems. His conception of that phenomenon, reality, may be too narrow to begin with, and secondly, he has often forgotten what his role with regard to it is. His only problem as a writer is to act upon the reader in such a way as to cause in him a release of understanding, or delight, or energy—the result of one thing only: the impact upon him of a story which is well told, by whatever means best suits the material. A writer does not solve "real" problems anyway; he makes the readers want to solve them.

Science fiction takes a swaggeringly inquisitive view of the world in which we happen to be. It has no particular awe for things as they merely seem—without specific investigation. As I have tried to suggest, science fiction, like other imaginative writing, has access to techniques adequate for expressing whatever scientific, or merely personal, conclusion one happens to come to—expressing them as fiction.

There may easily be a reaction against the more complex, the more fluid story, and writers may many times go back to telling a simpler and broader story, a story even which could take place in a flat world, or a world that stood still—but are they likely to go backward very convincingly when our whole picture of the physical universe, and of ourselves, is moving in this other direction?

Imaginative Fiction and Creative Imagination

by L. SPRAGUE DE CAMP

L. SPRAGUE DE CAMP *is a versatile person with a versatile pen. Since he wrote his first science fiction in 1937, over a hundred of his stories and articles have appeared in thirty-four scholarly and popular periodicals; ten of his works of fiction and two of his nonfiction have been published in hard covers. As this goes to press, his latest books are:* Lost Continents, *a study of the Atlantis theme; a paper-bound edition of his novel,* Rogue Queen; *a nonfiction collaboration with Willy Ley entitled* Lands Beyond.

Born in New York City in 1907, Mr. de Camp holds a B.S. *in Aeronautical Engineering from California Institute of Technology, and an* M.S. *in engineering and economics from Stevens Institute. He has worked as a surveyor, sawmill hand, draftsman, engineer, patent expert, teacher, editor, and lecturer. During World War II, he was a Lieutenant-Commander in the Navy.*

He works at home—a remade stable and coach house in the Philadelphia suburb of Wallingford, where he lives with his wife and two sons—and turns out some 250,000 words a year, almost all of which he sells. In his spare time, he plays an active part in several professional organizations and learned societies, reads fifty to a hundred books a year, and keeps up with a score of magazines.

THE COMPOSITION of a story is a story in itself, though seldom the kind of tale that a writer can sell. But it is a story nevertheless, and the hero or protagonist of this story is the writer's faculty of creative imagination. What is creative imagination, how does it work, and what are its results?

To begin with, creative imagination is the catalyst, the mysterious agent, of the fiction-writing process. It is spoken of in reverent tones at writers' conferences and in lectures and articles on How to Write. People who claim to have it sometimes use it as an affectation or as an excuse for behavior that might otherwise be deemed merely eccentric. But just what it *is* is a little harder to discover.

To ascertain what it is we might ask: is creative imagination restricted to writers? No; artists of all sorts, inventors, scientists, many craftsmen, promoters, advertisers, and even some political leaders have it: anybody, that is, who gives the world something new and different.

Can one write fiction without it? Sometimes, but the result is likely to be reviewed with such cold-potato phrases as "competent journalism." Is creative imagination a reliable or predictable human attribute like brown eyes? No; it crops up in the unlikeliest social settings; it disappears or goes on strike in the middle of a writer's career—perhaps to return, perhaps not. And when it becomes exhausted, as it usually does if the writer lives long enough, the writer finds himself willy-nilly writing the same story over and over.

And if creative imagination is important to the writer of conventional fiction, it is *a fortiori* essential to the author of imagina-

Imaginative Fiction and Creative Imagination

tive fiction—a term that includes both science fiction and fantasy.[1]

For whatever such a writer can do, he can hardly just report things as they are, and claim to have an imaginative story. Of course an unimaginative writer can plagiarize the works of his colleagues, but such conduct is no more approved in this field than in any other branch of fiction. And even the lowest-paying magazines of the genre take such imitative pieces only when they have to, preferring products of an able imagination when they can get them.

A few years ago my eminent colleague Bernard De Voto, in his admirable book *The World of Fiction,* asserted that the absolute essential for successful fiction-writing was neither profound erudition, nor painstaking research, nor warm human sympathy, nor technical writing skill, useful though all these qualities be. It was rather the ability to visualize one's characters, setting, and events so vividly and intensely that the reader was forced, whether he wished to or not, to share in this act of imagination. This quality is the one that I am discussing, and the fact that some have it and others do not explains why some writers otherwise not very skilled at their trade nevertheless attract a large or lasting readership.

How does creative imagination work in practice? Well, the writer's mind may be considered the focal point of a process in which data are taken from the real world as revealed by the senses

[1] In my usage, "imaginative fiction" includes the definite group of stories in the fiction of the modern Western world that are nonrealistic, imaginative, based upon assumptions contrary to everyday experience, often highly fanciful and often laid in settings remote in time and space from those of everyday life. Imaginative fiction can in turn be subdivided into "fantasy," comprising stories based upon supernatural assumptions [spirits, magic, life after death, et cetera] and "science fiction," based upon scientific or pseudo-scientific assumptions [space-travel, time-travel, extraterrestrial life, telepathy, robots, et cetera]. Some stories fall between the two sub-classes or combine attributes of both, and the genre as a whole shades off into historical fiction, satires, utopias, and so on. Other definitions have been proposed for these terms, but I think that my usage reflects the facts of the case as well as any.

and recombined into an imaginary narrative. (Please, let us assume that the world of the senses *is* the real world. If you believe that in addition to sensory data the mind also draws upon divine inspiration, universal consciousness, racial memory, or some other suppositious non-sensory factor, we shall have to agree to disagree.)

For creative imagination, whether it creates a story, a poem, a piece of music, a new gadget, a business enterprise, a scientific hypothesis, or a political party, does not really create anything out of nothing in the sense in which the Biblical Yahweh created heaven and earth. All that it does is to recombine elements that it has received through the senses into new and—it hopes—meaningful or useful combinations.

Actually, creative imagination seems to be nothing but the faculty of free association, highly developed. You may once have undergone a free-association test at the hands of a psychologist, who fired words at you while you responded with the first words that popped into your head. This test effects a rough classification of you, among other things, as an extravert or an introvert. If the former you tend to make conventional, obvious responses, but far-fetched, original, or unusual ones if the latter. So if an extravert hears "king" he will probably come back with "queen" or "ruler," whereas the introvert may come out with something like "lion" or "republic."

Now the person who possesses creative imagination is essentially one whose mind can, for every term or concept, quickly conjure up a large number and variety of associated terms, experimentally join them in a variety of possible combinations, and pick from these combinations those most pregnant with possibilities for the particular use that the thinker has in view. And it makes little difference to the final result whether the process takes place on the conscious or the unconscious level; whether the person deliberately joins his elements and compares the resulting combinations, or whether the finished optimum combination pops from the unconscious to the conscious level without the thinker's knowing where it came from. Usually both levels are involved at the same time, the unconscious more than the conscious.[2]

Of course, before a thinker can conjure up associations he has to have associations to conjure up—a storehouse of memories which he can use as a source for his combinations. If he is very young or has led a poor, circumscribed, uneventful life and has read little, his imagination will have little to build upon and his combinations will seem trite and feeble.

In fact, one of the most persistent handicaps of writers otherwise adequately equipped with imagination, a command of English, and a typewriter, is that they simply do not know enough. I do not mean grammar and punctuation (despite the singular multitude of writers and editors who see no flaw in the sentence, "He looked like he was dead,"—and not as a piece of dialect dialogue either). They do not know enough about their fellow man and the universe in which he lives to avoid glaring mistakes of fact and logic. One writer puts dinosaurs, which were air-breathing reptiles, at the bottom of the ocean. Another has his hero swing a fifty-pound sword, a feat beyond the thews even of Conan the Cimmerian. A third refers to an Oriental character named ibn-Hasan as "Ibn," which is like calling a man named Johnson, "Son."

Do I hear someone say that nobody but a pedant cares for such petty details, least of all the average reader? Well, Someone is mistaken, because even if the reader does not know about the weight of swords and the grammar of Arabic, such a lapse is likely to give him an uneasy feeling that something, he knows not what, is wrong. And pop! goes the illusion that the writer has been trying so hard to build up.

Care in details is particularly important in a story of imaginative fiction, because the reader's suspension of disbelief is under a greater strain to begin with in consequence of his having been

[2] This is not a new theory. It is merely associationist psychology, which goes back long before Freud. If you don't hear much about it today, the reason is not that it has been disproved but that it has become axiomatic and is taken for granted.

hauled from his own little world of dear familiarities to Mars, Atlantis, the millionth century, a parallel space-time continuum, or a divergent time-track. Therefore the least fallacy or inconsistency will cause it to snap like an over-taut rubber band.

But to return to creative imagination: in speaking of the young writer's lack of sources to draw upon, we touch the incongruous fact that most people's imaginative powers seem to reach a maximum around the time they attain their legal majority and thereafter slowly decline, whereas experience continues throughout life. Hence the common phenomenon of a writer who starts out with notably original ideas crudely expressed, and as he accumulates experience and acquires technique his writing becomes smoother and clearer but his ideas become progressively less original and more repetitious.

The things for us to consider in connection with creative imagination are, then, first the writer's sources and second what he does with them up to the point where he has a good approximation of a story either in his head or on paper. What he does with the story after that—polishing, inserting a wisecrack here and a bit of alliteration there, cutting and rewriting, typing a final draft, mailing it to editors and arguing over subsidiary rights—belongs in another department.

The writer's sources may (if we rule out divine inspiration and the like) be lumped together as "experience." And experience may in turn be classed as either personal or vicarious, the latter being what the writer has been told or has read or has seen on a motion-picture screen.

Personal experience has the virtue of being the more vivid and authentic of the two. There is no preparation for describing a battle or a typhoon or a lion hunt or a love affair that surpasses having experienced one. But personal experience has the disadvantage that unless one is a phenomenon like Winston Spencer Churchill it takes a lifetime to accumulate enough of it to make a good book, which leaves no time for learning to write. Hence the explorers, adventurers, intelligence agents, and such people who have fascinating stories to tell but who become finger-tied in front of a typewriter. Hence the ancient and more or less honorable trade of ghost-writer.

Now every piece of fiction ever written can be broken down into bits of the writer's experience, provided that we know enough about the writer. Even such imaginative achievements as Samuel Taylor Coleridge's "Kubla Khan" and "The Ancient Mariner" have been shown by John Livingston Lowes, in his erudite and fascinating piece of literary detective-work *The Road to Xanadu,* to have been derived from a number of old travel books that Coleridge had read, especially the works of Samuel Purchas, an early seventeenth-century English compiler of tales of exploration. Particular phrases used by Coleridge were traced down to a variety of sources: thus "Alph, the sacred river," comes from the Alpheios River in western Greece, about which many classical authors wrongly thought that it disappeared underground, flowed under the Adriatic through a tunnel, and reappeared as the spring Arethusa in Sicily. "His flashing eyes, his floating hair" is from a description in James Bruce's *Travels to Discover the Source of the Nile* of King Tecla Hainamout of Abyssinia (Ethiopia).

If we had equally good information on the reading of all the other imaginative writers, from Plato to Lovecraft, no doubt an equally thorough exegesis could be made in all cases. In fact, I have elsewhere[3] undertaken this very task for Plato's Atlantis story. While in Plato's case we are admittedly handicapped by the loss of nineteen-twentieths of the total classical literature, it can still be shown with a good degree of probability that Plato derived some of his ideas for this romance from Herodotus, some from Thucydides, some from Babylonian astrological theory, and so on.

In further comparing personal with vicarious experience as the writer's ultimate source, vicarious experience is even more im-

[3] In my *Lost Continents* (Prime Press) and Willy Ley's and my *Lands Beyond* (Rinehart & Company).

portant in the case of imaginative literature than in that of realistic fiction. The reason is that nobody can yet ship as a hand on a space ship to acquire the necessary first-hand knowledge, or travel into the future which the writer purports to describe. While I know of no survey of the reading habits of writers of imaginative fiction (a promising subject for one of the science-fiction fan organizations) I should guess, judging from the allusions that appear in the stories, that most of them are heavy readers. An ill-read science-fiction writer is at a great disadvantage unless he has some unusual compensating asset such as outstanding genius or an editor who will act as a silent collaborator.

Of course, any real experience that the writer has had he can and probably will use sooner or later. Thus Theodore Sturgeon used his one-time employment on earth-moving machinery in his "Killdozer." Malcolm Jameson exploited his naval experience in a number of stories. Professor Homer Nearing, Jr., employs his academic background in his hilarious tales of Professors Ransom and MacTate. And having worked in a sawmill, a correspondence school, a trade-journal publishing company, and an engineering laboratory, I have succeeded in insinuating all four backgrounds into my own stories. Unfortunately we do not live long enough to experience in person all the occupations and environments that we may wish to use in stories, and therefore have to fall back upon what we have heard or read.

In assembling his hypothetical future setting, the writer brings together elements from a variety of present-day sources. Suppose he wishes to describe life on a space ship. Though there are no space ships yet, the writer can work up a plausible illusion of one by using everything he knows about high-altitude rockets and astronautics as set forth in the works of Willy Ley and Arthur C. Clarke. For an idea of how passengers will pass their time—well, the present-day transoceanic liner seems to offer a plausible analogy, so he combines his rocket knowledge with what he has experienced or read about contemporary water ships. And the better a science-fiction writer he is the more convincing this synthesis will be.

If he is a good science-fictioneer, he takes into account the fact that, while space travel may have some elements in common with that of a liner, it will also differ from it profoundly in other respects. An analogy closer than the steamship, from the point of view of life on board, would perhaps be the submarine. If the writer is not so good he simply tosses the *Queen Elizabeth* out into space with her funnels converted into rocket tubes, and at least for the more sophisticated reader, away goes the illusion again.

In former times the vicarious experience of the writer of imaginative fiction consisted mainly of traditional myths and legends on one hand and extant scientific literature on the other. In Classical times scientific knowledge was slight, and imaginative writers like Plato, Loukianos, and Lucius Apuleius paid little attention to what there was.

Hence most of the earlier efforts in imaginative fiction, such as the Egyptian story of Setnau Khaemuast and Neferkaptah's ghost, Apuleius's *Golden Ass,* and the medieval romances of Geoffrey of Monmouth, Robert de Boron, and Heinrich von Veldeck would be classed as fantasies in the strict or supernatural sense. This type of literature has remained a fairly constant component of fiction from the earliest times to the present. Nowadays, while it still claims a modest but faithful readership, fantasy has been overshadowed by the enormous growth of its sister genre, science fiction, in the last century, ever since the Industrial Revolution has made technological change a constant, obvious, and inescapable feature of daily life.

The scientific bent of Western civilization, however, appeared as early as the Middle Ages and soon began to influence imaginative fiction. Thus in Sir Francis Bacon's utopian romance *The New Atlantis,* the author's Bensalemites are credited with what were then futuristic or visionary scientific achievements such as submarines and air conditioning.

The earlier writers, in drawing upon the science of their times, naturally drew upon its errors as well as its verities. Hence Loukianos's space travelers are wafted to the moon without space suits and without suffering from lack of air. Therefore if the science of a given time is badly mistaken in some regard, the imaginative fiction will be also. If our science fiction seems more plausible than that of our grandparents it is not that we are cleverer, but that our science has both learned and unlearned a lot of things since their time.

Another source used by writers of imaginative fiction is the work of their predecessors. This influence factor goes back to some of the earliest works in the genre. Thus Francis Bacon's *New Atlantis* is overtly inspired by Plato's original Atlantean romance.

In more recent times H. P. Lovecraft was strongly influenced by Poe and in turn influenced August Derleth. Robert E. Howard imitated Talbot Mundy and Harold Lamb. Clark Ashton Smith has been influenced by Lord Dunsany, and Ray Bradbury seems to have been affected by Hemingway and Steinbeck. A poll of candid writers would reveal a whole network of threads of influence. I confess to having been influenced by many writers, among them Burroughs, Dunsany, Eddison, Thorne Smith, and Wodehouse.

With the great growth of the imaginative genre in recent decades, this type of influence has probably increased among writers. In time this imitative factor may menace the entire genre by giving a feedback effect, causing the writers to work and rework each theme until they are merely threshing old straw. Other literary forms once dominant—the essay, the philosophical dialogue, and the long narrative poem—have gone down to virtual extinction, and the detective story seems now to be on the decline because the soil of experience on which it grows has been worked to death. Hence it is not incredible that imaginative fiction might some day suffer the same debacle.

Certainly one danger threatening science fiction is that the progress of science itself answers so many questions raised by science fiction, thereby removing one story idea after another from the domain of the speculative fictioneer. Fifty years ago airplanes were science fiction, and who knows what else may have been reduced to fact fifty years hence? Astronomical knowledge of Mars and Venus is already cramping the style of the storyteller, even before these planets have been visited, by revealing them as places where men could live only if bundled up in special protective equipment, unsuitable both for rescuing a beautiful princess from the nameless horror to which she is about to be sacrificed by a wicked high priest, and for making love to her afterwards. In fact, the princess herself gets more implausible all the time.

But for the present the genre of imaginative fiction, or to be more exact its science-fictional wing, is still expanding. And if the worse comes to the worst the writer can always remove his setting to other galaxies, which men seem unlikely ever to reach in fact, or fall back upon those equally unattainable fictional standbys, time travel and the parallel universe. Or one can confine oneself to supernatural fantasy which, being based upon assumptions admittedly contrary to fact, is safe from scientific assault.

So much for the sources of writers in general and of writers of imaginative fiction in particular. Let us now consider the actual creative process by which these sources are assembled into new combinations and beaten into new forms.

The gestative process works differently with different writers. The creator of Captain Hornblower recently pointed out that the adventure-story writer conceives an event or a train of events and then devises a character to fit them, whereas the nonadventure-story writer is apt to think up his character first and then let the character do what a person having that assumed personality would naturally do. As most stories of imaginative fiction belong in the adventure category, I suppose that most writers of science fiction use the former approach. The result is that most stories in the genre do not fall into that class of character-centered stories that many highly regarded literary critics, such as Orville Prescott of the *New York Times,* appear to regard as by far the worthiest type of fiction.

My own opinion is that, important though character is in stories and significant though character-centered stories be, the question of character is sometimes a wee bit overdone. A good character story can be extremely absorbing, but so can a good idea-centered or action-centered or setting-centered story. Moreover, when a story of character is badly written it can be dreadfully dull—at least as tedious as a bad story of one of the other types.

You may if you like conclude that is merely an expression of personal prejudice, and that if I could write better character stories myself I should esteem fiction of that type more highly. I shan't mind, because I think that most literary criticism, including my own, is largely subjective anyhow.

Then how does a writer compose his stories? Naturally I know my own system better than any other. I am likely to conceive a story first in the form of a problem: What would happen *if* . . . ? Or what would you do *if* you were . . . ?

Or I may conceive a story first in terms of its setting, as with *Divide and Rule* and the stories of the Viagens Interplanetarias, and then make up events and characters to go with it. While I think up plenty of characters—usually combining attributes of different people whom I have known—rarely do they themselves form the basis for a story. (The only one whom I can think of who did was Johnny Black, my erudite bear.) Rather they sit around in my idea file until a story comes along in which they can play an appropriate part. This file, I may add, is a real literal collection of typed sheets, for without it I should never be able to remember my good story ideas when I wanted them.

Other writers use different systems, but they all come down to a process of experimentally combining ideas until one combination clicks. As the process takes place mostly on the unconscious level, it cannot be closely controlled. All that the writer can do is to set favorable conditions for his unconscious to work and hope that it will do so. Then after he has sweated for days, consciously trying out hopeless-seeming combinations, the right combination may suddenly leap into his conscious mind, leaving him to wonder why he was so stupid as not to see such an obvious solution sooner.

With most writers this process requires a good deal of undisturbed time—many hours at a stretch without distractions. I have known writers who could write in odd moments, or who could work in the midst of a roaring party, but I do not think that they are typical.

A few years ago a colleague of mine who had been successful as a nonfiction writer, but who had also sold a little science fiction, got financially pinched—a condition characteristic of all writers some of the time and some writers all of the time—and asked my advice. I urged him to try more fiction. He had, he said, but it did no good; no ideas. How long did he try? Oh, a couple of hours each time.

I explained that it usually took me from one to two weeks to conceive and plot a short story, and from one to two and a half months to do the same for a novel. And I should, I suppose, be considered one of the more voluminous producers in the imaginative field, even if not in a class with Will Jenkins ("Murray Leinster") or with L. Ron Hubbard in his pre-Dianetic days.

The leisurely and capricious working habits of the creative imagination are a standard source of irritation to the wives of fiction-writers. For every so often the writer appears to go into a kind of trance. He sits around all day with a vacuous expression on his face and, though he seems to be doing absolutely nothing, he insists that he is working hard and must on no account be interrupted, for instance to help with the housework.

Well, what is the writer doing during this yogic trance to convert his experiences into story material? Not simply combining them at random as in an idle reverie; not if he wishes to lay a saleable story.

No, the imaginative process must, for fictional purposes, be disciplined to serve certain ends. And essentially the writer is trying to do three things: to entertain the reader, to express himself and his feelings, and to convey some idea or opinion.

Each of these objectives will of course vary according to the kind of experience that the writer is drawing upon, the techniques of entertaining that he favors, the personality that he is expressing, and the ideas that he is trying to put across. Nevertheless, the proportions in which these three ingredients are mixed will to some extent determine the type of story that results.

For instance, in Burroughs, Anderson, Kuttner, and Leinster the pure-entertainment element usually predominates. In Williamson, Bradbury, Sturgeon, Kornbluth, and Fowler Wright we get a strong flavor of the author's personality, wherefore we might call their tales "self-expression stories." And in Heinlein, Asimov, Piper, and Stapledon the element of deliberate extrapolation, of serious cerebration, is strong.

All these elements are no doubt to be found in all stories, and the proportions vary between tales by a given author. Thus while Leiber's Gray Mouser fantasies are the purest kind of straight-entertainment stories, his recent "Coming Attraction" and "Nice Girl with Five Husbands" are straight cerebral extrapolation without even a pretense of a plot.

Most authors, however, do tend to stress one element more than the others. An author who overstresses any one of them may get into trouble on that score. Thus a pure-entertainment story with neither ideological content nor personal feeling may be dismissed as a "contrived" or "formula" story. A story that is all self-expression may be so subjective as to become unintelligible, while one that is all information or opinion will be rejected by a reader looking for fictional escape as an inadequately disguised article.

Now to consider each of these three fictional elements in detail.

Firstly, the author is trying to amuse, intrigue, beguile, or thrill the reader. There are well-understood ways of doing this which you can find in books on how to write: by the "narrative hook" or "shooting the sheriff on the first page"; by cracking jokes and putting the characters through pratfalls; by providing a sympathetic protagonist for the reader to identify himself with; by appealing to pity, terror, indignation, patriotism, and other sentiments.

The appeal of humor, pathos, suspense, or horror is the same in imaginative fiction as elsewhere, but it works on different materials. Instead of feeling sorry for a downtrodden man, one pities a downtrodden robot or Martian. Instead of laughing at a man's public loss of his clothes, one laughs at his embarrassment upon arriving clad in an era where clothes are deemed indecent. And instead of panting on the trail of a Communist spy, one pants on the track of a Procyonian spy who is even more formidable because he can change himself into a bridge lamp or a bottle of catsup.

But imaginative fiction does differ in another respect from conventional fiction. In imaginative fiction, to a much greater degree than in other fiction, the writer appeals to the reader by means of the glamor of the exotic.

This may mean setting the story in the distant past, or in the future, or in other worlds. The writer may jog the reader's emotions by introducing the startling incongruity of an exotic element, such as people from another era or planet, into an otherwise humdrum realistic contemporary environment. Or he may cut loose from the here and now to transpor. the reader to times and places of limitless remoteness.

Surmising that to the reader the primitive, the ancient, or the medieval have glamor (because the reader was once a Boy Scout or imagined himself as d'Artagnan), the writer drags the reader into an environment where men fight with swords or stone axes. Or he appeals to the reader's omnipotence-wish by providing his protagonist with a ray gun or other invincible weapon, or enables him to blow up whole galaxies, or to move faster than light, or to travel in time or through extraspatial "dimensions."

Sometimes the writer proffers archaic and futuristic weapons and other trappings at the same time, as Burroughs did in his zestful if juvenile tales of Mars and Venus. The writer hopes that the reader's suspension of disbelief will not snap at the absurdity of fooling around with swords when one can drill one's foe with deadly Z-rays. (As readers of my stories know, I like a bit of swordplay too, but I always try to give it a rational basis.)

This persistence of antique elements in imaginative fiction merits a closer look. It may seem a little odd that a genre so largely devoted to the future should exploit such archaisms as pregunpowder weapons, hereditary monarchy, and all-powerful hierarchical religious cults.

There are two answers to this. One is that, while change is constant in human affairs, it takes place neither at uniform speed throughout all the elements of human culture, nor in a straight line in an easily discerned direction.

For instance, in our modern scientific world a majority of the earth's population still lives on a preindustrial or even a preliterate level. If you wish badly enough to have your brains beaten out with a stone ax you can arrange to do so by visiting the interior of New Guinea. And elsewhere such archaisms as hereditary monarchy not only survive but flourish. Moreover even in a highly scientific and industrialized element of Western culture such as warfare, the old survives beside the new. Thus the superscientific second world war with its long-range rockets and atomic bombs saw the use of such "obsolete" military expedients as swords, bows, horse cavalry, sailing ships, and war elephants.

Furthermore, instead of civilization's simply getting better and better in every way century by century, as our grandparents naively thought it might, a respectable school of philosophers from Plato to Spengler holds that civilization follows a cyclical tendency, rising from barbarism, passing through recognizable stages of growth, maturation, and decay, and finally sinking back into barbarism. The theory may or may not be right, but it is certainly more plausible than many that have been taken as assumptions for imaginative fiction.

It is therefore legitimate for writers about the future to assume that one or another former condition or institution may come again. After all, twenty-five years ago Western men were smugly congratulating themselves on having forever banished slavery and judicial torture from all but the most backward parts of the world. Now we know better.

The second explanation of the use of archaisms in imaginative fiction lies in the subtle appeal of such antiquities to the reader. One of the most persistent elements of the human mental outlook is the attraction or glamor of old times. Most cultures have had a myth of a heroic age, when mankind was young and all men were virile, all women beautiful, and all problems simple. The modern Western belief that ancient times were mostly hard, cruel, dreary, and unsanitary, while probably closer to the facts than the heroic-age concept, is a relatively new one. It is the obverse of the modern idea that perfection is to be sought, if anywhere, in the future as the result of scientific progress.

This complementary pair of ideas, of the wretchedness of the past and the possible glory of the future, arose during the last century and a half as the result of the Industrial Revolution on one hand and of the discoveries of anthropology and archeology about the actual ancestry and development of mankind on the other. Nevertheless, the older if less defensible concept of the heroic age persists as a sort of mental substratum. Hence the perennial popularity of low-cut historical novels, and hence the persistent use of antique elements by writers of imaginative fiction.

Thus many writers of imaginative fiction, including the present one, have tried their hands at stories of prehistoric life—say of the struggle between the Neanderthal and Cro-Magnon races for possession of postglacial Europe. These tales are not exactly historical fiction, because they deal with an era from which no historical facts survive; nor are they exactly science fiction, because they deal with a real human setting, and one without science unless the writer chooses to bring in some elementary discovery like that of fire. They are, however, usually classed as science fiction, as are another large group of stories: the lost-race adventure stories, wherein a nation of ancient Greeks, Egyptians, Norsemen, Aztecs, or Atlanteans is discovered still flourishing in some unexplored region. The stories of this last class, though popular in their day, are becoming rarer because the earth's surface has now been almost completely explored, so that it has become almost impossible to find a plausible site for such survivals. The same restriction applies to stories of the *Lost World* type, wherein an explorer finds an enclave swarming with leftover dinosaurs or ape-men.

Or the writer may boldly rewrite ancient history and prehistory to suit himself, or compose a story based upon ancient or primitive myths. Back in 1940 Fletcher Pratt and I with our *Roaring Trumpet* started a whole cycle of fantasies based upon Norse mythology. (Coincidentally, Lester Del Rey wrote one based upon the same theme at the same time, but, unfortunately for Lester, Pratt and I got our manuscript in to the editor first.) A couple of years ago there was a veritable plague of stories wherein the two leading characters turn out in the last paragraph to be Adam and Eve. And over fifty books, not to mention innumerable magazine stories, have been based upon Plato's tale of the lost Atlantis—the earliest real science-fiction story known to us.

To go back to some fictional prehistoric civilization like that of Atlantis or Lemuria gives the writer considerable advantage. If he wishes to write a fantasy, his spirits and spells seem more plausible in such a setting than in a familiar one. On the other hand if the writer intends to compose a science-fiction story he can assume that these ancients had a lost science, thus plausibly combining the appeal of supergadgetry with the glamor of antiquity.

Moreover, by going back to such an imaginary setting he protects himself against the criticism of informed readers who might otherwise catch him in technical errors. He need not fear what once happened to me. When my *Lest Darkness Fall* (laid in sixth-century Rome) appeared, a professor wrote me a kind letter of appreciation—which, however, pointed out that in one place a character speaking a phrase in the Gothic language used the nominative case where he should have used the vocative!

As an illustration, a young Texan writer named Robert E. Howard once wrote a fantasy called "The House of Arabu," eventually published in *Avon Fantasy Reader* under the wretched title of "The Witch from Hell's Kitchen." The story was laid in ancient Sumeria, and the hero was an Achaean mercenary soldier, a brawny barbarian of the type that Howard liked to imagine himself as being. The story failed to sell, at least until long after Howard's early suicide, but from its style and concepts Howard later developed his popular Conan series. This time, however, he threw the setting back into the Third Interglacial Period or thereabouts, taking elements from the whole ancient and medieval world and from Egyptian, Greek, Irish, Norse, and other mythologies to construct his gorgeously vivid if riotously anachronistic post-Atlantean but prehistoric Hyborian Age. Thus he at once avoided archeological pitfalls on one hand and gave himself ample elbow-room in which to play with eras and empires on the other.

Besides trying simply to entertain the reader, the writer is also expressing himself: his own sentiments, prejudices, personality, attitudes, desires, fears, and complexes. He *may* entertain the reader in so doing because the reader harbors similar mental elements and the writer strikes a responsive chord. If he strikes it in enough readers he may become known as a "great" writer.

Subjectivism is however a dangerous form of self-indulgence for a writer, as his own thoughts may prove less fascinating to others than to him, and if he gets into the habit he may find himself writing the same story over and over. Moreover, when the writer intrudes himself and his opinions (as opposed to the opinions of his characters) upon the stage of his story, as Victorian writers did openly with their "dear reader" asides, he risks showing up his characters as the puppets they are and the whole tale as the sham it is by destroying the reader's illusion.

On the other hand, the writer cannot help revealing himself to some degree even when he tries to be objective. For he expresses not only his conscious ideas but also his unconscious ones, based largely upon forgotten events of his early childhood.

Hence the curious recurrence of certain themes and characters in the work of many writers: the superman with the godlike arsenal of transcendental powers and extrasensory senses (van Vogt); the lonely leader, the natural aristocrat who has to boot the unappreciative clods around for their own good (Hubbard); the immature, irresponsible, impulsive adult-infantilist (Bradbury); the pitiful, pain-wracked old idealist who, despite every conceivable disaster, doggedly claws his way from crisis to crisis (Williamson); and so on.

Fortunately not all writers are like their characters. Nobody has seen a van Vogtean hyperman (I hope), and by all accounts Bradbury is a sober and responsible citizen, quite unlike the sentimental hoodlums whom he writes about.

Still, the fictional characters do represent a persistent complex of ideas or sentiments somewhere in the writer's mind: something that the writer is, or was, or would like to be, or is afraid of being. And that is one reason why these characters often appeal to readers, since the readers, too, carry around such complexes. We all have an infantile Bradburyan giggling down in our unconscious. Most of us have suppressed the creature. If we had not, the human race would all still be chasing each other through the woods with clubs and subsisting on a meager diet of berries and beetle-grubs. But this child-mind is still there, waiting for sufficient shock or strain or fatigue to weaken our adult grip on ourselves so that it can seize the helm and commit us to some frightful foolishness. Hence the violent if vaguely repellant emotional impact of Bradbury's stories.

Imaginative Fiction and Creative Imagination

The persistent fictional character need not even be a part of the writer. It may be some other person who at an impressionable age made a strong impression upon the writer for good or ill. This is perhaps the explanation of the slimy politicians and benighted bureaucrats on whom Leinster has long been waging a fictional war to the knife; or Bradbury's crass, brutal Philistines who fanatically strive to destroy everything beautiful and imaginative in the world; or Brackett's snarling, suspicious misanthropes; or the stupid, tyrannical, arrogant military officers of too many writers to list.

These last, of course, have become stock villains in war fiction of all kinds, imaginative or realistic; every writer who ever writhed under his father's dictation seems to find the "officer caste" a convenient scapegoat for his long-suppressed resentments. The reason does not seem to be that all officers are really such vile caricatures of humanity. From my own firsthand observations I should say that the percentage of bastards is no higher in military life than elsewhere. It only seems higher sometimes because when one of the bastards gets into a position of authority he can cause more grief to those under him than he could get away with in civilian life.

But I suspect that the real reason that so many writers compose diatribes against the armed services is that most writers belong to the individualistic, introverted, cerebrotonic, schizoid-intellectual type to begin with. And such a person finds military life with its lack of privacy, enforced uniformity, arbitrary rules, stultifying monotony, physical hardships, and other well-known conditions much harder to bear than does the average man. Some of the latter even *like* it.

Finally, the writer is trying to convey an idea to the reader. In the majority of science-fiction stories, the story is laid in the future, and the idea is what the writer thinks or hopes or fears that the future may bring forth.

The writer may be merely trying to give an objective opinion, based upon rational extrapolation from known facts, of how things will be in the next century, or how they might be on some other planet, given certain assumptions. During the last century the straight-information element predominated in stories to a sometimes intolerable degree. Thus Jules Verne provided his stories with an indefatigable lecturer and an inexhaustible listener so that the former could expound the science of the time to the latter a whole chapter at a stretch. Nowadays, one must be more subtle and work in one's information in the guise of action or casual snatches of speech; no Platonic lecture dialogues.

Or the writer may be trying to sway the reader to some opinion which he wishes him to adopt: for instance that Communism is worse than war and so should be fought, or conversely that it is preferable to war and should therefore be surrendered to. The writer may work on the reader by showing him the utopian world that will result from adopting the writer's program, or by describing horrors that will ensue if certain contemporary tendencies are not stopped. Perhaps this kind of proselytization should be classed as self-expression, as people's opinions are notoriously much more the result of emotional attitudes and subconscious factors, and much less the fruit of logical ratiocination, than they would like others to think.

Here the danger of lecturing the reader is even greater than in the case of the writer who is presenting facts. H. G. Wells ruined some otherwise good stories as fiction by taking time out for editorializing. The really clever writer appears to have no personal opinions at all; he is merely drawing inescapable inferences from well-established facts. If he lets himself go on some pet enthusiasm or antipathy he ceases to be a fiction writer and becomes a tractarian, and the reader, who in this noisy age is conditioned against homiletics, quickly gets bored and shuts the book. Furthermore, a writer who rides his pet passion on to the pages of his story is indulging in the same sort of subjectivism warned against above.

But let us consider the writers of imaginative fiction who have seriously tried to peer into the future, as this aspect of imaginative fiction is one of those that is most widely discussed. How successful has creative imagination been in revealing things to come?

No doubt you have heard of some of the prophets' successes. Both the Bacons, Roger and Francis, foresaw inventions that later came into use. Wasn't a patent denied on a periscope because Verne had accurately described one in *Twenty Thousand Leagues?* And there was that atomic-bomb story in *Astounding* that had the F.B.I. in a stew. . . .

However, when we look at the whole field of prophetic fiction the impression is somewhat different. It does little good to consider prophecies of the twenty-first and subsequent centuries, because that time has not yet arrived. But during the second half of the nineteenth century—or more accurately from 1880 to 1910 —prophetic stories began to appear in quantity for the first time, and many of them dealt with things as the writers thought they would be in the later twentieth century—that is, about now. In other words we can, for the first time in human history, see ourselves as our ancestors foresaw us. And what did they see?

A young man from a Swiss colony in Africa, Gabriel Weltstein, comes to New York to arrange for the sale of his colony's wool. The big city awes him: the glass-roofed streets, lit by magnetic lights and jammed with pedestrians; the municipal heating system which gets hot water from the depths of the earth; the pneumatic-tube network by which a subscriber can communicate almost instantly with any other in the city; the suicide houses where people are given a painless end. Overhead weave elevated railways and airlines. The latter are of two kinds: inverted monorail cars hung from a cable which is in turn suspended from captive balloons, and great electrically powered dirigible airships with sails for auxiliary power and parachute lifeboats.

When Gabriel sits down in a restaurant he sees a "mirror" like a television screen on which appears the menu. After making his choice he presses numbered buttons below the screen, and presently the table opens and his meal rises from below. When he presses another button a facsimile of the day's newspaper appears on the screen. The restaurant is cool even in a New York summer, because a balloon is tethered overhead by means of a double canvas tube through which hot air is evacuated from the restaurant to the stratosphere while cold air is sucked down from the heights to replace it.

At last comes the day when Gabriel snatches a beggar from under the hooves of the coach horses of one of the wicked world-ruling oligarchy of bankers. The beggar turns out to be a leader of the oppressed masses, and Gabriel is launched upon his adventures.

Such is the New York of the present time as described sixty years ago by Ignatius Donnelly in his prophetic novel *Caesar's Column,* which sold over a million copies.

The enthusiastic but uncritical Ignatius (1831-1901) is a significant figure in the history of imaginative fiction, for besides writing three novels in the genre he also popularized several pseudo-scientific theories which have been used in fiction. In *Atlantis: The Antediluvian World,* which ran through fifty editions and is still in print, he converted Plato's sunken continent from a speculation of scholars to a popular cult. In *Ragnarok* he revived the discredited theory of Count Carli and other eighteenth-century catastrophists that the earth had once been widely devastated by a collision with a comet, an idea more recently revived again by Zschaetzsch and Velikovsky. And in *The Great Cryptogram* he popularized the eccentric speculation that Sir Francis Bacon wrote the plays of William Shakespeare. He also led an active political career, becoming lieutenant-governor of Minnesota at twenty-eight, congressman, state senator, and one of the founders of the Populist Party.

Donnelly's three novels, *Caesar's Column, Dr. Huguet,* and *The Golden Bottle,* appeared in the early 1890's. The first deals with the uprising of the masses against a Jewish oligarchy. (Later Donnelly seems to have outgrown his anti-Jewish animus.) But

142

the masses have become so degraded by their servitude that they kill off their own more enlightened leaders, and the world sinks into barbarism. *Dr. Huguet* deals with the Negro problem by the familiar device of transposing souls. To make his hero appreciate the plight of the American Negro, Donnelly puts his soul into the body of one. And *The Golden Bottle* is an alchemical dream wherein the narrator is given a liquid that turns base metal to gold. By this power he becomes a financial titan and conquers and reforms the world.

Many of the prophetic stories of the period under discussion are pretty poor stuff by modern standards. Thus Edward Bellamy's *Looking Backward* (1888), a prophecy of an ideal socialist future which had an enormous sale at the time and, like *Atlantis,* is still in print, is unreadably dull. Bellamy puts his hero to sleep in 1887 and awakens him in 2000. After that all that happens is that the hero listens to interminable lectures on the social and economic organization of 2000.

Yet even the worst of these yarns sheds light on man's ability to foresee his future. We often hear of such successful prophecies: Jack London's *The Iron Heel* is cited as a forecast of Fascism and is said to have influenced the contemporary British Labour Party politician Aneurin Bevan.

But one cannot prove prophetic insight by citing successes alone, for if one makes enough guesses about the future of anything one will make some hits by luck. What of the failures? For instance, while Donnelly foresaw air travel, and while his pneumatic tubes and magnetic lights have analogues in the real world, he anticipated nothing corresponding to the automobile or the radio.

Many of these Victorian writers of futuristic novels devoted much space to the mechanical wonders of the future. They made some good hits and some even more remarkable misses. Even Bellamy, who paid little attention to technical matters, credited his future Americans with a device like Muzak.

We find the transatlantic telephone, the electric light, and the flashlight in *The King's Men* by Grant, O'Reilly, Dale, and Wheelwright (1884), a lively tale despite the extraordinary number of collaborators who wrote it. It is the story of an abortive conspiracy to restore King George V to the throne of the British Republic. This king is fat, foolish, and lecherous, quite different from the frigidly correct and conventional man who actually occupied the British throne under that title. But with all their improvements the authors still fill their twentieth-century scenes with horse-drawn carriages and servants in powdered wigs.

Or consider *A.D. 2000* by Lt. A. M. Fuller, USA (1890). Like Bellamy, Lieutenant Fuller puts his hero to sleep and awakens him in 2000, to find electric clocks like ours, a New York subway system not unlike the real one, and a national newspaper printed in many places at once by a "sympathetic telegraph"—a kind of radio-teletypewriter. Street traffic is a mixture of horse buggies and "electric drags"; underground pneumatic railways span the continent. Air travel is by dirigible balloon or airship, and the author sends his hero off to discover the North Pole in one.

Likewise Frank Stockton of lady-or-tiger fame, in *The Great Stone of Sardis* (1898) had the Pole reached by submarine, as Sir Hubert Wilkins once tried to do in fact. The story combines considerable creative imagination and Stockton's folksy humor with glaring logical lapses and a feeble knowledge of the science of Stockton's own time.

Several authors foresaw the wide use of aluminum—but at the same time forecast the ubiquity of moving sidewalks and monorail trains, which have not materialized. The latter were to be of two kinds: one suspended from an overhead rail like the real interurban line at Wupperthal in the Ruhr in Germany; the other stood on a single rail, kept upright by gyroscopes. The streamlined Diesel-electric train was not foreseen, though the Diesel engine was patented in 1892 and the streamlined train as early as 1865.

In general, pre-automobile authors missed the automobile completely, despite occasional mention of electric bicycles or the like.

Or, at least, they had no conception of the automobile's future importance in economics, social custom, city planning, road-building, and traffic management. They also missed motion pictures and the radio and related electrical communication (teletype, television, radar, et cetera).

In the matter of aircraft, some like Grant, Bellamy, and Stockton ignored them. Others mistakenly bet on the dirigible airship instead of the airplane. The prophets illustrated the principle that they are fairly safe with generalities, but their score gets progressively worse as they try to become more particular. H. G. Wells and Rudyard Kipling both tried their hands at detailed aeronautical prophecy with amusing results.

In *When the Sleeper Wakes* (1899) Wells awakens his "sleeper," Graham, about 2100. Graham's money has accumulated at compound interest until he owns most of the world, which is ruled in his name by a "Council" of trustees of his fortune. There are "aeroplanes" (large fast transport aircraft with wings in tandem, something like clipper ships with the masts and sails sticking out sidewise instead of up) and "aeropiles" (small insectlike fliers for private use). Their military power has never been developed because the Council stopped all war before they were perfected.

By 1907 aircraft had been reduced to reality, and in Wells's *The War in the Air,* published that year, Germany sets out to conquer the United States with a fleet of rigid airships of the type that Count Zeppelin had been developing. These craft are accompanied by a swarm of parasite airplanes or *Drachtenflieger* suspended from them as the U. S. Navy actually did with the unfortunate *Akron* and *Macon.*

First the Germans sink the American fleet with bombs from the airplanes. Then Wells's airships go on to destroy New York City and to seize strategic points about the nation. Meanwhile Britain and France attack Germany and an Asiatic empire attacks everybody. The Asiatics use flattened airships, like oversized flying saucers, and swarms of one-man ornithopters. The pilots of the latter alight and attack their antagonists with samurai swords —not so funny as it sounds, for in World War II Japanese aviators actually wore such swords in their cockpits, as Russian aviators are now said to climb into theirs with Cossack sabers.

Finally civilization is smashed and everything simmers down to barbarism—a favorite theme with Wells, who never realized that with the increase of powers of destruction has gone an almost as impressive growth in powers of organization and reconstruction.

In a later novel, *The World Set Free* (1914) Wells foresaw the destruction of cities by atomic bombs dropped (by hand) from airplanes. Despite this startling feat of prophetic insight, the work is much inferior as fiction. Civilization is saved from collapse when the King of England and the French Ambassador to the United States get together and call a conference of heads of nations to set up a world government, as people in real life have made two fumbling, half-hearted, and not very successful efforts to do.

Kipling's short "With the Night Mail" (1909) bets on the airship for long-range transportation, but assumes that its lift will be greatly increased by "Fleury's gas." Mechanically, Kipling's aircraft have little to do with modern airliners, though his description of aerial traffic control has a ring of reality. And being, like Wells, a natural storyteller, his tale is infinitely more readable than those of amateurs like Bellamy. None of these early aeronautical prophets foresaw the true nature of aerial combat. Their aircraft fight with rifles, or by ramming and boarding, or by grasping each other with steel jaws.

In the sphere of culture most prophetic novels are weak. Developments in the arts are largely ignored. Most of the writers assume us to be wearing the beards, stiff collars, and street-sweeping dresses of Victorian days. When the authors do hazard a clothes prophecy they are likely to content themselves with putting the men into knee-breeches. No doubt the writers of that time would be amazed to see an American summer street thronged with hatless, coatless, tieless men, and women in knee or calf-length dresses or even, in suburbs, in shorts and halters. They would be horrified by our bathing beaches, and the nudist movement would reduce them to gibbering incoherence.

While some of the prophets mentioned the emancipation of women, none grasped the lengths to which it has gone, with lady senators and colonels. They never dreamed of "good" women wearing cosmetics, smoking, swearing, and drinking—acts which in their day were restricted to what they called "unfortunate females." Their heroines shriek and swoon at the slightest shock in true Victorian tradition. None foresaw the most important Western cultural developments of late decades: the grotesque prohibition episode in America with its resulting rise in organized crime; the decline in the influence of religion; the rise in the living standards of most lower-income groups; and the stupendous rise in the rate of divorce and remarriage.

Well, not quite. Victor Rousseau (Emmanuel) in his *The Messiah of the Cylinder* (1917) foresaw a world ruled by an atheistic socialistic tyranny which encourages such horrors as divorce and birth control. However, the pious Christian Russians (of all nations) come to the rescue of the oppressed Good People, destroy the socialist armies in a war fought with death rays and airplanes with jaws, and restore the old-fashioned virtues.

Which brings us to political prophecies. The authors have tried everything. The world may be happy under a purified capitalism or groaning under a capitalist dictatorship. Sometimes socialism has effected a utopian millennium; sometimes it has engendered a tyranny as oppressive as that of the actual U.S.S.R. The prophets erred in seeking political simplicity, whereas reality has been infinitely various, inconsistent, and untidy. The authors have repeatedly made Great Britain into a republic or a socialist dictatorship, but none foresaw the mild bumbling democratic socialist monarchy that obtained there after World War II.

Several writers have annexed Canada and Mexico to the United States, to the annoyance of Canadians and Mexicans who think that they are doing all right and have no wish to join the *Yanquis*.

Usually the prophets (at least in American and British imaginative fiction) have either proclaimed or hoped for the triumph of democracy, with exceptions. That delightful old imperialist Kipling put the world under an irresponsible Aerial Board of Control, while Lieutenant Fuller reformed the United States along the lines that one would expect from a politically naive military man: he had a single political party and got rid of such disorderly manifestations of democracy as juries and labor unions.

And what of war? The earlier prophets failed to foresee the mechanization and complexity of modern warfare. While some introduced airplanes, most retained horse cavalry. The tank was foreseen only twice. One of them is well known: a short story by H. G. Wells ("The Land Ironclads," 1903) wherein a battle in a South African locale is won by a lot of machines like armored boxcars creeping forward on a multitude of wheels and shooting remote-controlled guns.

The other prevision was more remarkable, coming as it did from a man whose ideas were the opposite of scientific. It appeared in a novel, *The Great Red Dragon,* by Cyrus Reed Teed, founder of a cult called Koreshan Unity. This Teed (who called himself "Koresh"—Hebrew for "Cyrus") received a divine revelation in 1869 to the effect that the earth is a hollow sphere with us on the *inside.* In 1894 he set up a celibate, communistic community at Estero, Florida, where he reigned until his death in 1909 following a beating received from a non-admirer at a political meeting. As he had convinced his followers that he was immortal, they laid him out on a cypress plank on the banks of the Estero River and for some weeks awaited his resurrection. What with the heat and damp they soon had to pour the remains into a bathtub, and a hurricane washed away tub, corpse, and all.

In his novel, Teed described an American civil war wherein the army of the socialists beats that of the capitalists near Chicago by means of "automobile artillery chariots." Then the Japanese, having conquered the rest of the world, invade the United States which cannot stop them because its navy has been destroyed in the civil war. The American army is saved from annihilation in a great battle in New York State by a fleet of aircraft secretly prepared by the Koreshans, and in the end everybody is happy under a Koreshan theocracy.

For first-class war prophecies, however, we have to come down to later times: to Hector Bywater's *The Great Pacific War* (1925) and to Floyd Gibbons's *The Red Napoleon* (1929). Bywater, a British naval expert, told of an American-Japanese war of 1931-33. In many respects it followed the course of the real one: the Japanese took Guam and the Philippines; then we took Truk and Angaur, retook the Philippines, brought the Japanese fleet to bay, and defeated it.

Bywater, trying to be conservative, underestimated the range and striking power of modern fleets and vastly underestimated the power of the airplane. Amphibious operations and new warship construction play but little part in his war. In his preface he says:

"It would have been easy, for example, to bring the Japanese battle fleet to Hawaii . . . but to do so would have been to expose the narrative to the well-merited ridicule of informed critics."

Shades of Pearl Harbor! Of course, in 1931 the airplane was not so effective as a decade later, and landing craft had not even been invented. Moreover Bywater thought that the Japanese would be kind and chivalrous towards their prisoners, whereas they proved anything but.

Gibbons tells of the effort of Ivan Karakhan, Stalin's fictional successor, to conquer the world. During 1932-36 his armies overrun all the Old World and then, using the European and Japanese fleets, he hurls great expeditions across the oceans to Mexico and both coasts of Canada to attack the United States. If Bywater underestimated the possibilities of such operations, Gibbons greatly overestimated them. But his climactic naval battle is more nearly in accord with technical possibilities than Bywater's. The American surface fleet is outnumbered, but American superiority in submarines and airplanes turns the tide.

Gibbons's shortcomings are ideological rather than technical. In decrying the Red Menace he quite overlooked the Fascist Menace, destined to make an earlier attempt at world conquest. And his villain Karakhan calls for racial equality and the brotherhood of man, like an enlightened modern statesman, while Gibbons himself appeals to his readers' basest prejudices by ranting about "yellow hordes." Both Gibbons and Bywater thought that the Japanese-Americans of Hawaii would revolt, whereas actually in World War II they furnished the U. S. Army with its finest soldiers.

Thus the later Victorian prophetic story writers managed to be right in a few broad and simple respects in their prophecies of the latter half of the twentieth century. They foresaw that the world would become more mechanized, populous, and complicated; that socialism would grow and attain power in some countries; that faster transportation, especially by air, would affect men's lives.

As they became more specific and detailed, though, they went farther astray, and they overlooked some important developments: the automobile, radio, and moving picture; the internal-combustion engine in its many applications; prohibition, birth control, and widespread divorce; the fading away of the old Judeo-Christian nudity tabu; and so on. Their ratio of success is little if any greater than that to be expected by luck. It seems greater because we remember the successful forecasts and forget the failures.

Such being the case, what are the chances that present-day prophetic fiction will score any higher success ratio when the real future unfolds? It has been claimed that because our present-day writers have more advanced psychological and sociological sciences to draw upon, they should score much better than their bewhiskered predecessors.[4]

Well, for one thing, we must consider what we are talking about. If one means: will a higher percentage of the prophecies come true, considering the total mass of science fiction written? the answer is plainly no, because so many varied and mutually exclusive futures have been proposed. Moreover, many of these futures have not been those which the authors believed to be seriously likely, but were made deliberately fantastic (as in the case of the synthetic feudalisms in my *Divide and Rule* and *The Stolen Dormouse*) for the sake of a laugh or a dialectical point.

Now, obviously, if one writer foresees the man of 2052 A.D. as dancing naked with flowers in his hair about the lawns of a scientific-democratic utopia, while a second plunges him into superscientific interstellar warfare, a third has him writhing under the heel of a world despotism, and a fourth portrays him as cowering in troglodytic barbarism in the atom-blasted ruins of civilization, they cannot all be true at once. And so many guesses have been made that almost anything that happens is bound to have been foreseen. Even if by some horrid joke of nature space travel turns out to be flatly impossible, some writers have used that dismal but not negligible possibility as a basis for stories.

But suppose we mean: will the writers of today be shown to have been more accurate in making serious predictions, as opposed to fanciful futuristic speculations advanced to sell a story or an ideological bill of goods? Or will they transpire to have overlooked fewer real developments, as the Victorians overlooked the automobile and the Bikini bathing suit?

Well, neither question can really be answered until the time

[4] When several of the preceding pages were published as an article in *Galaxy Science Fiction* for February, 1952, Editor Gold added a couple of paragraphs that made it appear that I thought that present-day prophets *would* do much better. Now, I am not angry at anybody, but I should like it understood that this opinion is Horace's, not mine.

arrives. My own guess is that they may prove to have done a little better—but only a little. If they do not fail to foresee developments to such an extent, the reason is mainly quantitative: that so much more science fiction has been written that there is less chance that developments, even fantastic ones, have been missed altogether.

Well then, what is creative imagination and how is it used in composing imaginative fiction?

Creative imagination is the attribute that enables writers to compose original narratives, different from other and earlier stories. It appears to be a development of the faculty of free association, disciplined in a desired direction, and while it does not enable the possessor to create anything absolutely new, it does make it possible for him to recombine elements from his previous experience, both personal and vicarious, into new combinations. While creative imagination is important in all fiction writing, it is the *sine qua non* of imaginative fiction, which cannot effectively be performed without it at all.

Creative imagination works upon the writer's previous experience, personal and vicarious, and the effectiveness of the result depends upon the writer's mental power of combination and upon the richness and diversity of the experience that his imagination has to draw upon. In imaginative fiction vicarious experience—mainly wide reading—is relatively more important than in fiction of other kinds, because the stories by definition deal with themes and settings that do not exist in the everyday world of fact and which therefore cannot be experienced personally. But personal experience—knowledge of different social milieus, occupations, personality types, et cetera—is still valuable to the writer. In story writing as in law, ignorance is no excuse.

By means of his creative imagination the writer combines these elements from his experience into factors of plot, setting, and character which comprise a fictional narrative having a temporary illusion of reality and significance, even though, in imaginative fiction, the story be based upon non-factual or fanciful assumptions, and which a reader will find interesting, entertaining, or absorbing.

In effecting his combinations and composing his story, the writer is attempting simultaneously to do three things: to amuse or entertain the reader, to express his own personality and attitudes (even though unconsciously), and to convey to the reader some idea or opinion. In imaginative fiction this idea commonly extrapolates from known fact to the hypothetical unknown of the remote past, or the future, or worlds other than that which we know. Or the writer may assume a world in which the known laws of science are thrown out in favor of other laws, such as those of magic. In appealing to his prospective reader, the imaginative story writer plays upon the same sentiments that a writer of conventional fiction does, and in addition he appeals strongly to the glamor of the exotic, the appeal of the antique, and the desire to escape the limitations of everyday life.

Although such stories more often than not take the form of a narrative laid in the future, they should not be taken too seriously as prophecy of how the world will actually be. For one thing, many of them were not really intended as such, and for another, there is such an infinitude of assumptions upon which the writer can erect his imagined future, and so many of them have been employed to construct not one but a vast multitude of different and mutually exclusive fictitious futures.

The actual effect of creative imagination, in enabling writers to create these fictitious worlds, lies not in conferring upon them any mystical gift of prophecy whereby they can actually peer along the time-axis into the future. Rather it is that, by enabling them to construct such a variety of possible futures different from the present, they have accustomed the reader to the idea of inevitable change and of a host of possible alternative outcomes to present tendencies.

Therefore, no matter how the world makes out in the next few centuries, a large class of readers at least will not be too surprised at anything. They will have been through it all before in fictional form, and will not be too paralyzed with astonishment to try to cope with contingencies as they arise.

Science Fiction, Science,
and Modern Man

Social Science Fiction

by ISAAC ASIMOV

ISAAC ASIMOV, *who needs no introduction to science-fiction readers, is exactly thirty-three years older than this book, his birthday month coinciding with the month of its publication.*

In those years, he has accomplished a great deal. He has been writing for fourteen of them, and his science fiction—witness his fine Foundation series—has spanned millennia, the rise and fall of galactic empires, the birth and death of cultures and of sciences. He now has seventy titles to his credit (all science fiction), including six novels (one under a pseudonym). A seventh novel, The Currents of Space, will be out in February, 1953.

And that's not all. In 1948, Isaac Asimov took his PH.D. *in chemistry at Columbia; and he is now Assistant Professor of Biochemistry at Boston University School of Medicine. He is part author of a textbook in the field, Biochemistry and Human Metabolism (Williams & Wilkins, 1952).*

Dr. Asimov is married, has a two-year-old son, and lives in Massachusetts.

SCIENCE FICTION is an undefined term in the sense that there is no generally agreed-upon definition of it. To be sure, there are probably hundreds of individual definitions but that is as bad as none at all. Worse, perhaps, since one's own definition gets in the way of an understanding of the next man's viewpoint. In this book, for instance, we have eleven different essayists on the subject, no two of whom, probably, would agree exactly on what it was they were discussing.

Under the circumstances, I think it best to make a personal definition here. As I am writing this without having read the other contributions, there is the chance of possible duplication. I'll risk that.

I should stress that my own definition is not necessarily better than the next man's or more valid or more inclusive or more precise. It simply expresses my way of thinking and will serve to lend a framework to this chapter.

About a year ago, I wrote an article for *The Writer* which I called "Other Worlds to Conquer." In it, I defined science fiction as follows: *Science fiction is that branch of literature which is concerned with the impact of scientific advance upon human beings.*

I intend to stick to that definition here, with a single slight modification which I will come to in a moment. I find intellectual satisfaction in the definition because it places the emphasis not upon science but upon human beings. After all, science (and everything else as well) is important to us only as it affects human beings.

The modification I wish to make in the definition is made necessary by the fact that it narrows the boundaries of science fiction to a greater extent than most people are willing to see it narrowed.

158

For that reason, I would like to say that my definition applies not to "science fiction" but to a subdivision of the field which I find it convenient to speak of as "social science fiction."

It is my opinion that social science fiction is the only branch of science fiction that is sociologically significant, and that those stories, which are generally accepted as science fiction (at least to the point where skilled editors accept them for inclusion in their science-fiction magazines) but do not fall within the definition I have given above, are *not* significant, however amusing they may be and however excellent as pieces of fiction.

This is a broad statement and may even sound a bit snobbish. But then the general purpose of this chapter is to give my opinions on the influence of society upon science fiction and science fiction upon society, so I am prepared to explain my stand at considerable length.

I

It is rather fashionable among some connoisseurs of science fiction to stress its age. This is partly the result of a thoroughly natural desire to lend an air of respectability to a class of literature that is often the target of laughter and sneers from those who picture it in terms of comic strips and horror movies.

August Derleth, for instance, one of the most able and indefatigable anthologists in the entire field of fantasy, has collected a volume called *Beyond Time and Space* (Pellegrini and Cudahy, 1950), which he has subtitled *A Compendium of Science-Fiction Through the Ages.* In it, he traces back his own conception of science fiction some 2400 years to Plato. The Platonic selection is, of course, the Atlantis story from the dialogue, "Critias." Selections are also included from More's *Utopia,* Rabelais' *Gargantua,* and Swift's *Gulliver's Travels.*

The anthology is one of the best and most fascinating in the field. Nevertheless, I think that Derleth is overzealous. The attraction of great names notwithstanding, science fiction, even at its broadest, cannot logically be traced further back in time than the period in which the western world became aware of the significance of the Industrial Revolution.

What about Plato's Atlantis, then? What about More's Utopia and Swift's Lilliput, Brobdingnag and Laputa? They represent superlative feats of imagination, but they do not have the *intent* of science fiction. They are social satires. The societies they describe are not intended to have meaning in themselves but are a reflection, usually a derogatory one, of the societies in which the authors lived.

Let's give this type of literature a name for convenience's sake. Let's call it *social fiction,* and define it in this way: *Social fiction is that branch of literature which moralizes about a current society through the device of dealing with a fictitious society.*

This is really an inevitable category of fiction if we consider that at most periods of human history, it was more than a little dangerous to analyze the then-prevalent society with too probing a finger and too curious an eye. It was far safer to show the reader his own image in a distorting mirror, hoping that sooner or later he would turn from the grotesque reflection to himself with the sobering thought that it *was* a reflection and, after all, not such an inaccurate one.

There is nothing in the definition of social fiction which limits the nature of the fictitious society. It can be a very realistic one, or it can be a fantastic one involving men on the moon, six-inch-high pygmies or intelligent horses. The presence of these *outré* overtones does not of itself convert social fiction into science fiction. It is, I repeat, a question of intent.

Social fiction, whatever the nature of its fictitious society, has its eye fixed on the current society. It pictures life not as it will be or as it might be or as it could be, but as it *should* be or as it *should not* be.

Science fiction, on the other hand, is really concerned with the fictitious society it pictures. It becomes not merely a lesson to us, a text from which to draw a moral, but something that bears the possibility of importance in its own right. When does science fiction become conceivable then? When the minds of mankind are so oriented by circumstance that it becomes reasonable to them that any society other than the one in which they live can be conceived of, if not in the present, then at least in the future.

This may sound startling. Surely it is obvious that more than one kind of society is possible. You have only to look about you to see India, China, the South Seas; only to look back in time to see pagan Rome and pharaonic Egypt.

But that is only because we live in an era of widespread education, rapid transportation and universal communication. Go back two hundred years and Earth expands into a tremendous, shadowy unknown while the horizon of the average individual shrinks to the village in which he is born, lives and dies.

Until the middle of the eighteenth century, the dominant factor in human history was stasis. Empires rose and empires fell. Conquerors flashed across the world stage. Barbarians thundered in from the steppes. To the peasant on his farm, generally speaking, it all meant nothing. The generations went on.

The "changes" that seem so impressive in the history books, the rise of this city or that, the fall of this empire or that, are really not changes to the average man. A given individual might have the current of his life turned awry if a war band clattered through his patch of farming ground, or if pestilence struck, or famine ground him. If he survived, however, he was back in the old place, and if in a large city a hundred miles away, a new king reigned, he heard it only by rumor and it meant nothing.

To a man who lived his life as his father had done and all his father's fathers as far back as his knowledge went, it would inevitably seem that there was a "natural order" of things. This natural order was prescribed either by the innate qualities of the human being and his world (if we listen to the Greek thinkers) or it was imposed by the greater wisdom of some supernatural being (if we listen to the Judean thinkers). In either case, it could neither be fought nor changed.

In such a world, science might exist, but its potentialities for social change would be understood only by a few, and that with difficulty. To the ancient Greeks, for instance, science was not the study of the blind laws that governed the motions of matter and its components. Instead, it was simply an aspect of beauty. Its final aim was purely and statically intellectual. By greater understanding, the educated Greek hoped to appreciate the design of the universe, almost as though it were a geometric figure conceived by a divine mathematician, rather than a handy device which impious man could seize and use to increase his own comfort.

Greek science was abstract geometry; Pythagorean studies of the mystical values of number; Platonic and Aristotelian speculations on the existence of "ideals," on the true nature of "virtue." Beautiful it was, but sterile, also.

To have viewed science as a means by which mankind could control his environment and deliberately change social structure would have made a marked man of one, a crackpot, a possible blasphemer. Plato, on being asked by an aspiring student as to the usefulness of geometry, gave him a coin that he might not feel he had gained nothing from the study, and ordered him to begone. A man who wanted practical applications was no true scientist.

It was the lack of social insight and not the lack of scientific ability that prevented Greece from initiating the Industrial Revolution two thousand years early. L. Sprague de Camp, in a brilliant commentary on the science of the Hellenistic age ("The Sea-King's Armored Division," *Astounding Science Fiction*, September-October, 1941) describes how close to it they were.

This is not to say that there was *no* change in human society until the mid-eighteenth century. Obviously mankind advanced continuously from the stone axe to gunpowder and from a hollowed-out tree trunk to the full-rigged ship. But the advance was slow in comparison to the passing of the generations.

Probably the first single event in history which affected the general population in a fundamental manner with sufficient quickness and intensity to be unmistakable to all was the French Revolution of 1789-1799. This phenomenon differed from previous rapid changes, such as Alexander's blitzkrieg against the Persian Empire, in that the alterations that resulted applied not to a thin Macedonian aristocracy, but to the entire French population from King Louis to Jacques Bonhomme.

It seemed like the end of the world to most of Europe. By the time the Revolution and its Napoleonic sequel had come to an end, the social structure of Europe had been changed radically in the space of *less than one generation*. The statesmen at the Congress of Vienna did their best to wipe out those changes, to restore the "natural order" of things, to replace the omelet within the eggshell. They failed, of course.

It is obvious then, that if science fiction is to deal with fictitious societies as possessing potential reality rather than as being nothing more than let's-pretend object lessons, it must be post-Napoleonic. Before 1789 human society didn't change as far as the average man was concerned and it was silly, even wicked, to suppose it could. After 1815, it was obvious to any educated man that human society not only could change but that it did.

Before passing on to the post-Napoleonic world, however, it might be well to forestall certain doubts that may exist in the reader's mind as to the true priority of the French Revolution as a recognizable rapid-fire social disintegrator. There have, for instance, been numerous religious revolutions in world history. Usually they are slow, but the Lutheran Reformation, two centuries before the French Revolution, was certainly rapid enough. In one generation, the religious map of Europe changed and was never the same again. Despite a series of wars, as vicious as any in history, the Reformation was another omelet that would not re-enter the egg.

Nevertheless, religious revolutions, important though they are, cannot be creators of nonstatic societies. Each new religion, however scornful of the claims to absolute knowledge and absolute authority on the part of the older faith, is firm in the belief that now, at least, the truth *has* been found, and that there is no ground for any further innovations.

Politico-economic revolutions are only slightly less emotion-ridden than are religious revolutions and there is little to choose in bitterness between them, but there is this important difference. A religious stasis is accepted by its devotees as having been ordained by a god or gods, and therefore not to be questioned by man. Not one jot or tittle of the law may be changed till all is fulfilled. Political stases, however, are ordained by men; none of their devotees can deny that. And it is easier to gainsay men, however great, than gods, however small.

Nevertheless, this difference does not seem sufficient to support my argument. Is there another difference between the time of Luther and Calvin and the times of Robespierre and Napoleon? The answer is, yes, the centuries involved—the sixteenth in one case and the eighteenth in the other.

Actually, the French Revolution itself was not primary. Underlying it lay centuries of slow changes in the fabric of society—changes of which most men were unaware. But from the nadir of western society—the tenth century—and through the Renaissance the *rate* of change had been steadily and continuously increasing. In the eighteenth century, the rate bounced forward tremendously. With the French Revolution, it became completely obvious.

To start the era of change with the French Revolution is therefore merely a handy way of pegging a date. The fundamental consideration is that about 1800, the tide of hastening change due to the scientific and industrial development of western society had become a colossal current that swept all other competing factors into discard.

In the eighteenth century, the Industrial Revolution began in England. It not only began, it was drastically stimulated by events on the Continent. The necessity of fighting France, then twice as populous, heavily militarized, and, eventually, the controller of all Europe from Madrid to Moscow, forced England's economy into hot-house growth. In 1815 after twenty years of continuous warfare, she was stronger and richer in relation to the rest of the world than ever before or since.

II

Even today it is not entirely plain to many people that scientific-economic change is the master and political change the servant. From 1789 to 1900, we changed from Louis XVI to the Third French Republic; from George III to Victoria; from George Washington to William McKinley; but we also changed from the stagecoach to the railroad; from the sailboat to the steamboat; from Buffon to Darwin and from Lavoisier's discovery of the nature of oxidation to Becquerel's discovery of the fact of radio-activity.

You may wonder how one can balance the Emancipation Proclamation against the electric light and the Bill of Rights against the X-ray tube, but we are not making moral judgments or comparisons here. We are trying to look the facts of social change in the face. Consider the political changes in our own generation. The rise and fall of Nazi Germany, with its World War II enclosure, took place in a round dozen years. Forty years ago the word "Fascism" did not exist. In less than forty years, Communism grew from a splinter group in the Socialist left to the predominant code of thinking of one third of the world. And today we live, surrounded by a cold war of a type few could have anticipated ten years ago.

Tremendous! It seems more cosmic, more world-shaking than the scientific and technological changes in the same period of time: things like the rise and decline of radio, the growth of the automobile, the coming of television and sound movies, jet planes and radar. The only scientific innovation that perhaps really impresses us is the atomic bomb.

Yet consider! Imagine a world in which Communism suddenly ceased to be. It would be a different world, wouldn't it? Your life would be changed, perhaps drastically (if you were an aeronautical engineer, for instance). Now imagine a world in which the automobile ceased to be. I feel certain that your life would experience a greater *immediate* change in that case. In other words, while changes in political affairs often hit us at an abstract and rarefied level, technological changes always hit home, right in the bread basket.

Then, too, technological changes lie at the root of political change. It was the developing Industrial Revolution that placed western Europe so far ahead of the rest of the world, that it could control all of it from China to Patagonia, either by outright political rule or by indirect economic mastery. Even the railroads of the United States were built as the result of the investments of European capitalists. And it is the Industrial Revolution spreading outward to America first, then to Russia, and now to China and India, that has shaken and is destroying European hegemony. Forty years ago, Russia couldn't build its own railroads without help. Today it is building jet planes we suspect of being better than ours. The world wags away, and these days the wagging is so rapid as to be a blur.

How did this new factor of social change enter western literature? In three ways, which we may list.

1) Through adoption in the field of social fiction. After all, the social satirists were describing fictitious societies. Why not one in which the obviously advancing technology advanced still further? Bellamy wrote *Looking Backward* and Wells wrote *The Shape of Things to Come*. But these were still social fiction. The writer's eye was still on the present. He was using science to help him point his moral, to shape his warning, or to help point the way. We might, if we wished to be whimsical about it, call this sort of thing enriched social fiction, since a moribund literary form was revitalized through the addition of a sprinkling of science, much as white flour is "enriched" with various vitamins. This type of literature is still with us today and the authors who engage in it are far from being unrespected. I point to Huxley's *Brave New World* and the quite recent *1984* of Orwell. But it is

a blind alley. We cannot forever face the future only as the present's object lesson; we must look at it as the future, something as valid as the present. We may not like it, but there it is.

2) Through adoption in the field of Gothic horror fiction. The terrifying tale of the supernatural (or, usually, subnatural) is as old as literature, and to adopt the mysteries of science as an aid to horror was an inevitable development. *Frankenstein* is one of the first and certainly one of the most successful of its kind. That genre has lived through the decades also. Its recent representatives include the works of Merritt and Lovecraft.

3) Finally, around scientific advance there developed—there *had* to develop—a new and specialized literature, peculiar to itself. Let us now, therefore, make a new and very broad definition of science fiction. *Science fiction is that branch of literature which deals with a fictitious society, differing from our own chiefly in the nature or extent of its technological development.*

This is a very broad definition. Since nothing is said about whether or not this fictitious society is intended to be a possibly real one or is merely composed as a lesson to present humanity, it even includes "social fiction plus science." (My personal impulse is to add a clause to the definition to the effect that the fictitious society is not advanced for the purpose of conscious moralization—but such a limitation would conflict with the ideas of those science-fiction enthusiasts who consider the works of Stanton A. Coblentz, for instance, as science fiction.)

We have now reached the point of the foundation of science fiction. Before we pass on to a new section in which we consider the development and differentiation of science fiction, I would like to rephrase briefly the reason for its beginnings. I can do it in one sentence.

Technological advance, rapid with respect to the passing of the generations, is a new factor in human history, a factor that marks off the last few generations of mankind from all the generations that preceded, and science fiction is the literary response to that new factor.

III

The history of science fiction can be divided into four eras: 1) 1815-1926; 2) 1926-1938; 3) 1938-1945; and 4) 1945-present.

The first era, a long, amorphous one, may be termed "primitive." It was a primitive era because although the concept of science fiction had been born, the economic basis for the support of science-fiction writers did not yet exist. It may seem a detestably commercial attitude to take toward art, but before any extensive literature can exist, some method must be found for feeding, clothing, and sheltering the practitioners while they create the literature.

Until 1926, science fiction possessed no regular outlet. Individual science-fiction stories had to find a literary home in periodicals devoted to general literature. Such periodicals could absorb only a limited quantity of experimental material. Individuals of towering stature, a Jules Verne or an H. G. Wells, might publish these fantastic stories about trips to the moon but no young writer, still clumsy with his words, could think of specializing in science fiction unless he were quite content to make his living some other way while doing so. No large class of science-fiction specialists, such as exists today, could possibly have existed before 1926. The economic basis for it was lacking.

In 1926, Hugo Gernsback founded *Amazing Stories*. He had edited magazines previously which published science fiction among other things, but *Amazing Stories* was devoted exclusively to science fiction. What this meant, put in its baldest terms, was this: allowing six stories per issue, seventy-two science-fiction stories could be published each year. A corollary was that with the success of *Amazing Stories*, other publishers would take the risk. Within five years two more magazines, *Science Wonder Stories* and *Astounding Stories*, were out.

It is quite reasonable, therefore, to call the second era of science fiction from 1926 to 1938, the "Gernsback Era."

It is interesting that in the very early days of *Amazing Stories*, the poverty of the field was such that Gernsback devoted himself to reprinting H. G. Wells. It was only gradually that young authors developed to whom science fiction was the primary and, sometimes, exclusive means of literary expression; authors such as Edmond Hamilton and Jack Williamson, to name two who, a quarter of a century later, are still publishing.

But now we have a fundamental change. Social fiction (which may be considered a sort of ancestor of science fiction, as alchemy is to chemistry) was essentially an extremely mature fiction. Only men of mature thought would be expected to appreciate either the satire or the moralization. (What does a youngster make of *Gulliver's Travels?* He considers it an English *Sindbad*.)

Science fiction, on the other hand, entered a domain that belonged almost exclusively to the young at that time, even to the adolescent. This *had* to be. A new literature, devoted to the principle that change was continuous, inevitable and even desirable, had to find its devotees among those to whom change was not something frightening; to the young, in other words.

To the youngster, born in the midst of this change, more change was only natural. They could hardly wait for it. The airplane had been invented; it was already old stuff; the next step is the rocket-ship; what are we waiting for? Well, we have radio; where's television; what's the delay?

This meant that science fiction had to lose most of its adult qualities, which were already well developed in the work of such a primitive master as Wells. (The word "primitive" is by no means to be taken as a derogatory term. I am merely placing Wells in time, setting him down as belonging to the "primitive era" because he wrote his science fiction before 1926.)

As most of the readers and many of the writers were in their teens, it was not reasonable to expect many stories containing social and economic complexities to be written, and even less reasonable to expect the few that were to be appreciated. In the place of such things there came again the epic individual who is the hallmark of primitive literature; the hero of infinite resource and daring, lacking completely the imaginative intellect that can conjure up horror and produce terror. The d'Artagnan sword and the Hickock six-shooter were thrown away and discarded and, in their place, there came the Hawk Carse-Richard Seaton hero with his ray gun and space ship.

The "adventure science fiction" dominated science fiction during the Gernsback Era. Please do not think that by this I imply that there are sharp boundaries in anything I discuss. Adventure science fiction existed before 1926 and it continued to exist after 1938. The point is that never has it dominated the field as it did between those two dates.

Among the connoisseurs of today, adventure science fiction is spoken of, with a certain flavor of disapproval, as "space opera"—the term being analogous to the contemptuous "horse opera" applied to the run-of-the-mill "western." There is perhaps a little unjust snobbery in this.

In the first place, space opera within the limitations of its own field can reach a high pitch of excellence. Edward E. Smith and John W. Campbell brought this type of story to its heights. With the entire cosmos as their field they streaked their heroes from star to star and from galaxy to galaxy. No homesickness intruded, no fear, no human weaknesses, no petty quarrels, no passion—only gigantic wars and conquests, tremendous victories and gargantuan dangers boldly disposed of.

Make no mistake. They were exciting reading.

Even today, many magazines specialize in adventure science fiction, and this is not an evil thing, or even particularly undesirable. The youngsters of today can't plunge head first into a complex adult story. They must begin with adventure, i.e., space opera. But space opera, unlike horse opera, is not a dead end. The youngster may grow out of the science-fiction habit altogether as he almost invariably grows away from Hopalong Cassidy, but he may also graduate into the more complex varieties of science fiction.

Another kind of science fiction that was important during the

Gernsback era was the reverse of adventure science fiction. If the youngsters wanted their blood and thunder they also wanted their science, and so story after story came out in which that stock character, the irascible, eccentric (or even mad) scientist explained his inventions and discoveries in interminable double-talk.

We might call this "gadget science fiction," and dismiss further consideration of it here, since it becomes more important in the next era of science fiction.

IV

In 1938, John W. Campbell became editor of *Astounding Stories*. If Gernsback is the father of science fiction, Campbell is the father of "social science fiction"; that is, the branch of science fiction which really lives up to my original definition: (*Social*) *science fiction is that branch of literature which is concerned with the impact of scientific advance upon human beings.*

It would be wise to pause at this point. I have mentioned three varieties of science fiction now: adventure science fiction, gadget science fiction, and social science fiction. Definitions are all right but it won't hurt, and it would probably help considerably, if I come up with a few examples.

Let us suppose it is 1880 and we have a series of three writers who are each interested in writing a story of the future about an imaginary vehicle that can move without horses by some internal source of power; a horseless carriage, in other words. We might even make up a word and call it an automobile.

Writer X spends most of his time describing how the machine would run, explaining the workings of an internal-combustion engine, painting a word-picture of the struggles of the inventor, who after numerous failures, comes up with a successful model. The climax of the yarn is the drama of the machine, chugging its way along at the gigantic speed of twenty miles an hour between a double crowd of cheering admirers, possibly beating a horse and carriage which have been challenged to a race. This is gadget science fiction.

Writer Y invents the automobile in a hurry, but now there is a gang of ruthless crooks intent on stealing this valuable invention. First they steal the inventor's beautiful daughter, whom they threaten with every dire eventuality but rape (in these adventure stories, girls exist to be rescued and have no other uses). The inventor's young assistant goes to the rescue. He can accomplish his purpose only by the use of the newly perfected automobile. He dashes into the desert at an unheard of speed of twenty miles an hour to pick up the girl who otherwise would have died of thirst if he had relied on a horse, however rapid and sustained the horse's gallop. This is adventure science fiction.

Writer Z has the automobile already perfected. A society exists in which it is already a problem. Because of the automobile, a gigantic oil industry has grown up, highways have been paved across the nation, America has become a land of travelers, cities have spread out into suburbs and—what do we do about automobile accidents? Men, women, and children are being killed by automobiles faster than by artillery shells or airplane bombs. What can be done? What is the solution? This is social science fiction.

I leave it to the reader to decide which is the most mature and which (this is 1880, remember) is the most socially significant. Keep in mind the fact that social science fiction is not easy to write. It is easy to predict an automobile in 1880; it is very hard to predict a traffic problem. The former is really only an extrapolation of the railroad. The latter is something completely novel and unexpected.

In any case, it was this social science fiction that Campbell encouraged. A new group of writers grew up about him: Robert A. Heinlein, L. Sprague de Camp, A. E. van Vogt, Theodore Sturgeon and many others. Older writers such as Jack Williamson and Henry Kuttner changed their styles to suit the times. (I might mention as an aside that I sold my first story to Campbell only a few months after he became editor.)

What, specifically, did Campbell do? First and foremost, he de-emphasized the nonhuman and nonsocial in science fiction.

Science fiction became more than a personal battle between an all-good hero and an all-bad villain. The mad scientist, the irascible old scientist, the beautiful daughter of the scientist, the cardboard menace from alien worlds, the robot who is a Frankenstein monster—all were discarded. In their place, Campbell wanted business men, space-ship crewmen, young engineers, housewives, robots that were logical machines.

He got them.

Again the dividing line is not sharp. Science fiction with real characters existed before Campbell, notably in the stories written by Stanley G. Weinbaum in his short, meteoric career. His first story, *A Martian Odyssey* is, in my own opinion, the first example of modern social science fiction. It dealt with an alien race not inferior to Earthmen; not superior; merely different. He got across that sense of difference. His environment was not merely grotesque or merely horrible. It was different, naturally different. The scene was Mars and it felt like Mars, not like a horror movie. Most of all, his people talked like people and acted and felt like people. *A Martian Odyssey* appeared in 1934 in *Wonder Stories*. The editor—give him credit—was Charles R. Hornig.

The importance of Campbell is that he was not content to let Weinbaums spring up accidentally. He looked for them. He encouraged them. It is that which makes the years 1938-1945 the "Campbell Era."

Campbell also brought to the field an increasing rigor as far as scientific background was concerned. In the cut, thrust, and slash style of adventure science fiction, science which was inaccurate or even ridiculous in terms of what was actually known at the time frequently found a place. The better writers of the type, the aforementioned E. E. Smith and Campbell himself, were too well-trained in science (Smith has a doctorate in chemistry and Campbell is a physics-major graduate of M.I.T.) to offend badly in this way, but hordes of lesser lights dealt with such things as a hollow Earth, inhabited within; atoms that were really miniature solar systems and inhabited; Mars that was pictured as having

Earth gravity, atmosphere and temperature, with Earthlike inhabitants.

Although the stories written about such central ideas are often vastly entertaining, they remain completely fallacious. The Earth is *not* hollow. The atom is *not* a miniature solar system. Mars is very different from Earth and could not support Earth life.

The reader may seriously question my concern over such discrepancies. Does not all science fiction involve the fantastic? Yes, but there is a great difference between taking liberties with the unlikely and taking liberties with the impossible. The liberties allowed legitimate science fiction are so great that there is no need to drag in outright impossibilities, and there is an important social reason why it should not.

Science fiction aspires now to be more than a literature for youngsters. To appeal to adults, to gain serious consideration in our society, it must not offend reason. It must be coherent with the life we know in the sense that it does not contradict that which is known to be uncontradictable. A historical novel, to take an example from another field, might include a dozen thoroughly fictitious characters for the Civil War era, but it can't describe Stephen A. Douglas as president of the United States. It can make General Grant do many things he never did, but it can't make him surrender at Appomattox.

I will give my reasons later in this essay for thinking it important that science fiction be accepted with respect by society in general for the good not only of science fiction, but of society.

Two qualifications to my last argument must be made. It must not be thought that all writers of adventure science fiction are necessarily given to bad science. I have already mentioned Smith and Campbell. I want to emphasize the point and advance L. Sprague de Camp as an example. De Camp is one of the best, perhaps *the* best of the contemporary practitioners of the derring-do-and-sword-play school of science fiction. He is also one of the most meticulous men in the field when it comes to excluding known scientific impossibilities. Much more meticulous, for instance, than myself, though I do more preaching about it.

The second qualification has a name. That name is Ray Bradbury. Bradbury has written scores of stories about Mars. He gives Mars an Earthlike temperature, an Earthlike atmosphere and Earthlike people, sometimes down to tuxedoes and pocket-handkerchiefs. His stories reek with scientific incongruity. But he gets away with it. Not only does he get away with it, but, among the general population, he is by far the most popular science-fiction writer and regularly appears in such magazines as the *Saturday Evening Post*.

In my opinion, Bradbury gets away with it because he does not really write science fiction. He is a writer of social fiction. His "Mars" is but the mirror held up to Earth. His stories do not depict possible futures; they are warnings and moral lessons aimed at the present. Because Bradbury believes that our present society is headed for chaos and barbarism unless it changes its present course (he may well be right), his warnings are jeremiads. This has led some critics to the superficial belief that the man is simply "morbid" or that he has a "death wish." Nonsense! He is simply writing social fiction.

It is not my wish to imply that the creation of social science fiction was a complete tour de force on the part of Campbell. It was true that he had the wisdom to see and respond to a new demand, but the fact of fundamental importance is that the demand existed.

After all, twelve years had passed. The boy of fifteen who had read *Skylark of Space* in 1928 and was overwhelmed by it was now twenty-five and longing for the "good old days." He no longer enjoyed science fiction and remembered the past with nostalgia because he thought the stories were better. They weren't. He had merely been ten years younger. To satisfy the veterans of science fiction, to take into account the steadily increasing average age of the readers, to prevent the older enthusiasts from falling away as similar grownups fell away from Edgar Rice Burroughs and Zane Grey, science fiction had to mature with its readers. Fortunately, it did.

V

In 1945, the atom bomb was dropped on Hiroshima and a fourth stage of science fiction was ushered in.

Why? Primarily because the atom bomb put a new light on science fiction. Until 1945, it was only too easy to dismiss science fiction as "weird stuff," as "horror stories," as "comic-strip things."

"Do you read that stuff?" people would say.

The great popularity of such strips as *Buck Rogers, Flash Gordon* and *Superman* made it easy for people to categorize all science fiction as juvenile. The lurid covers of many of the science-fiction magazines did not help. As a result, many adults who would have enjoyed and appreciated science fiction did not, because it never occured to them to try it.

And then a weapon right out of science fiction ends World War II and changes the balance of power on Earth. It is time for a sober look at the crackpots, so-called, who have been talking about atom bombs at a time when no one but a few specialists in nuclear physics even thought they were possible.

The result was that more people tasted science fiction and found they liked it. As the reading public suddenly grew larger, science fiction became "respectable." Publishing houses such as Doubleday and Simon & Schuster began putting out science-fiction books regularly and with no attempt at "diluting" them in any mistaken belief that the book-buying public was not yet ready for the straight stuff. In addition, science-fiction magazines other than Campbell's *Astounding Science Fiction* (both newcomers and old reliables) began shifting their story policy in the direction of Campbell's.

In 1950, Horace L. Gold brought out *Galaxy Science Fiction* which, from the very beginning, published only advanced social science fiction so that with the first issue it was accepted by most fans as sharing top honors with *Astounding*.

Campbell is still editor of *Astounding* and still a tremendous force in the field, but because he is no longer the lone champion of social science fiction, the era since 1945 cannot be tabbed with his name, or any name. It must simply be called the "atomic era."

VI

Now it is time to look closely at social science fiction. Having isolated it as one of three types of science fiction, and the *one* type with social significance, the question next comes up whether social science fiction is a precise term or whether within it there are also subdivisions.

Neither alternative, in my opinion, is quite correct. Social science fiction is not a precise term but neither is it old enough to have developed a clear-cut subdifferentiation. Instead it consists of a broad continuous spectrum. If we consider the two extremes of the spectrum, we will seem to be treating two widely different types of story, but we will have to keep it continuously in mind that one extreme shades imperceptibly into the other and no man can point and say, "Here is the dividing line." (To a lesser extent this is true of the broader categories of adventure, gadget, and social science fiction; also of the still broader categories of social fiction and science fiction.)

Despite what I have just said, I cannot resist the temptation to give the two extremes names. Names are dangerous because they imply neat categories. Nevertheless, I hope you will humor me in this respect. I could call the extremes conservative and radical; realistic and romantic; simple and complex. I'll use none of these. Instead, I'll use the terms "chess game" and "chess puzzle" which are more picturesque than any of these but, in my opinion, more accurate as well.

A chess game has the following important characteristics: 1) it begins with a fixed number of pieces in a fixed position, and

2) the pieces change their positions according to a fixed set of rules.

A chess puzzle differs from a game in that although the second point holds, the first breaks down. A chess puzzle begins with any number of pieces (up to and including the full amount used in a game) placed in any arrangement that does not break the fundamental rules of chess.

It is important to remember that in the case of the puzzle, the original position is not necessarily one that is likely to be arrived at in the ordinary course of a game. In fact, in the vast majority of cases, a pair of chess players would have to be most ingeniously insane to arrive at the sort of position that would make a good puzzle.

How is this analogous to the spectrum of social science fiction? Point 2, which is held in common by games and puzzles, i.e., the rules by which the pieces move, may be equated with the motions and impulses of humanity: hate, love, fear, suspicion, passion, hunger, lust and so on. Presumably, these will not change while mankind remains Homo sapiens. Stories can be written about "supermen" or intellectual mutants. They may even be written about alien species or robots that do not share these fundamental human drives. However, they must still be written by a very human author and addressed to a very human audience. If the characters are not recognizably human in these respects it is difficult or impossible to treat them adequately or to please the audience with them.

(One exception—and virtually any generalization about science fiction has a dozen exceptions—is Olaf Stapledon's *Odd John*. This is the story of a superman who is so skilfully drawn that he really seems both nonhuman and superhuman. Being only human myself, I didn't like Odd John—the character, that is, not the story, which I thoroughly enjoyed—any more than a chimpanzee could like a human being if he were capable of really understanding the gulf of mental difference that separated himself from man.)

Point 1 of the chess-game—chess-puzzle dichotomy can be equated with the fundamental socio-economic environment of humanity. The type of story that corresponds to the chess game with its fixed starting position is that which assumes the socio-economic environment we now possess. That is: a city culture as opposed to a village culture; an agricultural economy as opposed to a nomadic or hunting economy; a family system as opposed to a tribal system. Add to these certain newer fashions which have become so ingrained in our own ways of thinking that any deviation has become abhorrent. For instance: heterosexual relationships as the sexual norm; monogamy; a mild, formal and passionless monotheism; taboos against cannibalism and incest; and so on.

With this starting position fixed, it is then only necessary to play the "chess game" according to the rules. The only modification from our own society is that certain technological innovations are allowed. Atomic power may have replaced coal and oil as these once replaced wood. Robots may have been developed. Interstellar travel may be commonplace. But people are still our kind of people with our way of thinking about things.

In the purest form of the chess-game type of social science fiction it is frequently found convenient to take advantage of the fact that "history repeats itself." Why shouldn't it? Given the same rules and the same starting position, the element of repetition must obtrude.

As a result, a whole class of "Galactic Empire" stories has arisen. The Galactic Empire, or its equivalent, is usually simply the Roman or British Empire written large, and the events that transpire can be equated without too much difficulty with analogous events that took place in past history.

I have a personal leaning toward this type of story and have written a few myself. My first novel, *Pebble in the Sky* (Doubleday, 1950), dealt with an Earth, ravaged by radioactivity, despised by its neighbors, but dreaming of its glorious past and certain of its special mission in the future. Most thoughtful readers had no difficulty in recognizing the fact that I was retelling the history of Rome and Judea. I even had Earth governed by an Imperial Procurator.

I wrote other stories, the germs of whose ideas I derived from the histories of Justinian and Belisarius, Tamerlane and Bajazet, John and Pope Innocent III. Naturally they were told in my own way and departed from their historical counterparts whenever it pleased me to have them depart. It was simply that I was following the chess-game theory in which all games start from the same point.

(I do not wish to imply that I am the only writer of such stories, or even the most important such writer. Robert A. Heinlein has specialized in this field and is widely considered to be the most proficient. Of the younger writers, one name which I pick at random is Poul Anderson who did an excellent job of chess-gaming in "The Helping Hand.")

Not everyone approves of this sort of thing. Damon Knight, one of the best and brightest of our postwar crop of social science fiction writers, and a devotee of the chess-puzzle variety, took particular issue with it in an article he wrote for an amateur science-fiction "fan magazine." His thesis was that history did *not* repeat itself.

Whether it does or does not repeat itself depends, of course, on what you mean by repetition. The same people never live twice, the same wars are never fought twice, the same conditions never occur *exactly* twice. Nevertheless, similar broad responses frequently occur under similar broad stimuli. If you stand far away from the great and variegated story of man and squint your eyes so that you drown out the details and see only the broad blocks of color, various repetitive patterns do appear.

We have, for instance, the alternation of city domination and nomad domination in the early days of Near-Eastern civilization; the pattern by which a dynasty or a nation or an empire establishes itself under a strong individual (usually destroying, in the process, a more aristocratic dynasty, a wealthier nation, a more civilized empire), maintains itself through a few harsh reigns or centuries, reaches a peak of luxury and magnificence and then declines to fall victim to another dynasty, nation, or empire.

However, I shall not try to repeat in detail what Toynbee has said in six volumes.

But, after all, how useful are these repetitions of extremely broad sweeps? Fiction to have a real interest must deal with specific happenings—and how specifically can history repeat? The answer is, in my opinion, that it can repeat with surprising specificity.

If you don't mind, now, I would like to present some examples. I have wanted to do this for years and now that the opportunity has come I do not intend to wait for a second knock. I will present, in bare outline, a certain passage of history, in which key words or phrases will be represented by dashes. I invite the reader to fill in the dashes before he looks at my own "solution" at the end of the passage.

VII

Sample: *The Revolution*

In the ——(1)—— Century, the European nation of ——(2)—— was in a shaky state. In the previous century, it had reached a peak of military glory under the monarch ——(3)——, under whose leadership the nation defeated the attempts of ——(4)—— to gain hegemony over Europe. Since then, the fortunes of the nation had declined, military defeats had been suffered and finances had grown nearly impossible.

The current king ——(5)—— was not noted for either firmness of character or brilliance of intellect. He was noted chiefly for the fact that, in a dissolute court, he maintained a spotlessly moral private life. He was well-meaning and amiable and had none of the sexuality and despotic instinct of his illustrious predecessor ——(6)—— who had a long and successful reign.

The king was, at least in the beginning, liked by the people who, however, bitterly distrusted Queen ——(7)—— who was of foreign extraction and, indeed, was of the ——(8)—— nation whom the people had thought of as enemies for generations. The queen was the stronger personality of the two, the less willing to compromise with the people and the more contemptuous of them.

Despite the resources of the nation, which were ample, and the taxes, which were ample, the government lacked money, partly because of waste and inefficiency and partly because of the——(9) —— war.

Although the nation had been notoriously loyal to its sovereigns in previous centuries, it now rose in violent revolt. At first mildly radical policies prevailed under the influence of such personalities as ——(10)——. As the revolution proceeded, however, it grew more violent. Some of the original architects of the revolution ware forced into exile, for example, ——(11)——. Others, as the revolution grew more violent, paid with their lives. Two of these, among numerous examples, are ——(12)—— and ——(13) ——. Eventually, a strong government was formed under ——(14) ——. The king was eventually executed, an act which shocked all of Europe.

What shocked some people even more were the measures taken against the established ——(15)—— church of the nation.

Although the rest of Europe would gladly have intervened to put down this dangerous new government and re-establish legitimacy and order, they were not in a position to do so efficiently. There was difficulty in coming to a common decision as to a means of action. In addition, much of Europe was disorganized because of the great ——(16)—— which was just coming to a conclusion.

Half-hearted attempts at intervention failed though they aroused the bitter resentment of the revolutionary government which was quick to respond. Its people became suddenly formidable. Against its foreign foes ——(17)—— it won unexpected victories that, for a time, established its government securely, and, in fact, made of it a menace to the rest of Europe. Eventually, however, the revolution came to an end and after an interlude of domination under General ––(18)–– the heir of the executed king returned to his kingdom as ––(19)––.

I doubt that any reader will not have definite ideas as to which nation and what period in its history I am talking about. Some, perhaps, are thinking that I may be talking of either of two nations. Actually, I am thinking of three. This is the way the blanks could be filled in:

	A	B	C
(1)	17th	18th	20th
(2)	England	France	Russia
(3)	Elizabeth I	Louis XIV	Alexander I
(4)	Philip II of Spain	(not applicable)	Napoleon I of France
(5)	Charles I	Louis XVI	Nicholas II
(6)	Henry VIII	Louis XIV	Peter I
(7)	Henrietta Maria	Marie Antoinette	Alexandra
(8)	French	Austrian	German
(9)	(not applicable)	American Revolution	World War I
(10)	Pym	Mirabeau	Kerensky
(11)	(not applicable)	Lafayette	Trotsky (later)
(12)	(not applicable)	Desmoulins	Zinoviev (later)
(13)	(not applicable)	Danton	Bukharin (later)
(14)	Cromwell	Robespierre	Lenin
(15)	Anglican	Roman Catholic	Orthodox
(16)	Thirty Years War	(not applicable)	World War I
(17)	Holland	Austria	Germany
(18)	Monk	Bonaparte	(not applicable)
(19)	Charles II	Louis XVIII	(not applicable)

I maintain that this is not bad. To be sure the comparisons can only go so far. Lafayette and Trotsky are in no way comparable except that both went into exile and, more strongly still, General Monk and General Bonaparte are completely different except insofar as one succeeded Richard Cromwell and preceded Charles II, and the other succeeded the Directorate and preceded Louis XVIII.

Now does this prove that history always repeats itself? No, but it shows that it is legitimate to extrapolate from the past because sometimes such extrapolations are fairly close to what happens.

Suppose that in 1910 a science-fiction writer wished to lay a story of the future in Russia and, after a shrewd consideration of the conditions then prevailing, decided to have its social background one of revolution. If he were a believer in the chess-game theory he would have used the French Revolution as a framework to keep himself from overstepping the rules of the game.

And he would have done pretty well, if he had done so. Of course, he might have had the Tsarevich Alexius returning to his throne in 1930, and he might have had the ragged Red Army *not* defeated at Warsaw in 1920, but advancing to the Seine before it could be stopped by combined Anglo-American forces (a contingency that may have been premature rather than entirely wrong). Otherwise, it would sound well.

Is this a freak case? Have I just picked out the one case of duplication (or rather triplication) in history, in order to back up my own argument? Not at all. I could find many others. This example could itself have been almost indefinitely extended with parallels all along the line. I might even have, as a particular tour de force, attempted a five-way correlation between Philip II of Spain, Louis XIV of France, Napoleon of France, William II of Germany and Hitler of Germany. But it is time to leave the chess-game variety of social science fiction and pass on to the chess puzzles.

VIII

In chess puzzles the starting position can be adjusted to the will of the puzzle composer. Analogously, in chess-puzzle social science fiction, the initial society in which the characters move can be as the author pleases. Ordinarily, the society is distinct from our own in one or more fundamental ways, though usually it can be viewed as possibly having originated from our society by some radical development or overgrowth of some aspect of our way of life. The heterogeneity of this type of literature is such that it can be explained satisfactorily only by examples.

Fritz Leiber, in an extraordinarily powerful story, "Coming

184

Attraction," postulates an American society in which social disintegration is nearly complete. America is covered with patches of radioactive destruction as a result of a recently concluded atomic war. Women wear masks in public since sexual fixation has traveled from the breasts and hips to the face. Women wrestlers have become a recognized social caste and are more proficient than their male counterparts. The society reeks with a semi-accepted sado-masochism.

The reader is at once repelled by the story and strongly attracted. He is horrified at the society, moved by its reality and profoundly disturbed at the realization that it is an extrapolation of some of the worst features of our present way of life.

Another imagined society occurs in Wyman Guin's "Beyond Bedlam." Here we have a society in which schizoid personality is the accepted norm. It is, in fact, the compulsory norm. Each body is controlled by two minds and personalities, not simultaneously, but alternately for five-day periods. The two mind-controlled bodies bear no relationship to each other. A single person in alternate five-day periods may have two different occupations, two different wives, two different statuses in society and so on. The postulation states further that by forcing split personality on humanity, the eternal struggle between the half-formed personalities within men and women can no longer find its outlet in war and destruction. The two personalites are released, freed of one another, and may go their way in peace.

Guin goes further in this story than a mere statement of a schizoid society. He writes about a situation that is natural, perhaps inevitable, in such a society, but which is alien to us. He gives us an insight into life in a changed society that, in an abstract sense, is very valuable to those of us who expect inevitable change. The story deals with a man who has fallen in love with his wife's alter ego, who has in turn fallen in love with him. In the society of "Beyond Bedlam" this is evil, disgusting and immoral. The struggles and dilemmas of the two star-crossed lovers are followed to the inevitable tragic ending.

It is as though a Roman writer of the Augustan age told a story of a future society in which color distinctions were important, and in which a man found himself hopelessly in love with a girl whose skin tinge was slightly different.

Both "Beyond Bedlam" and "Coming Attraction" appeared in *Galaxy Science Fiction*. This is not to imply that chess-puzzle social science fiction does not appear in *Astounding Science Fiction*. In that magazine, I can cite William Tenn's "Firewater" as an excellent recent example. Nevertheless, due perhaps to the differing personalities of the two editors, the chess-game variety is slightly more prominent in *Astounding*, and the chess-puzzle variety in *Galaxy*.

Two more examples. (It is difficult to know where to stop.) Eric Frank Russell's story "—And Then There Were None" in *Astounding Science Fiction* dealt with a society in which individualism was carried to its logical extreme. Each man did exactly what he wished and no more. Efforts to persuade him to do otherwise were met with a grim, and effective, passive resistance. The other is *Rogue Queen* by L. Sprague de Camp, which has appeared in book form only (Doubleday), and which deals with a quasi-human society whose manner of living is akin to that of the bees, i.e., one functioning female per economic unit, a relatively small number of functioning males, and a large majority of non-functioning females.

I have now followed the divisions and subdivisions of science fiction as far as I can and I must pause to remind the reader of a statement I made at the very beginning of this chapter. All that you have read represents a strictly personal organization of the subject. I do not pretend that there is any objective truth in it or even that any sizable portion of science-fiction readers agree with me. It may well be that almost all disagree with me.

Even if we can suppose that in some way I can persuade most or all readers to accept my classification of the field, there would still be wide disagreement as to which story belongs where. To me, for instance, the stories of A. E. van Vogt are gadget science fiction since van Vogt uses Korzybskian semantics as a "mental-variety" gadget around which to build his story, much as George O. Smith used his "physical-variety" gadgets to build his Venus Equilateral stories. To others A. E. van Vogt is social science fiction.

Again, some readers are beginning to take the attitude that any story dealing in Galactic sweeps is automatically "space opera." They will include in the category such examples of adventure science fiction as *Galactic Patrol* by E. E. Smith, gadget science fiction such as *Weapon Shops of Isher* by A. E. van Vogt, and social science fiction of the chess-game variety, such as *The Stars, Like Dust* . . . by myself. To my own way of thinking that broadens the term, space opera, to the point where it is almost co-extensive with science fiction. I therefore disapprove of this tendency. To others this may seem very logical and right, on the other hand.

Since there is no way for any of us to establish absolute truth, if, indeed, such an animal exists, our only alternative is to consider the various classifications presented to us and make that decision among them which pleases us most. The one that pleases me most is the one I've presented here.

IX

Having until now considered the effect of society upon science fiction, its genesis and development, it remains to consider the reverse of the proposition: the effect, actual or potential, of science fiction upon society.

This may seem rather bumptious of me. Can a literary form such as science fiction seriously be considered to have any likely effect upon society? Is it not simply a form of escape literature, simply a kind of entertainment?

If it were, that would be no disgrace. Any human being has the right to relax and get his mind off his dreary surroundings, particularly today, when dreariness is a universal factor. As the tailor said, when reproached for taking a month to make a suit when

God had created the world in only six days: "Feel the material of this suit and then come to the window and take a look at this phooey world."

The world today certainly does seem phooey, and it would be a harsh and self-righteous man indeed who could quarrel with the natural desire of an individual to look the other way. Unfortunately, the fact remains that we've got to face our problems at least part of the time. We have to live in the world and be part of it. Worse still, our children will have to also.

But *is* science fiction *only* escape literature? Is it similar in this respect to the western story which describes a world that has not existed these fifty years and probably never existed in the manner made familiar to our cap-pistol-toting children? Is it similar to the love story that lifts our typists and housewives into an imaginary world of synthetic passion purified by the Post-Office Department of any trace of true-to-life sex? Is it similar to the mystery story designed to present the *aficionado* with incredible amounts of make-believe danger and violence within the safe confines of an easy chair?

Superficially, science fiction is similar to these. In one way, however, it is vitally different. It treats not of a make-believe past or a make-believe present. It treats of a make-believe future.

The importance of this difference rests in the fact that a make-believe past or present must exist side-by-side with a known and actual past or present. A make-believe future has no known competitor. It can serve as a nucleus for serious thought without the distracting thought that it is a *known* falseness.

But is there a value in considering make-believe futures? I think so. For the first time in history, the future is a complete puzzle even in its most general aspects. There used to be the consolation, that even though we, as individuals, might die, life would continue, spring would come, flowers would bud. But now we have brought ourselves to such a pass that we wonder whether the planet itself might not die with us.

We've *got* to think about the future now. For the first time in history, the future cannot be left to take care of itself; it must be thought about.

But what can science fiction do about it? It can first, and most important, accustom the reader to the notion of change. The force of change is all about us, it is the essence of our society. Science fiction is the literature of social change, and it treats social change as the norm.

This is important. Resistance to change is, next to the desire for self-preservation, perhaps the most deeply ingrained behavior pattern in the human being. A child will not sleep in a strange crib. A man's digestion is upset if he eats at an unusual time.

In broader terms, you cannot reasonably expect any individual who has attained years of maturity and a place in society which seems natural to him (whether that place be stockbroker or dishwasher) to accept cheerfully any change that alters his place into a new and unaccustomed one.

I once did some library work for a sociology professor (in those days I had to work my way through college) who was writing a book on social resistance to technological change. It was a fascinating and frustrating experience. The priestly caste of primitive civilizations, for instance, fought any attempt to establish a system of writing. Once writing was established, they used all their influence to resist any simplification that would make writing more available to the general population. Naturally, that would weaken their own influence as the repositories of tribal wisdom. The introduction of the iron plow was met with the cry that iron would poison the soil. The use of coal for fuel purposes was opposed by the theory that the fumes would poison the air. Fulton's steamboat, the observers said, would never start. Once started, they knew it would never stop. The airplane, as Simon Newcombe (an eminent astronomer) proved mathematically, was an impossibility. No engine could be designed strong enough to lift a machine aloft which was capable of carrying a man. The

Wright brothers flew at Kitty Hawk, and Newcombe changed his mind. All right, he said, *one* man. But no airplane, he insisted, would ever carry more than one man.

The dislike for technological innovations that upset the even comfort of a carefully-designed rut extends with even greater force to social customs. Even the skeleton of a custom of which the pith has long since rotted away remains untouchable.

But is change valuable? Is it even necessary?

In the study of evolution, it turns out that organisms which do not change to meet a changing environment become extinct. Organisms, on the other hand, which find themselves an unchanging environment, find themselves also in blind alleys with no possibility of future advancement.

Human societies, history shows, must also grow and develop or they will suffer. There is no standing still.

Examples can be presented. Two occur to me. In the eighteenth and nineteenth centuries, Europe was presented with the necessity of change. A new industrialism was upsetting the old peasant culture, bringing to the fore two new classes: the industrial employer and the industrial employee. The former became more important than the old landowning aristocracy; the latter, more important than the generally inarticulate peasantry.

Nowhere in Europe was this gathering change popular among those who were getting along perfectly well under the old system. On the Continent of Europe, the landowners resisted the change manfully. They would not and did not give in to change. They *fought* change.

Did they *stop* change? They did not. Resistance welled further and further up the dam formed by the unyielding breasts of the old aristocracy. Then when the dam buckled, the flood was infinitely worse than it would have been had it never been built. From 1789 to 1917 a series of revolutions shook and convulsed Europe.

In England, however, the landowning squirearchy retreated (often unwillingly, it is true) step by step, inch by inch, giving in here, giving in there. The result? Where in Europe, out-side of England, is there such a secure throne, such a secure peerage?

Much the same may be said of the small Scandinavian coun-tries and of Switzerland. Here, however, it is not so remarkable. Small countries may vegetate, unaffected by the stress of large world movements, except where it is forced upon them by invad-ing armies. England, however, was subject at all times to the pressures and risks devolving upon a great power. (How much of her fortune is due to the twenty-two miles separating Dover and Calais?)

Another example! Our western culture hit the Far East with a thunderous roar one hundred years ago. The Far East, with a civi-lization of its own that was superior in many respects to ours, fought it bitterly and unsuccessfully, since our own civilization happened to possess one advantage worth all the rest—a superior technology. China rejected the technology along with all the rest of our culture. She would not compromise. She would not yield. She would not change.

The result? She lost anyway and what she would not give was taken by force.

Japan also retained her culture, but she had the wisdom to bow to the necessity of change. She accepted our technology. The re-sult was that in fifty years she not only became a great power in her own right, respected by all the other great powers, but she was even able to join in the exploitation of China, and outdo all the rest.

Now a fictitious example! Suppose that in the 1840's, the Amer-ican South had come to the conclusion that the world tide was against chattel slavery and had decided to make the best of a bad bargain by selling its slaves to the government and then rehiring them on the open labor market. Suppose that the North had de-cided that if matters went as they were, things would only end in a big catastrophe, and that they might as well contribute to the buying of the slaves and their subsequent liberation.

It might have cost money—but not 1 per cent of what the Civil War cost. The South would still have its labor supply, as it has now. Without the memory of a costly war and a costlier reconstruction, without the sense of a regional humiliation, without the sense of being picked on and kicked about, the South eventually might have come to feel less lordly about the color line.

What am I advocating? A doctrine of an irresistible *Wave of the Future, à la* Anne Morrow Lindbergh? Not at all.

I am saying this: it is useless to attempt to solve the tremendous problems of our times by adopting one of only two attitudes. Either to resist change, any change, and hold savagely to the status quo, or to advocate change, a certain change, and no other change. Neither of these views is flexible. Both are static. The result of a collision of such views is almost always disastrous.

I say there must be a third group, one which realizes that the status is not and cannot be quo forever, but which also realizes that the exact nature of the change which will best suit the currently changing social and economic forces may not be guessed at very far in advance.

Franklin Delano Roosevelt's New Deal represented such a third group. He broke with the brute capitalism of the 'twenties, yet did not accept a doctrinaire socialism. Roosevelt frankly and unashamedly experimented. He stated in one of his fireside chats that he liked to try *something*. If it worked, fine; if not, he tried something else.

I cannot help but wonder if a maturely developed sense of social experimentation may not some day bear as much fruit for society as physical experimentation has done for science.

Certainly, there is a good deal of this notion in science fiction. Its authors, as a matter of course, present their readers with new societies, with possible futures and consequences. It is social experimentation on paper; social guesses plucked out of air.

And this is the great service of science fiction. To accustom the reader to the possibility of change, to have him think along various lines—perhaps very daring lines. Why not? In the world, as

it wags today, there is precious little to lose. We face the
atom. . . .

x

So far, the contribution of science fiction seems to be an entirely passive one. It says "Change!" but it doesn't say how. It
says "Go!" but it doesn't say where.

As I have already pointed out, it is service enough merely to
say "change" and "go." It would be nice, however, if science fiction could be said to point actively in a worthwhile direction. It
would seem that it cannot. It presents a thousand possible futures
and there is no way of telling which of these will resemble the
real future or even whether any of them will resemble the real
future.

Unless, that is, we can find any way in which most of the futures presented resemble one another. There is such a way. The
large majority of the futures presented in science fiction involve
a broader stage for the drama of life. The one world of Earth is
expanded to a whole series of worlds, sometimes to millions of
worlds. Other intelligences may exist or they may not, but at least
the inanimate universe with which man struggles is stupendously
expanded.

The result of that is that to science-fiction readers Earth becomes small and relatively unimportant. A subdivision smaller
than Earth becomes even harder to focus upon.

There was some tendency, for instance, during World War
II, to write science-fiction stories in which Nazis or Japanese were
the villains. Such stories don't tend to be successful. They're too
topical.

It is as though science fiction, dealing, as it does, with solar
systems, cannot adjust itself conveniently down the scale to the
villainies of a single country on this small world.

This is not because science-fiction writers are internationalists
as a group, or because they have a more enlightened and all-in-
clusive outlook, are less patriotic or less given to sectional passions

and race prejudice. They are human, as human as other people. I do not wish to imply that any effect science fiction has upon society is the result of conscious effort on the part of those who write it.

Using this present case as an example, writers ignore the sub-divisions of mankind because the nature and scope of science fiction is such that anything less than the "Earthman" doesn't make much sense.

Whatever the reason for it, science fiction is serving a specific and important function. By ignoring "racial" divisions among men it is moving in a direction the rest of our culture must move in out of sheer self-defense.

There has always been hostility between the "us guys" and the "you guys." This hostility, however, need not flare into violence. I was brought up in Brooklyn, but for some reason I was a New York Giant fan. (I still am.) I hated the Dodger fans and they hated me, but it was a business hate. When we weren't discussing baseball, we were friends.

My state is better than your state, my city than your city, my block than your block, and my father can lick your father. It's all very normal. When your own group shines, you shine by reflected glory. When dear old Siwash wins a football game, all the Siwash alumni get drunk—although their only connection with their alma mater might have been a dismal four-year record of rejected education.

Where does this me-you rivalry stop being exhilarating and start being dangerous? When it coincides with a fixed belief that "you" are an inferior human being and "I" am a superior human being.

Just at the time that the western European powers began to expand across land and sea and to collide with societies other than their own, they also began to develop their superior material technology. Not only were the American Indians, the African Negroes, the Asiatic Indians and Chinese, the South Sea Malays and the Australian aborigines heathen and therefore inferior by divine fiat; they were unable to stand up to our gunfire and there-fore inferior by natural law.

This division of mankind into whites (particularly Nordic whites) and everybody else was safe only as long as western Europe (and its cultural appendages in America and Australia) maintained their technological superiority.

But the superiority is no longer being maintained. In 1905, the Russians suffered the humiliation of being defeated by the yellow-skinned Japanese. But the rest of the white world took it calmly enough; after all, the Russians were half-Tartar and very backward for a theoretically white nation.

Then, in 1941 and 1942, Japan inflicted defeats upon British, French, Dutch, and American troops, the pick and cream of the white world. Even Japan's final defeat did not abolish the shock her initial victories communicated to the entire nonwhite world.

So times have changed and race prejudice is becoming a dan-gerous anachronism. We are treating with an outmoded emo-tional attitude a group of humans who outnumber us badly and who are drawing abreast of us technologically. For selfish reasons alone we should be wiser than we are. (And on moral grounds we never did have a leg to stand on.)

Science fiction, insofar as it tends to think of humanity as a unit and to face humanity, white, black, and yellow alike, with common dangers and common tasks, which must be pushed to a common victory, serves the world well, and America particu-larly well.

XI

I have written longer than I intended and more circuitously. I would like to make up for that by ending with a three-point sum-mary:

1. For the first time in history mankind is faced with a rap-idly changing society, due to the advent of modern technology.

2. Science fiction is a form of literature that has grown out of this fact.

3. The contribution science fiction can make to society is that of accustoming its readers to the thought of the inevitability of continuing change and the necessity of directing and shaping that change rather than opposing it blindly or blindly permitting it to overwhelm us.

Science Fiction: Preparation for the Age of Space

by ARTHUR C. CLARKE

ARTHUR C. CLARKE *writes of travel into space both as a scientist and as a science-fiction writer. As a scientist, he has published two books dealing with the subject:* Interplanetary Flight, *and* The Exploration of Space *(a somewhat less technical work which was a Book-of-the-Month Club choice for July 1952, and the first book of its sort so chosen). As a science-fiction writer, he has three novels currently in print in the United States and in his native England:* Prelude to Space, The Sands of Mars, *and* Islands in the Sky. *In addition, he is the author of scientific papers on radar, electronics, and (of course) space travel, as well as of many short stories.*

Mr. Clarke was born in Somerset. During the war, as a technical officer in the Royal Air Force, he was in charge of the first experimental Ground-Controlled Approach unit. Afterwards, he took his B.Sc., with First Class Honors in Physics and Chemistry, at King's College in the University of London, and spent a year as assistant editor of Physics Abstracts. *Then he began to give his entire attention to broadcasting and writing.*

Mr. Clarke is a Fellow of the Royal Astronomical Society, and he has served as Chairman of the British Interplanetary Society since 1949.

IT CAN HARDLY be doubted that, of all the themes used in science fiction, that of space travel is by far the most prominent. Indeed, to the public the two ideas are now practically synonymous and the very phrase "science fiction" immediately conjures up in most minds thoughts of space ships and extraterrestrial monsters.

This state of affairs is no mere accident of literary taste (ignoring the vexed question as to how many of these stories can be considered as literature at all). That we are now upon the verge of crossing space is almost universally realized. What is not realized is the part that science fiction—using this term in its widest sense—has played in this development. For we have in the space-travel story something that may well be unique in literature—a type of fiction which by its persistence and steady evolution has had a major effect upon the affairs of the world. Upon the affairs, indeed, of more worlds than one, as the next few centuries may prove.

In most cases, of course, the writers of these stories were aiming at nothing more than entertainment (and here I would like it to be understood that I am not one of those who always prefix the word "entertainment" with the derogatory adjective "mere"). Other writers had political axes to grind and used their stories— as did Dean Swift—to satirize existing states of affairs. Very few indeed, until the last few decades, treated the theme realistically as a serious scientific project. Yet although the "technical" as opposed to the purely "literary" space-travel story is a recent development, all these tales have contributed something to the present state of astronautics. At the very least, they inspired the imaginations of countless readers and made them conscious of the fact that there are other worlds than ours. That consciousness was, clearly, essential before any serious work on space flight could begin. The fact that interplanetary travel is no longer a matter for derision is not only due to the scientists and engineers. The fiction writers prepared the way for them. Even Flash Gordon will be worth a sympathetic footnote when the full history of the subject is written—on the principle that there is no such thing as *bad* publicity.

A Gallup Poll of leading rocket engineers and astronautically-inclined scientists would, I have little doubt, show that most of them received their initial infection from such sources. And there have been many examples of astronauts who have turned novelist in order to propagate their ideas. It is not generally known that a considerable section of Hermann Oberth's largely mathematical *Wege zur Raumschiffahrt,* which laid the foundations of the science, consists of extracts "from one of my unpublished novels." Quite recently a still more striking instance was provided by Dr. Wernher von Braun, probably the world's leading rocket engineer. Dr. von Braun has published the results of his researches on a Martian expedition in two forms—a purely technical book and a work of fiction based upon this.

There has as yet been no really comprehensive treatment of the space-travel story from the modern viewpoint. The two best-known books on the subject, though useful, have major short-comings. Marjorie Nicolson's *Voyages to the Moon* (1948) stops at the moment when the interplanetary story begins to get interesting, i.e., at the end of the eighteenth century. It is obvious, also, that Miss Nicolson regards the subject chiefly as an amusing exercise of the imagination, and not as something with imminent and incalculable consequences to the human race. J. O. Bailey's *Pilgrims Through Space and Time* (1947) is more up-to-date, though its coverage is rather patchy and unrepresentative. Unfortunately the author's lack of scientific knowledge sometimes produces odd results, as, for instance, when he quotes a description of an already existing piece of equipment as an example of pseudo-scientific jargon.

It is obvious that the somewhat conflicting talents needed for an authoritative survey of the space-travel story are seldom likely to be combined in a single person. (I have met only one man with Master's degrees in literature *and* science, and the less said about his career the better.) Certainly I don't pretend to have the necessary equipment: all I have attempted to do in this essay is to pick out those ideas and themes in the interplanetary story that have struck my fancy or which seem to me relevant to our present conceptions of astronautics. I have also concerned myself primarily with the technical content of these tales; their literary merits, such as they are, have not been considered here. This means that I shall say practically nothing about some of the finest of all interplanetary romances—such as Stapledon's *Last and First Men* or C. S. Lewis's *Out of the Silent Planet,* which were concerned with social or philosophical rather than technical ideas, but will deal largely with stories at a far lower literary stratum, such as Verne's *From the Earth to the Moon.* Perhaps this self-denial is only appropriate on the part of one who some time ago sacrificed his own amateur status in this field.

The first problem encountered in this survey is that of classification. My interest now being mainly concerned with techniques, I cannot use the simple and obvious historical approach and discuss stories of space travel in their chronological sequence. Instead, I have divided them into two main groups which for convenience may be labeled "mechanistic" and "nonmechanistic." In stories of the first class, some engine or technical device, more or less plausible according to the science of the time, is used to bridge space. The second class contains all those stories in which dreams, supernormal intervention, psychic forces or the like are invoked. This includes most of the very earliest works, but the division cuts across any historical sequence, since some of the best stories of our own era belong to this category.

Science Fiction: Preparation for the Age of Space

SUPERNATURAL VOYAGES

It is somewhat curious that the first truly *scientific* moon voyage invoked supernatural forces. This was the *Somnium* (1643) written by no less a man than Kepler, to whom astronomy and hence astronautics owe almost as much as to Newton himself. To the modern mind, Kepler presents something of a paradox. The discoverer of the laws governing the motion of planets—and therefore of space ships—he was both a scientist and a mystic; his background may be judged by the fact that his own mother barely escaped execution for sorcery.

In the *Somnium,* which was not published until after his death, Kepler employed demons to carry his hero to the Moon, but he was careful to make the point that as one leaves the Earth the air becomes rarefied and breathing can only be carried out by "sponges moistened and applied to the nostrils." Even more significant is Kepler's remark that as the voyage progressed it would no longer be necessary to use any force for propulsion. Thus three hundred years ago, before the discovery of the law of gravitation, Kepler had foreseen two of the most important features of space flight. His description of the Moon, based on the new knowledge revealed by the telescope, was also as accurate as possible, though he assumed the existence of water, air and life. It is interesting to note that the *Somnium* influenced H. G. Wells, who mentions its ideas in *The First Men in the Moon.*

At the end of Kepler's book, it is revealed that the whole adventure is a dream—an annoying device which has been used all too often in fantastic literature, particularly in stories of this kind. Equally common is the idea that in some trancelike state one's mind, or even one's body, could travel across space to other worlds, not limited, perhaps, by the miserable speed at which light is forced to crawl along. This device was used in Stapledon's *Star Maker* (1937), C. S. Lewis's *Perelandra* (1944) and in David Lindsay's remarkable but little-known work *A Voyage to Arcturus* (1920). Descending a few orders of magnitude in the literary scale, it was also employed by the late Edgar Rice Burroughs to transport John Carter, Prince of Helium, to the blood-stained little planet into whose population he was to make such serious inroads.

Before the age of science, there was good reason to employ such paraphysical means of conveyance because they seemed as plausible as any other in times when an air-borne broomstick would have excited far less surprise than many of the objects we are accustomed to seeing in the sky. On the other hand, when a modern writer uses such means it must not be imagined that he is too lazy to think of anything better; he may have very good reasons for his choice. There are, indeed, few alternatives if one wants to write a story of cosmic scope, yet assumes that the speed of light can never be exceeded. Some of the most thoughtful of recent authors (such as Jack Williamson in his novel —*And Searching Mind* [1948]) have suggested that in the long run purely mechanical solutions to the problem of space flight will be superseded by paraphysical ones. How far one is prepared to grant this possibility depends on one's assessment of Dr. Rhine's latest work (see, for example, *New Frontiers of the Mind*). It will certainly be an irony of fate if the giant space ships of the next millennia belong to the childhood of the Universe—if, after all, Kepler has the last laugh.

USE OF NATURAL AGENCIES

In the earliest times, writers who wished their stories to have a certain plausibility, or did not approve of trafficking with supernatural powers—transactions in which, however carefully one read the contract, there always seemed to be some unsuspected penalty clause—often used natural agencies to convey their heroes to the Moon. (It was, of course, almost always the Moon. We tend to forget that the discovery that the other planets were actually worlds, and not mere points of light on the celestial sphere, is relatively recent. It was not known, for example, to Shakespeare, although it had been *guessed* by some of the Greeks.)

Science Fiction: Preparation for the Age of Space

Natural forces were invoked in the earliest of all stories of space travel, the misleadingly entitled *True History (Vera Historia)* written by Lucian of Samos in A.D. 160. In this book the hero's ship, cruising in the dangerous and unexplored region beyond the Pillars of Hercules, was caught in a whirlwind and deposited on the Moon. It is true that no one ever has much good to say of the weather round the Bay of Biscay, but this must have been an even rougher passage than usual.

It is an astonishing fact that though Lucian wrote two stories on this theme (his second, *Icaromenippus*, we shall come across later) no one bothered to imitate him for 1,500 years. (Though it is, I suppose, no more astonishing than the fact that for even longer men possessed ships yet never sailed them westwards. Perhaps Lucian's first story scared them back into the Mediterranean.) At any rate, it was not until after the death of Kepler and the appearance of the *Somnium* that the first English story of a lunar trip appeared—Bishop Godwin's *Man in the Moone* (1638). Godwin's hero, Domingo Gonsales, flew to the Moon on a flimsy raft towed by trained swans. Gonsales had no intention of traveling to the Moon, but accidents will happen even in the best circles, and when he made an emergency take-off to escape from brigands he did not realize that his swans were in the habit of hibernating on our satellite. Gonsales' journey lasted twelve days, and he appears to have had no difficulty with respiration on the way; he did, however, notice the disappearance of weight—though this happened when he was still quite close to the Earth. Such a view of the short-range nature of gravity, one might point out, is still quite common even among educated laymen today.

The most ingenious use of natural forces was, I think, that employed by Cyrano de Bergerac in his *Voyages to the Moon and Sun* (1656). In the first of his several interplanetary expeditions, the motive power was provided by vials of dew round his waist, for Cyrano very logically argued that as the Sun sucked up the dew in the morning, it would carry him up with it. In other voyages, to which we will refer later, Cyrano used more scientific means and, quite accidentally, made some remarkably accurate predictions.

The last story which I shall mention in this group is Verne's *Hector Servadac* (1877), in which a comet grazes the Earth, scoops up Hector and his servant, and takes them on a trip around the solar system. As they explore the comet they come across bits of the Earth which it has acquired in the collision, some of them still inhabited. A fragment of the Rock of Gibraltar is discovered, occupied by two Englishmen playing chess and, according to Verne, unaware of their predicament. I doubt this; it seems much more likely that they knew perfectly well that they were on a comet but had come to a crucial point in the game and refused to be distracted by trivialities.

SUBTLE ENGINES[1]

So much for pure fancy. With the development of the scientific method in the seventeenth and eighteenth centuries, and the fuller understanding of what interplanetary travel really implied, authors went to greater and greater efforts to give their stories some basis of plausibility, and as a result the first primitive space ships began to appear in the literature. They were, naturally, not much like the space ships of today's fiction; but we had better not be too supercilious, for some of our own conceptions may seem almost as quaint a century or so from now.

The first mechanical attempts at flight—in the atmosphere or above it—were of course made with artificial wings. Since the early writers did not realize that the air extended only for a few miles from the Earth, they assumed that if one could fly at all then it would only be a matter of a little extra effort to go to the Moon. Lucian of Samos used this idea in his second story, *Icaromenippus,* where his hero removed one wing from a vulture and one from an eagle, and, despite the resultant asymmetric

---

[1] I am borrowing, without permission but at least not without acknowledgment, this delightful phrase from Mr. C. S. Lewis.

thrust, succeeded in reaching not only the Moon but also the Sun.

To Cyrano de Bergerac, however, must go the credit both for first applying the rocket to space travel and, much more astonishing, for inventing the ram-jet—a priority which I do not think has hitherto been recognized. In his trip to the Moon (the first attempt, that using bottles of dew, had been unsuccessful and he had come down in Canada) Cyrano took off from the Earth in a "flying chariot" festooned with firecrackers. No detailed description of the apparatus is available, but from what we now know of rocket mass-ratios and exhaust velocities the performance is most remarkable.

Cyrano's last attempt at interplanetary flight is, I think, the most interesting and the most scientific. The flying machine he evolved consisted of a large, light box, quite airtight except for a hole at either end, and built of convex burning-glasses to focus the sunlight into its interior. As a result, the heated air in the chamber would expand and escape through one nozzle, continually being replenished through the other. As Cyrano put it:

> I foresaw very well, that the vacuity that would happen in the icosahedron, by reason of the sunbeams, united by the concave glasses, would, to fill up the space, attract a great abundance of air, whereby my box would be carried up; and that proportionable as I mounted, the rushing wind that should force it through the hole, could not rise to the roof, but that furiously penetrating the machine, it must needs force it up on high.

Making allowance for the quaintness of the language, this is surprisingly like some kind of ram-jet. However, Cyrano's speculations were no more than brilliant flukes, for he had no real understanding of the forces he was trying to describe, and indeed his idea that "Nature abhors a vacuum" made him imagine that

it would be the air rushing into the *lower* orifice that would pro-
pel his vehicle upwards! But he did at least realize that the thrust
would fall off with altitude!

With the discovery of the nonmechanical forces of electricity
and magnetism, new possibilities were opened up to writers, but
on the whole they seemed to take little advantage of them. Cyrano
—who seems to have tried everything once—did make the prophet
Elijah ascend to Heaven by taking a lodestone and a "very
light machine of iron," sitting in the latter, and throwing the
lodestone into the air. The iron chariot was then attracted to the
stone, and the prophet repeated the operation until, presumably,
St. Peter was able to give him a helping hand.

The most famous of all magnetically driven vehicles is, of
course, Swift's flying island of Laputa, four and one-half miles in
diameter, which was propelled by an enormous lodestone, pointed
to give any required direction of flight. Laputa, however, lies
outside our terms of reference as it was earthbound and could
never fly very far from the mainland beneath it.

The use of magnetism also reminds me of a much later story
which I remember reading many years ago, *The Conquest of the
Moon* by A. Laune (1894). In this an iron mountain was
turned into a vast electromagnet for the purpose of pulling down
the Moon. I suppose this would count as some sort of interplanetary voyage, though it was certainly a spectacular case of the
mountain coming to Mahomet.

The devices mentioned in this section can be classed as "engines" since they do represent deliberate attempts to cross space
by *mechanical* means, however crazy the actual suggestions were
in detail. Towards the end of the eighteenth century, writers became more cautious in describing what we should now call space
ships, possibly because the public was becoming sufficiently well-
educated to see through the proposals they put forward (though
looking at some of the things we read in the daily press nowadays
this hardly seems a sufficient explanation) and possibly because
the invention of the balloon in 1783 had turned attention towards

navigation of the atmosphere rather than the remoter parts of the Universe. Whatever the reason, the nineteenth century was well under way before the interplanetary story got into its stride again, and steadily proliferated until it now seems that there are very few corners of the cosmos which are not pretty thoroughly explored. In the last century, also, the types of propulsion which are still in common fictional use began to establish themselves and to be worked out in some detail. They fall into three main classes—projectile, antigravity, and rocket—each of which we will now illustrate by some typical examples.

SPACE GUNS

The idea of the space gun does not, as is generally believed, originate with Jules Verne although he provides us with the most famous—or notorious—specimen of its class. According to Professor Nicolson, the conception first appears in print as early as 1728 in a little-known book by one Murtagh McDermot called, rather originally, *A Trip to the Moon*. McDermot traveled to the Moon by rocket, after the style of Cyrano de Bergerac, but came back in true Jules Verne fashion after inducing the selenites to dig a great hole containing seven thousand barrels of gunpowder. (One can only suggest that he must have had a very glib and persuasive tongue to talk the local inhabitants into doing all this work for him; but one also notes that he was Irish.) Here is McDermot's description of the project:

> We already know, said I, the Height of the Moon's Atmosphere, and know how much Gun-powder will raise a Ball of any Weight to any Height. Now I design to place myself in the Middle of ten wooden Vessels, placed one within another, with the Outermost strongly hooped with Iron, to prevent its breaking. This I will place over 7,000 Barrels of Powder, which I know will raise me to the Top of the Atmosphere . . . But before I blow myself up, I'll provide myself with a large pair of Wings, which I will

fasten to my Arms in my Resting-place, by the help of which I will fly down to the Earth.

The last item provides a distinctly modern touch, with its hint of braking ellipses and hypersonic glides back into the atmosphere.

Jules Verne's *From the Earth to the Moon* appeared in 1865, and its sequel *Round the Moon* in 1870. It is difficult to say just how seriously Verne took the idea of his mammoth cannon, because so much of the story is facetiously written. But he went to a good deal of trouble to check his astronomical facts and figures, and had the ballistics of the projectile worked out by his brother-in-law, a professor of mathematics. Probably he believed that if such a gun could be built, it might be capable of sending a projectile to the Moon, but it seems unlikely that he seriously imagined that any of the occupants would have survived the shock of take-off.

The "Columbiad," as it was christened, was a 900-foot vertical barrel sunk in the ground in Florida. It weighed 68,040 tons and was packed with 400,000 pounds of guncotton (then a new explosive) and the cylindrical shell was made of the recently discovered wonder metal, aluminum. It cost $5,446,675, which in those times was quite a lot of money, though nowadays, of course, it wouldn't keep a nuclear physicist in heavy hydrogen.

Ignoring the impossibility of its actual launching, Verne's projectile must be considered as the first really scientifically conceived space vessel. It had hydraulic shock absorbers, air-conditioning plant, padded walls with windows deeply set in them, and similar arrangements which we now accept as commonplace in any well-ordered space ship. I need hardly say, however, that the gun itself would not have produced the results predicted by Verne. Willy Ley, in his *Rockets and Space-Travel*, disposes of it pretty thoroughly. Not only would the initial acceleration of some 40,000 gravities have converted the occupants into practically mono-molecular films in a few microseconds, but the projectile itself would have been destroyed before leaving the barrel owing to the air in its path. It's of some interest to note that both Oberth and von Pirquet have attempted to see if there are any conditions under which a space gun could operate (for example, by building it on a very high mountain and evacuating the barrel to reduce air resistance). Even in these circumstances, however, the project seems impossible.

Verne's gun was not by any means the last of its kind and scarcely less famous was that devised by H. G. Wells for his film *Things to Come* (1936). This caused the British Interplanetary Society much annoyance at the time, it being generally felt that Wells had let the side down badly. The explanation may be that Wells was never very much interested in science *qua* science; he explicitly denied attempting technological prophecy, and was always more interested in the impact of science on society. Certainly his space gun was no more impracticable than his antigravity screens, which we will discuss later, yet they aroused no such ire, though the law of the conservation of energy was really quite well understood in 1900. Still, there were no interplanetary societies in those days.

Two much more plausible attempts to use the space gun (in conjunction with rocket propulsion) have appeared in this century. One is in J. B. S. Haldane's essay "The Last Judgment" (from *Possible Worlds*, 1927), but a more thorough treatment was made in the interesting book *Zero to Eighty* (1937), written by the well-known electrical engineer E. F. Northrup under the improbable name "Akkad Pseudoman." This book, thinly disguised as fiction and apparently containing some real autobiographical material, was really a serious attempt to show that space travel could be achieved. Certainly it must be the only interplanetary romance with a forty-page mathematical appendix and photographs of the models constructed to test the theories involved!

Northrup, being a practical scientist, realized that human beings could only survive being shot from a gun if the barrel was made immensely long and the acceleration correspondingly reduced, though sustained for a longer period of time. He therefore used an electromagnetic gun (details of frequency, phase, etc., are discussed at some length) stretching for 200 kilometers along Mt. Popocatepetl. Even this did not give the full velocity of escape, and the final impulse was provided by rockets.

We do not often come across space guns in these more sophisticated days, for their fundamental disadvantages are too clearly recognized and are quite unavoidable. Traveling at five gravities acceleration, one must cover a distance of over a thousand kilometers before reaching escape velocity, and any practical launching device could be only a fraction of this in length, producing a proportionally small fraction of the required velocity. A track a hundred kilometers long, for example, would produce only a tenth of escape velocity at five gravities acceleration.

It does not necessarily follow, however, that space guns will *never* be used, for they may well come into their own for one particular but very important application where they can be employed under ideal conditions. I refer to the projection of fuel from a *lunar* base to space ships orbiting either the Moon or the Earth, where the required initial velocity is relatively small and there would be no restrictions set by air resistance or acceleration.[2]

ANTIGRAVITY

I am not sure who has the credit, or otherwise, for inventing antigravity, but the earliest reference to this popular method of propulsion seems to be in J. Atterley's *Voyage to the Moon* published in 1827. Atterley was the pen name of Professor George Tucker, under whom Edgar Allen Poe studied at the University of Virginia, and his work had a considerable influence on Poe's own satirical moon voyage, "The Incredible Adventures of Hans Pfaal" (1835)—not one of that great writer's more successful

[2] I have analyzed the theory and performance of the lunar-based launcher in *Journal of the British Interplanetary Society*, 9 (Nov. 1950).

efforts. Atterley's hero encounters a metal with a tendency to fly away from the Earth (how any of it has managed to stay on this planet neither Atterley nor his numerous successors ever explains) and by coating a vessel with it he is able to make a journey to the Moon.

This idea, of course, foreshadows that developed much more fully in Wells' *First Men in the Moon* (1901), which is still perhaps the greatest of all interplanetary stories despite its inevitable "dating." Wells' "Cavorite" was, as most of you will recall, a substance impenetrable to gravity just as a sheet of metal is to light. Consequently one had only to build a sphere—or rather a polyhedron—coated with it to fly away from the Earth. Control could be effected by rolling up sections of the Cavorite towards the body which one wished to approach. So much simpler than these noisy and alarmingly energetic rockets!

I do not suppose that Wells had ever come across Atterley's book, but I cannot help wondering if he knew of Kurd Lasswitz' *Auf Zwei Planeten* (1897), which has long been very popular in Germany and is now being translated by Willy Ley. This is undoubtedly one of the most important of all interplanetary romances. Not only does it include such ideas as antigravity, but explosive propulsion systems ("repulsors"—the word later used by the "Verein für Raumschiffahrt" to describe its own early rockets) and, most surprising of all, space stations! All these details were worked out with great care by the author, who was a professor of mathematics at Jena.

As another of the countless users of antigravity—though not for space travel—I cannot forbear to mention no less a scientist than Professor Simon Newcombe. Professor Newcombe's famous article "proving" that heavier-than-air flight was impossible has often been quoted against him. It is something of a surprise, therefore, to discover that he was the author of a novel with the quaint title *His Wisdom, the Defender* (1900), in which he described how airplanes, employing an antigravitational substance named "etherine," might be used as a means of abolishing war. Once again, I fear, the Professor proved himself a rather poor prophet!

It is hardly necessary to mention any of the innumerable other stories which have used the apparently plausible device of anti-gravity in some way or other. And it is hardly necessary to say that it won't work—at least in the way that Wells and Co. described it. There is, it is true, no fundamental objection to a substance which is repelled by gravity so that it tends to fly away from the Earth, and such a substance could, in principle, be used to lift a space ship. But in that case it would take work *to pull it down again*—exactly as much work, in fact, as would be required to lift an equivalent mass of normal matter to the same altitude. Thus the only way the travelers could return, or could land on another planet, would be to jettison their antigravitational material.

An antigravity screen, as opposed to a substance which gravity repels—is quite a different proposition and can be ruled out of court at once on first principles. A little examination will show that it involves a paradox of the "What happens when an irresistible force meets an immovable object?" category. If such a screen could exist, and could be used in the manner so often described, one need only place it under a heavy object, let this rise to a considerable height, remove the screen and let the object fall—thus obtaining a source of perpetual energy! Looking at it from another angle, Willy Ley has pointed out what a paradoxical situation such a material would produce. Imagine that one had a sheet of it nailed down on the floor. Above it, by definition, there would be no gravity, and therefore the space here would have the same gravitational potential as a point millions of miles from the Earth. Thus to step the few inches from *outside* the sheet on to its surface would require just as much effort as jumping clean off the Earth!

It must be emphasized, however, that there is no fundamental objection to an antigravity device which is driven by some appropriate source of energy, and therefore does not produce something for nothing. Presumably this covers those innumerable stories in which the release of atomic power provides propulsion through an unspecified "space-drive." The chances are that one day it will; but at the moment it shows no signs of behaving in such a convenient manner.

ROCKETS

As we have already mentioned, Cyrano de Bergerac was the first writer to use the rocket for interplanetary travel. Cyrano, of course, had no idea of the rocket's peculiar virtues (or, for that matter, its considerable vices) so he cannot be given much credit for the invention. Nor, I am afraid, can this passage from Defoe's *Consolidator* (1705) be regarded as more than a pure fluke, though it is certainly an uncannily accurate description of a liquid propellant rocket motor: ". . . and as the bodies were made of Lunar Earth, which would bear the Fire, the Cavities were filled with an ambient Flame, which fed on a certain Spirit, deposited in a proper quantity to last out the Voyage. . . ."

I wonder what would happen if one of our rocket engineers specified "lunar Earth" for a combustion chamber lining. It might be worth trying.

Although the rocket, or some other form of "firework," was often mentioned in the space-travel story, it was not until late in the nineteenth century that it began to become prominent. Verne used it in his *Round the Moon* (1870) to alter the orbit of his projectile, and understood clearly enough that the rocket was the only means of propulsion that would operate in space; but it never occurred to him to use it for the whole voyage.

Nowadays, of course, it is exceptional to find an interplanetary vessel which is not driven by rockets, and there is no point in listing the modern stories which have used it. As the work of Oberth and the German experimenters became more widely known, so a class of painstakingly accurate stories sprang up— some, indeed, being little more than thinly disguised textbooks. The German writers (Valier, Gail, etc.) were good at this sort of thing, and some of their works appeared in translation in early issues of *Wonder Stories*. I need hardly say that few of these tales were of much literary merit, but they are still very interesting from the historical point of view. One of the few stories which, as I remember it, did have a fairly elaborate and convincing technical background without damage to its entertainment value was Laurence Manning's "Wreck of the Asteroid" (*Wonder Stories,* Dec. 1932–Feb. 1933). Manning was an early member of the American Interplanetary Society, as it was then. He once introduced the rocket exhaust equation, complete with root signs and awkward exponents, into one of his stories—no doubt to the annoyance of *Wonder Stories'* compositor!

The almost universal acceptance of the rocket has left writers little room for ingenuity and one space ship is now very much like another. Very few of them have much resemblance to the ships which, unfortunately, we will have to build for the first voyages into space. Fuel tankage and similar inconveniences do not bother the science-fiction writer—still less the science-fiction artist, who gaily runs rows of portholes the whole length of the hull, and depicts thousand-ton rockets racing low over exotic landscapes with no visible means of support.

Going right out on a limb which Time will probably saw off behind me, I have suggested (in *The Exploration of Space*) that the space ship of the next century will be so much unlike our contemporary pictures that we wouldn't recognize one if we saw it. Certainly if orbital refueling techniques are developed as we expect them to be, then the space ships designed for true interplanetary flight would never land on any world, or even enter an atmosphere, and so would have no streamlining or control surfaces. Indeed, their natural shape would be spherical, but as the necessity for atomic shielding might rule this out, I have—until I change my mind again—suggested that a dumbbell arrangement has much to recommend it, since the radioactive power plant could then be placed far away from the living quarters.

Science Fiction: Preparation for the Age of Space

MISCELLANEOUS SPACE SHIPS

In addition to the main categories discussed above, there are also those space ships whose classification might well defy even the genius who once entered, on an auctioneer's catalogue, these successive entries: "Lot 56: 1 box oddments. Lot 57: 1 box miscellaneous oddments."

In this "miscellaneous" class are all those vehicles propelled by unspecified rays, tractor beams, fields of force, overdrives, underdrives and just plain drives. Some authors, however, have made serious attempts to evolve new methods of propulsion which at least do no violence to accepted physics, and I would like briefly to mention one or two of these ideas.

Consider a cylinder full of gas. All the molecules of the gas, according to the kinetic theory, are dashing hither and thither at hundreds of meters a second, but because there are so many trillions of them, all moving at random, the motions cancel out and there is no resultant tendency for movement. It is not impossible, in theory, that by the laws of chance all the molecules might decide to move in the same direction simultaneously, if one waited long enough. It would have to be quite a wait; according to my very rough calculations, there is about one chance in 10^{22} that all the molecules in a liter of gas would have even a small component of motion in common; and this is almost a dead cert against the even more astronomically remote possibility that they would have absolutely *identical* directions of movement.

Much of science and technology, however, depends on arranging things—stacking the cards, as it were—so that some operation, not normally probable, becomes in fact the one that actually happens. If therefore by some means of external persuasion one could induce all the molecules in a gas to co-operate and move in the same direction, presumably the container would move too, with anything that was attached to it. In the process, the gas would have to supply heat to maintain the movement.

It is difficult to imagine a more attractive way of converting heat into motion, but I fancy that somewhere along the line that old bogey, the Second Law of Thermodynamics, will step in and show that it can't be done. The system would certainly be ideal for running space ships among the inner planets, where there is always plenty of heat available from the Sun!

This idea was evolved about twenty years ago by John W. Campbell, Jr., now the editor of *Astounding Science Fiction*—which since his advent has become much more scientific than astounding. Some years later Campbell also produced a number of ingenious space ships which operated on the principles of wave mechanics and uncertainty. In the Uncertainty Theory, a particle cannot be said to have a fixed position in space but has a very small, though finite, probability of being anywhere in the universe. All you had to do, therefore, to get an instantaneous mode of transport, was to manipulate the Heisenberg equations until you were more likely to be somewhere else than where you started, and hey presto!

Finally, a word about ships which don't travel through space so much as make space move past them. It has often been suggested that two points which are a long way apart in our universe may be quite close in some higher, non-Euclidean or multidimensional space. As an example of this, consider the shape which can be made by taking a strip of paper, giving it a twist of 180 degrees, and then joining the ends—so that you have a loop with a kink in it. You can get from a point on the paper to a point separated from it by the thickness of the material either by going all the way round the loop (if one is restricted to movement in the surface of the material) or by traveling a fraction of an inch through the paper (if one is allowed to move off in another dimension). So the Andromeda Nebula may be a million light years away in our space—but only across the road if we knew the right direction in which to move. Needless to say many science-fiction writers have found this direction; and perhaps one day science may do the same.

Science Fiction: Preparation for the Age of Space

THE SPACE STATION

For some reason, the space station has attracted very few writers, probably because it is still, to most people, such a novel idea, whose possibilities and implications are not yet fully understood. No doubt we may expect an increasing number of stories on this theme in the near future, and when the first orbital rockets are set up it may for a while become one of the main preoccupations of contemporary science fiction.

It is generally supposed that the idea of the space station was first put forward by von Pirquet, Noordung and others in the 1920's. Hence it is extremely surprising to discover a story on the subject as long ago as 1870. Unfortunately, the only information I have about Edward Everett Hale's "The Brick Moon" is a short note in Bailey's *Pilgrims Through Space and Time*. According to this, a group of men decided that it would be of great assistance to navigation if the Earth had a second moon, so they decided to construct one. (This also is a surprisingly modern idea. It was put forward quite recently by Dr. Sadler, Superintendent of the Nautical Almanac Office, in an address to the Royal Astronomical Association [*Occasional Notes of the Royal Astronomical Association, No. 13, Sept. 1949*]. Until coming across this work of Hale's, I was under the impression that Dr. Sadler had discovered a completely new use for the space station.)

The artificial moon was to be projected upwards by being released at the required speed from the rim of an enormous rotating wheel, and one would very much like to have the engineering details of this remarkable device!

I suppose that one reason why the space station has been neglected is that it is such a nuisance to have to stop and build one, and most writers are in a hurry to get on to the planets. But the space station has a good many possibilities that have not yet been fully exploited. Quite recently, in *Astounding Science Fiction*, Hal Vincent (who I believe has a training in astrophysics) wrote an interesting story called "Fire-Proof" around the

217

idea that it would be impossible to have a freely burning flame in a space station, since there would be no convection to take away the products of combustion. This fact has recently been demonstrated experimentally by the German physicist Ramsauer by the simple device of filming a candle in a freely falling chamber. This seems to be an interesting case of two people arriving simultaneously at the same rather novel idea.

CONCLUSION

I have now come to the point where the road branches into countless byways, all so tempting that I dare not venture down any of them for more than a few paces. It would be entertaining to consider the secondary features of the space-travel story: to analyze, for example, the types of social system encountered on other worlds, the difficulties of communication (so often conveniently overcome by telepathy) and, above all, the reactions of extra-terrestrial beings to their unexpected visitors. It is, regrettably, true to say that these reactions are usually hostile—or else overbearingly supercilious. The behavior of the terrestrials themselves often leaves much to be desired, for in next to no time they usually get mixed up in local politics of an all-too-familiar type. Recently, the Russian *Literaturnaya Gazyeta* lowered its sights from T. S. Eliot, Stephen Spender and Co. to launch a salvo at American science-fiction magazines. These deplorable publications, it was pointed out, almost invariably assumed that civilizations on other worlds would be capitalistic and that Big Business would still reign supreme when we reached the stars. If one discounts the somewhat intemperate language in which the attack was couched, one must admit much truth in the charge. There are few things indeed in human society which are immutably fixed, and it would certainly be strange if the dinosaurs of the Victorian economic jungle survived into the age of interplanetary travel. I feel fairly certain that Big Business will have some unpleasant shocks if it expects to make much money out of astronautics—and though the *Literaturnaya Gazyeta* may be right in thinking that the social systems of other worlds won't be capitalistic, it seems equally improbable that they will be run on strictly Marxist lines!

I would like to end this survey of certain aspects of the interplanetary story by considering a point which is of peculiar interest at the present point in time. What, we may ask, will happen to these tales when space travel actually begins? Will they become extinct?

A test case has already risen in connection with atomic power. Five years ago fiction was still being published about the first release of nuclear energy; though it is no longer possible to write stories with this particular theme, nuclear energy is still a familiar subject in science fiction. Similarly, when space travel is achieved, the frontier will merely shift outwards, and I think we can rely on the ingenuity of the authors to keep always a few jumps ahead of history. And how much more material they will have on which to base their tales! It should never be forgotten that without some foundation of reality, science fiction would be impossible, and therefore exact knowledge is the friend, not the enemy, of fancy and imagination. It was only possible to write stories about the Martians when science had discovered that a certain moving point of light was a world. By the time science has proved or disproved the existence of the Martians, it will have provided hundreds of other interesting and less accessible worlds for the authors to get busy with.

So perhaps the interplanetary story will never lose its appeal, even if a time should come at last when all the cosmos has been explored and there are no more universes to beckon men outwards across infinity. If our descendants in that age are remotely human, and still indulge in art and science and similar nursery games, I think that they will not altogether abandon the theme of interplanetary flight—though their approach to it will be very different from ours.

To us, the interplanetary story provides a glimpse of the wonders whose dawn we shall see but of whose full glories we can only guess. To them, on the other hand, it will tell of ambitions achieved, of things completed and done countless aeons ago. They may sometimes look back, perhaps a little wistfully, to the splendid, dangerous ages when the frontiers were being driven outwards across space, when no one knew what marvel or what terror the next returning ship might bring—when, for good or evil, the barriers set between the peoples of the Universe were irrevocably breached. With all things achieved, all knowledge safely harvested, what more, indeed, will there be for them to do, as the lights of the last stars sink slowly towards evening, but to go back into history and relive again the great adventures of their remote and legendary past?

Yet I believe we have the better bargain; for all these things are still ahead of us.

Science Fiction and Sanity in an Age of Crisis

by PHILIP WYLIE

PHILIP WYLIE *is widely known as a philosopher and psychologist; his criticisms of contemporary man and his society have appeared in such books as* Generation of Vipers. *He is also a writer of fiction and science fiction as well as science fantasy; with Edwin Balmer, he wrote* When Worlds Collide, *recently made into a motion picture; his end-of-the-world story,* "Blunder," *originally printed by* Collier's, *has appeared in many anthologies; others of his science-fiction novels are* The Murderer Invisible, Gladiator, *and in a recent but more fantastic vein,* The Disappearance.

IT HAS BECOME trite to point out that, when an atomic bomb was detonated over Hiroshima and the news was spread abroad, the only considerable group of Americans who understood what it meant consisted of kids. The kids were held to be those who read science-fiction magazines, books and so-called comic books. To be sure, science-fiction magazines have been in existence for a long while, and the "kids" who read the early ones, like myself, are in their forties or fifties. And science-fiction novels, in a sense, are older than civilization. Even modern science fiction has quite a history. Jules Verne is long dead; shortly after Einstein made his first formulations, the brilliant H. G. Wells produced a book based on atomic bomb warfare. Still, the assumption was that only young people currently engaged in reading about imaginary atomic marvels were able to comprehend the marvel of the Manhattan Project.

In any case, it is certain beyond any doubt that most adults, including nearly every single member of Congress, hadn't the foggiest idea of the meaning of such terms as "nuclear fission" or "chain reaction." It is also axiomatic that, wherever a subject with vast *emotional* content comes to public notice, and whenever the public lack realistic or scientific data on the subject, a *mythology* is created by the people as a substitute for truth. That is not even a subjective assertion; visible behavior demonstrates it every day. If something is seen in the sky that nobody appears able to explain that "something" begins to "appear" all over the world, in countless forms, doing different things. Nevertheless (since the "something" is unknown and hence frightening in a very alarming epoch) a myth is immediately created—it is a "flying saucer," extra-terrestrial, inhabited by nonhuman "people" with superhuman intelligence—and so on, through the whole, silly and familiar event.

Yet the *need to know* every factual detail about every object or scientific concept likely to be emotion-packed and of wide public concern is not merely evident but forms the basis of the *idea of democracy*. In a dictatorship, of whichever hand, the need of the people to know is not great. If what they do not know alarms them, the State can punish enough of them for panicky behavior to calm the rest or at least to make the rest assume the outward semblance of calm. But in a democracy, the people must *know*—or the democratic process dissolves, by its very definition.

For we hold that a majority of any people properly informed will reach appropriate decisions. On that assumption rests our form of government. Without it, there can be no political freedom —hence no actual freedom of any sort. This great idea was evolved principally in Greece, following the reforms of Solon and Clisthenes. It died out under the dogmatic pressures of the early Christians which, in turn, produced the Dark Ages. It was restored by the Renaissance, revolutions in industry, and so on, a few hundred years ago and reached its full flourish in numerous nations in the eighteenth century.

At that time, any citizen and voter with a mere decade of current education had a reasonable comprehension of nearly all the main lines, and all the relevant lines, of contemporary knowledge and speculation. He (or she) was, indeed, "properly informed." He (or she) was therefore, by democracy's basic assumption, capable of making realistic and forward-looking decisions upon all matters of public import. The democratic idea was then workable and men enjoyed unparalleled measures of personal liberty.

The formula of freedom does not apply today. In the last century, mere factual knowledge has piled up so rapidly that men, including the very scientists who have piled it up, hold it to be impossible for any solitary person to have a good general knowledge of all the fundamental facts and processes in all the sciences

223

and their branches. Furthermore, science proceeds in two fashions: by blind pragmatism and by speculation followed by careful checking. If the pragmatic facts cannot be poured into any single human head—the speculations that outreach facts will be far beyond individual competence; for all such speculations about the Unknown rise from the Known.

The result is that we live today (and most of our savants agree we will be henceforward forever obliged to go on living) in a world where it is impossible to have a completely informed minority—let alone a thoroughly knowledgeable majority. It follows as inevitably as freeze in zero weather that the people are incapable as a whole of making appropriate decisions. It follows, too, that even the scientists are incapable of invariably making appropriate decisions on all topics for all men: they are specialists. They have confessed and even asserted the principle of general uneducability based on the thesis that there's too much to learn. Hence the judgments of any particular astrophysicist, for instance, in a matter of, say, public health, may be as irrelevant, as uninformed and as mistaken as an opinion on the same subject offered by an uneducated baseball player. And the vote of a great surgeon on, say, a matter of flood control, may fall as stupidly, as asininely, as the ballot of a moron.

The near-total ignorance of Congress in the matter of the structure of the atom in the year 1945 is a case in point. Brien McMahon, Chairman of the Joint Congressional Committee on Atomic Energy and Senator from Connecticut, once told this author that, on the day the announcement was made of the use of the atomic weapon, he had no lucid understanding of the technical aspect of the bomb. All he had was an intuition—an emotional sensation—that the bomb was of the utmost importance. However, unlike most members of Congress, he refused immediately to plan on the basis of mere emotions, loyalties, prejudices and so on. Instead, since his vacation began that day, he accompanied into the Maine woods a chemist of his acquaintance. He took along books. For a month, he "briefed" himself intensively on nuclear physics and related topics, with the result that when he returned to Congress he had a powerful grasp of the subject, and more than that: he had a plan for dealing with atomic problems which he opposed to the then-existing scheme: the May-Johnson Bill, which would have turned over atomic science, lock, stock, and barrel, to the military. The McMahon Bill—because of one intelligent man's effort to learn—became the law of our land.

It was undoubtedly as "good" or as "liberal" a piece of legislation as the American citizens in Congress could be made to accept at that time. Why? The correct answer to that "Why?" is, today, self-evident to many persons and becoming plainer to more as time passes. But it was evident to very few in 1945 and 1946. So far as this writer is aware, he, alone, was the only American author who argued (in *Collier's* magazine and in syndicated newspaper columns) for measures utterly different from any Congress had in mind and who, at that early date, predicted the current era of terror and peril in the event that the notions of Congress became law. For those "notions" were of the "flying saucer" variety. They were not evidence of thinking at all. Their content was emotional. Their interpretation was mythical. The Congressmen were not able to take into consideration the principle upon which democracy depends for the simple reason that they did not understand physics as a science, science as a method, and the atomic detail.

Congress (you will remember) assumed that the atomic bomb was "secret" and the knowledge by which it had been created was a "military" secret. (So did the generals and admirals in the Pentagon, who knew no more about nucleonics than the senators and representatives.) Congress, in 1945, assumed that the Soviets would be unable to "solve the riddle of atomic energy" for another twenty or fifty years. In vain, the atomic scientists argued that all this was balderdash. In vain, they pointed out, beginning with Smyth in his famed *Report,* that Russia had access to the basic data, and brilliant physicists besides. Congress decided to "keep atomic energy secret." Of course, we have since learned that the Soviets were hard at work on the development of A-bombs by the middle of the war and Congress was as near to nutty in its speculations and beliefs as men can get without chewing rugs.

What Congress did, in essence, was to try to remove a large branch of simple, physical knowledge and science from general human cognizance. Atomic physics was thus ordained by law an official secret of a few men of science and a few military men—to keep Russia and Russians ignorant. Of course, the Russians already knew—the whole world of science already knew—most of the facts which Congress suddenly proclaimed secret. And the Soviets swiftly managed, through Klaus Fuchs and others, to penetrate further secret details—by espionage—a certainty Congress ignored, since it acted as if the passage of its fiat would prevent such crime. But the bitter fact that, by legislation, Congress had for the first time denied to the people of the American democracy access to abstract knowledge did not occur to Congress or—if it did—failed to alarm Congress.

Thus, in 1946, through ignorance alone, the representatives of the American people set aside the fundamental process of democracy and, in a real sense, junked the Constitution. The Supreme Court was not asked to test the law but it is likely the Court would have failed, also, at that time, to see what had happened. Overnight, the American kids studying arithmetic could pursue it only so far. Beyond the point where it concerned physics, it was no longer knowledge entitled to free expression—it was secret. Overnight, the youngsters working with chemistry apparatus in laboratories found they could no longer learn all that science. The opportunity to become "properly informed" was taken away; thousands of years of effort to emancipate the human mind were, once again, crushed under a tyranny—in the American case, of "defense."

It was obvious to the very few who were willing and able to think rationally of the situation that other parts of other sciences would gradually go under the federal ban. They did. It was plain to the right–reader of human history and behavior that a vast and growing secrecy in government would continually expand into lesser (and even into irrelevant) areas, for secrecy is a cancer among free men, always. The cancer grew. As these lines are written, the President of the United States, in flat contradiction to the expressed sense of our Constitution, has implied he has the power to seize the press. At this same time, newspaper editors in annual convention are worrying over a sickly spread of censorship, closed meetings, and secrecy into such doings as the conversations of the selectmen in village councils and the meetings of small town school boards. Meantime in Washington, a presidential edict has given every bureau the power, in the diffuse name of "security," to withhold from the electorate any facts any bureau chooses to withhold.

All this should and could have been foreseen in 1945 and 1946, when the original matter of scientific "secrecy" was discussed. For the United States of America could not then, or ever, become a nation where science, or any part of science, was put under lock and key—without abandoning both democracy and liberty. The refusal of the Soviets to enter into a free, open and inspected world of science should have been regarded as a direct, hostile and intolerable blow to American liberty—one to be met with ultimatum if other means failed. The very few who saw that need were tarred as "warmongers" by the ignorance-ridden and fear-driven majority and even the physicists (!) failed to see that our national philosophy was being throttled. They regarded any thought of using force, not as the final, absolute necessity for a people wishing to stay free, but as a sicklier thing they called "preventive war." In the glare of the atomic blast, all USA was blinded to its history, its meaning and its ideals.

Today, as a direct result, the nation in which we live is no longer "governed by the people"—or even by their elected representatives. For Congressmen do not have the "clearance" which entitles them to the facts—and even if they had the clearance, they would not have the intellectual capacity to assimilate and assay the facts. We are no longer permitted to know for what purposes the gigantic tax assessment upon us all is spent. We do not know what our government knows of the arms and plans of our potential battlefield enemy. We do not know what the foreign policy is—or if one exists worthy of the name—or on what new ideal (since democracy no longer prevails) it may be based. In many vital areas we, the American people, are as uninformed as the citizens behind Russia's Iron Curtain. Indeed, from the practical and actual viewpoint, USA is nowadays a quasi-dictatorship. For it so happens that only one elected American can be told all the facts: the President. Without a fight, *without knowing what we did*, we Americans abandoned freedom as a philosophy. It is not surprising the direct result is that we live in terror or insecurity, in anxiety or in a fatuous state of apathy, according to our personal knowledge and private nature.

For, by voluntarily cutting ourselves off from science we have left no modus vivendi for ourselves save by the invention of fables and myths—fables like flying saucers and myths like the notion that the Soviets couldn't crack the "atomic secret" for twenty—or fifty—years. Thus the dawn of the atomic age is coincident with the greatest social blackout since the descending Dark Ages closed down on the knowledge of the Greeks and Romans.

Again, why? Even though most Americans can never expect to understand, say, the mathematics upon which the atomic bomb is based, there is a vast difference between (a) having such information publicly available and known to anyone who wishes to learn it and possesses the ability to learn it, and (b) outlawing such data for the general public. Under the former condition, a people is potentially and theoretically free; under it, even an uninformed population gets intellectual and reassuring impressions of proper means for deciding political problems through open and public discussions on the part of those who do understand every matter in detail. But under the latter condition, which now prevails, the public—accustomed to liberty or its constant potentiality, absolute freedom of knowledge—suddenly realizes freedom has vanished. For now, even the people who do understand can't talk. No sensible impression of situations can be gathered by the naive from the debates of the learned. The philosophy that was the mainstay not just of liberty but of human individuation and self-assurance is gone. The era that will follow *must* be one of constant crisis—and *negative* crisis—since the positive sensations as well as positive facts have been taken away. That is what has happened—a tragedy of fantastic magnitude, all the worse for not being generally and consciously perceived—to a nation in which only "the kids" had any inkling of atomic facts so soon put under the steel wraps of military security. It is a deluded, objective kind of security, gained at the expense of the very foundations of the intellectual and emotional security of the American people—and, just incidentally, as a result, of all the peoples of Earth.

II

It may be asked what all this has to do with *science fiction*— and even with science fiction and sanity. Obviously, the majority of the American people are not science-fiction buffs; neither are the majority of Americans Congressmen. Besides—though less obviously—it does not follow necessarily that even if the whole population read and understood and enthused over science fiction, the attitudes connoted above, which cost us our freedom, would have been altered in any fashion. For the fact cited at the opening of this argument—that only kids, in the main, understood the A-bomb—does not signify that their elders, given the same under- standing, would have made a wiser, braver and more far-sighted resolution of the great crisis that rose when the Soviets blocked all hope of scientific freedom without war, or, at least, our willing- ness again to go to war to stay free. The children and young peo- ple referred to here understood the mechanics of atomic bombs, more or less, and far better than the grownups, by and large. That is all. They had *not* been prepared by science fiction to contem- plate the *responsibilities at stake and the ideals involved*. Hence, the fundamental questions of this essay are the following:

Is science fiction truly educational? Does it, so to speak, present not only facts, and logical extrapolation therefrom, but tend to augment the reader's *ability to reason?* Or does science fiction, by muddling fact with fancy, tend to delude and addle the mind? Has science fiction any sort of *obligation,* aside from the task of entertaining anybody in any fashion the author deems profitable for himself? Or—put another way: does science fiction *owe anything* to the exalted standards of science itself? In short, does science fiction augment or aberrate human sanity in this age?

It will be held here that science fiction potentially can abet human wisdom but that the bulk of its present production has the opposite effect.

We have come to realize that mere factual knowledge is worthless by itself. Facts, however penetrative and productive, will serve the Hitlers and Stalins of this world as readily as free peoples. Yet the orientation of our public and our higher education for many decades has steadily tended toward the erroneous direction that comes from the assumption that specialization in one field of multitudinous facts constitutes "education." This is hardly the case, as has been indicated here by the statement that an accomplished physicist may be no more able to appraise a problem in public health than a baseball player who, perhaps, never got past the fifth grade. We have produced, through the means of what we consider very high education, a large group of persons who are ultra-knowing in one or two special fields and—often— ultra-ignorant in the remaining hundreds of fields. In that process, we have lost all sight, educationally, of the most fundamental teaching of all—the inculcation of an understanding of the principle upon which our national entity (and all our past national "success") has been founded. And science fiction has played its ancillary part in the tragedy.

Long ago, before there was any real science or any awareness of the nature of "fiction," men compounded tales of heroes and gods who achieved nth-degree extensions of their sensory faculties. The strength of Hercules was as the strength of modern machines. The speed of Mercury was as the speed of the plane and the telegram. The ability of Circe to see things happening far away might have been owing to the witch's possession of a television set. Thor's hammer was like an A-bomb. A hundred old heroes and gods could fly—many disastrously, like Icarus and Phaëthon. Legendary heroes could hear things going on at a distance of vast leagues, even as you and I hear over the telephone. The list is literally endless—a list of magic tricks invented by every barbaric people and every ancient nation—a list of mythological characters who could "do" miraculously what we have later on so painfully learned to do, each man for himself, with machines, but in actuality.

These old myths were the substance or the personification of what corresponded in ancient peoples to what is today *religion*. But science, as we know, has not itself been of religious value to the devout and doctrinal. It has not yet found "God" amongst the galaxies. It has not touched any Heaven with radar or beamed communications to any angels or demons. Nevertheless it has built up, *through science fiction*, a vast body of *legend* that corresponds to those old legends which are, as the psychologists have shown, still the hidden substance of so much of modern religious doctrine. The venerable myths were merely an imaginary picturization of all that the various ancient peoples hoped to do or yearned to do—or, of course, feared might be done to them! Science fiction, by exactly the same process, takes what we know for certain, or for a reasonable certainty, and, by going on from there, expresses what we hope and yearn to achieve, as well as what we dread in the light of the things we now know.

This process—the teleological yearning from what is merely wanted toward what is not yet known or not yet available—was surely the basis of the start of religious thought. Out of it, step by step, man evolved his whole philosophy. And if the contributions of idol-worshipping pagans were horrendous and shocking, they nevertheless played a part by leading on to later, magnificent contributions, such as, for instance, the Golden Rule. Science itself is religious in form, though not in content: it hews steadfastly to the highest subjective principle man has so far been able widely to adopt: absolute inner honesty toward outer objects. This is, essentially, a mere transposition of the subjective teachings of Jesus to the outer world. Many authors have said, rightly, in the opinion of this one, that true science was impossible before the teachings and ideals of Jesus had been disseminated.

It is, therefore, the quasi-religious, the certainly philosophical aspect of the "modern mythology" that is science fiction, which leads many commentators to assume its function is ipso facto for the general good. That assumption does follow, *providing* the example of science fiction in question actually represents at least some part of a formulation, process or philosophy that stands for what is "best" or "truest" or "highest" or "most complete" in all of science. The early myths were certainly both effective and affective: you can hardly find one that we have not turned into steel, vacuum tubes and whizzing electrons today. Hence the presumption that present "myths" will automatically lead men onward—and upward.

There is, however, a difference between the two. The old myths formed a complete although naive grouping of the natural and real hopes and fears of everybody. But our latter-day, self-conscious science fictions rarely exhibit a comparable inclusiveness. Early man proceeded to imagine from his feelings and his yearnings. Modern imaginers proceed, as a rule, not from the total needs or total dreads of their societies, but, simply, from their private hankerings and alarms. Early man had, as the "scientific" basis for his "science fiction," nothing more than a knowledge of his body: his running feet, lifting back, hearing ears, throwing arm—along with the capacities of the bodies of animals and the behavior of the elements seen in the incomprehended raw. But modern men have at their disposal a body of knowledge (which they regard as unassimilable for any one person) but, as has been suggested here, *no guiding, general principle*.

Thus, to the ancient Scandinavian, it would have been wonderful to have a hammer like Thor's. But, because the old Nordics were close enough to instinct to remember its workings, they knew there were no absolutes in human nature and no unopposable, solitary forces. Thor therefore had his weaknesses—as when he failed to wrestle Death to the earth—as did the other mythological powerhouses. Achilles' heel is the Greek parallel.

To the modern writer of science fiction, however, these *psychologically valid factors* are unknown. Save when such writers intuitively copy the ancient myth-makers, they have no sense of the importance of myth as allegory—or of the *balance* required by all such extrapolation, if it is to remain congruent with human nature past, present and future. Hence the bulk of their offerings, *unlike* the old legends, contains no germ of human truth whatsoever. So it is a great mistake to identify science fiction with mythology and from the identification to deduce the deep benefit of the former. Indeed, as shall be suggested, the intellectual aegis under which most current science fiction is written suggests that its very depersonalization represents a kind of insanity—a loss of contact with reality . . . in this case, with human reality.

There are some exceptions, to be sure. H. G. Wells' *The Shape of Things to Come* perceived that man's first greeting to the atomic age would be one of frenzy—that fear would lead to war—war to catastrophe—catastrophe to civilized rout—and only after that, would the wise among the surviving few endeavor to put together the human fragments on a basis of a philosophy loftier than the raging terrors of the interim. (As a "civilization" we are starkly and plainly well into this dire expectation and exhibiting the emotional build-up that went before Wells' calamity.)

Even more strikingly, Olav Stapledon, in *Odd John,* has sensed how modern, "scientific" man has failed to develop (by the same means of integrity and painful, slow empiricism) a science of himself and his motives adequate to match his objective science and so to conduct him securely through such crises as the present imbalance. In *Odd John,* the very few "superior" people who did possess that much sense, imagination, knowledge and

insight were first forced to find each other in a world of comparative nitwits, next obliged to set up a truly rational and scientific
society on a remote island, and, finally, under attack by a battle
fleet dispatched from a stupid and interfering world (which they
could easily have destroyed) these superior but still entirely human beings became so discouraged that they gave up their intention to create and promulgate a paradise for all men—and
destroyed *themselves*. The book was written long before groups
of busybodies publicly attempted to call a ten-year "moratorium"
on scientific research. It was composed a very long time before
the Congress of the United States (for all practical purposes and
democratic aims) actually *did* call such a moratorium for the entire Earth.

As we sit in our urban homes today—and tonight—the lack of
philosophy expressed in *Odd John* has loaded the engines of
destruction foretold in *The Shape of Things to Come*. One
small blunder, or one rageful afternoon in Washington or in the
Kremlin, involving only a few men, could bring the world awake
tomorrow morning with its hundred greatest cities smashed flat,
aflame and radioactive and tens of millions of the burned, mad,
horrified, starving and hysterical, surging on defenseless country-
sides the world around. All the cities might follow in the ensuing
weeks. This situation grows more homicidal with each passing
year, in a ratio almost geometrical, and there is not a sign or symptom of its abatement, anywhere.

Certainly, if science fiction plays any large part in leading the
minds of men toward new goals, the goals toward which it has
led most of its addicts to date are more evil than those of their less
well-informed forebears. Even among those authors of current
science fiction who assert that, for a quarter of a century or more,
science has been their passion, one does not find a deep and new
insight, based on any science. Rather, their orientation leads most
frequently to wild adventure, wanton genocide on alien planets,
gigantic destruction and a piddling phantasmagoria of impossible
nonsense. One needs only to read the contents of half a dozen

234

representative magazines and anthologies to recognize the fact. The fiction is of a perverse order in that it departs from what is scientifically known of man's nature. The science is most commonly employed either ignorantly or for sadistic melodrama. Thus the very writers who claim a long and philosophical intimacy with science and pronounce themselves leaders of the developing future and inspirers of youth, do not know sciences enough to take their privilege with any sense of real responsibility.

They are nearly all ignorant of one area of science as large as all the rest: psychology. They have neither factual knowledge nor insight into that science which deals with subjectivity. Their factual knowledge—even when they have any real knowledge whatever (and some of the writers are renowned men of science) —is limited to a square or two of the universe, a category or two of gadgets, a few cross-sections of objective data. Their own motives, fears, hopes, temper, values and imaginings remain unweighed and obscure. Yet, without a science of such matters, what they write is irresponsible, in the sense that it pretends to be "modern" whereas it is contemporary *in detail only*—and inevitably, *in meaning,* archaic. What they are attempting to accomplish, then, is not what the Greeks or the Norsemen or the Indians accomplished for themselves in their time and their frames of reference—although they claim it to be, often enough. They but create a new and sinister folklore, in which the latest facts from Massachusetts Institute of Technology are superimposed on a human insight hardly more developed than that of Bushmen.

III

It is for that reason Superman and Buck Rogers have given as frequent and severe nightmares to America's youth as the hoods and assassins who infest another area of American entertainment. Science fiction as a whole has made it possible for millions of adult Americans uncritically to accept the idea that the earth is being visited by men from outer space in dish-shaped ships.

Books, magazines and aggregations of individuals, all representative of presumptively sober and responsible citizens, have been emboldened to give the lie to the Air Force, on their private recognizance. This psychologically *toxic* effect has been the most conspicious, so far, of science fiction. It has undoubtedly led many a young boy into scientific fields (where, as has been said, he possibly remained an undisturbed bigot in all areas save his own); but science fiction has contributed little information to the general public concerning humanity. On the contrary, under the reckless outpouring of purple exploit, it has probably made the public more credulous and befuddled than ever. And it has certainly destroyed much of the stable skepticism once present in the population—as was shown years ago by the Jersey panic which Orson Welles and his radio Martians so absurdly precipitated. Now, with the air-raid sirens of every big city in America set to sound warning, at a moment's notice, of the approach of atomic bombs, of the bacteria of a new sort of war, of nerve gases, of fusing hydrogen isotopes and heaven alone knows what else— the average citizen, oriented in the irresponsible myths of science fiction, can be thrown into a tizzy by an odd glimpse of Venus, a high balloon, or, likely, flyspecks on his walls—if he's told the Russians precipitated them there.

Our judgment of things and situations has been shattered. To be sure, seven years of federal secrecy in science have added a huge quantum of fear and credulity to that nation-wide neurosis. But the roots of the disease lie in the modern *mythology* of science rather than in scientific information itself—or even in the withholding of such information. The average person knows "a lot" could happen any time. He has no appropriate way, any longer, of determining what is possible and what is not—what is likely—and what is not, although "secrecy" has not yet, at least, alienated him from reality to any such degree. The *myths of science fiction* produced the alienated condition by their irresponsibility, their psychological wantonness and their abuse of logic and reality.

236

Science Fiction and Sanity in an Age of Crisis

Most science fiction is trash, ill-conceived and badly written. Little distinction is made between stories that are scientifically probable (or, at least, conceivable) and stories called "pure fantasy" that have no purity as such. Every fantasy, impossible though it may be from the standpoint of "happenability," has an effect. And unless fantasy either consciously or intuitively states a complete philosophical hypothesis or truth, its only effect on the reader will be one of shock—like the shock occasioned by hearing a horrid account of a nightmare from someone else. Readers who consider themselves beyond the point at which they can be "shocked" in that sense, usually are unaware that their *unconscious minds* respond, often enough, in a way opposite to the fashion in which they *think*. All those (few) readers who do understand the subconscious, will see in the savage, silly amorality of the usual science-fiction fantasy a symptom of our general, mental disorder.

For whenever the imagination is allowed full play by a contemporary mind too naive to see the *implications* of the plots, situations, characters, action and symbols it conjures up, what is produced is merely a sample of the neurotic personality almost universal in this age. By all such process, the brain is deliberately detached from reason. Most brains, furthermore, lack instruction and education in the vast knowledge of mind and personality that lies, largely unused, in the files of modern science. The story planner who works in that now-obsolete fashion therefore has recourse to nothing save archaic and subaware material, such as bad dreams are made of. To clap a "happy ending" on a tale in which (say) whole planets-full of hostile Zoogoos have been radioactively exterminated by an aggressive American hero, is merely to set ringing echoes of our primitive hatreds and the inevitably accompanying creep of primordial fears.

To our common American way of "thinking" (since the lowest denominator of the most popular tales reflects that way) the universe is ninety or more per cent dangerous and hostile. Most space ships plunge across their abysses into combat with, or captivity, menace or torture by, brainy beasts of fathomless indecency. (We appear to trust brains less than knives in our own hands!) And where the universe is seen as benign, the quality is paternal: i.e., some mighty superman (as in the recent motion picture, *The Day the Earth Stood Still*) lands on earth (or is joined afar by "earthlings") and sets aright everything that galls, frightens, worries or enrages the author. So, we have not individuated as persons or as a species. We either battle madly and without asking why, against a world we hate and resent, or else we maintain through adulthood an infantile attitude—expecting a "deity" of some sort—or a Man from Mars to fix things up the while we do as we damned please.

Such is a sampling of the "psychology" of the ordinary science-fiction story. There are, it must be repeated, a few exceptions and all of them, if written articulately enough, have become classics.

Men like Freud, Adler, Jung, Toynbee and many more have shown the nature and the overwhelming importance of the myth to man. To Freud (if some oversimplification may be permitted here) random myths are infantile efforts to recapture situations that have no place in the mature mind. Often compulsive, always, in such cases, symptomatic, fantasies carry the lusts and hates of the cradle into the grown-up years. To Adler, invented legends attempt to compensate for a sense of insecurity, doubt of self, and inferiority feelings. To Jung and to Toynbee, myths are the philosophical stuff upon which whole societies are built; and when a given set of myths decays or becomes obsolete in the face of reality, it is a sign the believing and practicing society is doomed.

Our science fiction, as has been indicated, shows a regressive mythological bent; as has also been suggested, where it evades the rules of science and draws on the imagination without regard to logic or knowledge, it is obsolete. The fact that hardly a handful of science-fiction authors have any knowledge of the discoveries of the psychologists indicts the rest as obsolete for this age of crisis. It indicts, equally, the physical scientists themselves, for their pronunciamentos concerning everything *but* their sciences are as unlearned, the reader will recall and perceive, as the cosmic opinions that used to be uttered for the press by the late, great Babe Ruth.

So—all unconsciously—the majority of us who write from time to time a fiction of science, have devoted ourselves to the science of things and stayed kindergarten-ignorant of the science of human beings. It is not a timely or intelligent functioning, in a world where data for a more contemporary performance is available.

The proper function of the science-fiction author—the myth-maker of the twentieth century—would be to learn the science of the mind's workings and therewith to plan his work (as many "serious" writers do) so it will represent in *meaning* the known significance of man. Logical extrapolations from existing laws and scientific hypotheses should be woven into tales congruent not with our unconscious hostilities and fears but with the hope of a subjective integration to match the integrated knowledge we have of the outer world. Pure fantasies should be rendered truly pure—and every ending, "happy" or ironic, ought to describe a process of personality and conform to facts of inner experience.

For the reader not only projects himself into each tale he encounters, but he considers it, whether he is aware of the fact or not, from the allegorical standpoint. It becomes a parable to him and even though he forgets the detail, its lesson (implication) remains in him as a "feeling." If the lesson be no more than that the universe, including man, is a great zoo of horrible beasts, his subsequent responses will be such as we see on every hand, these days: fugue, flight, aggression, and panic like the one Orson Welles precipitated, or a slug-nutty apathy such as overcomes pigs in mazes too difficult for their insight—"hysteria," in short, the kind that characterizes most Americans this very day. For while we know our cities can be swept away overnight and may be, few of us will even prepare for the onslaught, or make ready to defend ourselves or pick up our wounded and bury our dead. We prefer to take a mocking or guiltily recessive view of our own "Civil Defense"!

We science-fiction writers—most of us—have taught the people a little knowledge, but such a little and in such a blurred and reckless fashion that it constitutes true and factual information in the minds of very few. More than that, we have taught the people to be afraid—because most of *us* are afraid, and do not realize it. That man is a positive force, evolving and maturing, responsible for his acts and able if he will to deal with their consequences, we have not said.

The Greeks and all the others had no means of appraising their myths or of evaluating the religion founded on those myths. Yet their myths add up to a concept more civilized, more mature, more positively inspiring than the mythology of our times. And we are the more barbarous because of our relative decline. We might be able to set ourselves and the clock of our evolution some thousands of years *ahead*, if the myth-makers took upon themselves the responsibility for learning the science of the mind and the personality. Indeed, after thumbing through several bookfuls of their efforts, this author feels that most of them should commence the procedure by submitting to psychoanalysis! Alas. . . .

Many will take umbrage at what has been said here; let them. Let the case rest on the future, on, say, the approaching atomic war. If it comes, we shall see how far our decerebrated rashness will carry us back toward primordial behavior. Then we shall see what men are made of. And afterward, as the survivors collect the pieces, they will perhaps be obliged to study man inside and discover how paranoid and how schizoid he has been for how many, many, many battling, tedious generations, simply because he has stubbornly gone on trying to conquer himself by conquering others and trying to conquer the world instead of trying to comprehend it.

This one author, however, believing as he does in liberty and above all else in freedom of knowledge (since all other liberties, by democratic definition, rise from an informed majority) would *compel* no one to rearrange his mind in a fashion suitable to his era. Men cannot be *compelled* to behave intelligently; any effort in that direction leads to madness. They can only be urged or advised or offered the instruction, in such matters as a deepening of their consciousness and a reforming of their ideals. . . .

Not long ago, standing on Frenchman's Flat, I watched an atomic bomb unfold its awesome surge of intolerable, white light. With such a glory in our hands I thought it time to stop acting like painted Indians. Time to restore freedom of knowledge on the face of the earth by whatever measures and sacrifices are necessary. Time, with freedom restored, to go out to learn and woo the universe—not lob hot metal at it. And the first step in this engaging adventure, this beginning of maturity in our species, would be to correct the myths, to bring them up-to-date, to discover in the front part of our brains the meaning of that old instinct of evolution which has brought life the long way from amoebas to you and me, and then to write down the discovery in allegories which would fill men with justified hope, rather than ignorant, personal fear.

Until now, men have always first employed their new discoveries as methods to injure their fellow men and only after one or more wars, adopted them to creative purposes. Would to God we could avoid the process this time!

It's our problem, I believe, and we could solve it if we but would!

Science Fiction, Morals, and Religion

by GERALD HEARD

GERALD HEARD *is a writer of many talents. Born in London, England, in 1889, he was educated at Cambridge, taking his degrees in history and doing postgraduate work in philosophy. Today, he is widely known in several different fields of fiction, as well as for his works on social evolution and history.*

Mr. Heard's mystery novels include A Taste For Honey *and* Reply Paid. *Among his fantasies are* The Great Fog and Other Weird Tales, The Lost Cavern, *and* The Black Fox. *He has written a number of science-fiction stories, and a science-fiction novel,* The Doppelgangers.

As far as nonfiction is concerned, it is necessary only to mention his study of the saucer sightings, Is Another World Watching?, *his* A History of Morals, 1900-1950, *and that very delightful book,* Gabriel and the Creatures.

In 1929 and 1930, Mr. Heard was editor of The Realist, *a monthly of scientific humanism, and from 1930 through 1934 he was commentator on current science for the British Broadcasting Corporation. He now resides in Southern California.*

Science fiction and morals-religion! Surely this is a grotesque assignment. Science fiction is escapism. Stalin, the puritan potentate, has said so. The Soviet has condemned these opium fantasies of a decadent capitalism. Fiction was never approved of by the moralist—it smacked of lying. Science was always making trouble for religion because it questioned theology.

And in science fiction's first phase it might have been admitted that ancient dogma and latest fantasy, moral rules and imaginary extravaganzas had nothing to do with each other. Science fiction was the extrapolation of science's wildest hopes and speculations. Science was then (as a corpus and a corporation) mainly an interest in the machine. It was the man in the machine (instead of the *deus ex machina*) that was to be "the master of things." And his answer to the Pascaline query, "May not the heart have reasons of which the mind is ignorant?" was the reply of the other French mathematician of a century later, "I have no need of such hypotheses." The universe is a vast machine and those therefore who would explore it will get furthest by and in machines.

Of course, H. G. Wells, who is a founding father of our fantasy, being a romantic socialist and for his "Fabian" years under G. B. Shaw's Emergent Evolution, was aware of Shaw's strange literary godfather, the Samuel Butler of Erewhon—Erewhon the inverted Utopia wherein man turned against the machines. Wells also once remarked that his own favorite story was "The Door in the Wall"—a tale both metaphysical and moral. But most readers decided that Jules Verne had a case when he claimed that Wells was a "deviationist," bringing into the purity of a world to be made manageable by instruments huge cloudy symbols of a high romance!

Romance, in the inhibited nineteenth century, could only find a place in science fiction as an effeminate desire for private petting which when thwarted spurred men "from all the littleness of love" out to real adventure. The most famous of all Verne's characters is Captain Nemo—the man who has chosen to call himself "no one"—the romantic who literally plunges into the abyss to drown his sorrow, where, in his super-submarine the *Nautilus*, he prowls the sunless deeps, not darker than his gloom, until, his rival unwittingly sailing over his lair, Nemo runs the rival's ship right through with his lancelike craft and sends his foe to the bottom.

Nor was there any change in the contemptuous indifference with which all serious-minded people regarded science fiction in the post-Verne period, when, extending the range but not adding to the variety, Mars became the target instead of the moon. With sub-adolescents (much keener on a car than on a mate) space-shooting in super-rockets, morality didn't arise and religion was decently escorted to rest beyond the limits of the space-time continuum. The young hero of course in the end killed the Martian monster and married the maid from Venus. But that was the merely conventional epilogue of the ancient fairytale—"They married and lived happily ever after." The heart of the matter lay in the mortal risks run and the breath-taking, hair-raising hazards of steeplechasing among the stars and death-dodging with the aerolites. And when the young Twenties of the twentieth century emerged with its passport to freedom signed by Freud, that only rendered still colder than the abyss the disapproval with which conventional morals and traditional religion regarded science fiction. The hot rod, the hot boy and the hot girl were crudely extrapolated into the hotter space jet in which, in exhibitionistically hot space suits, the two perfervid kids skid, clamped together, through sub-zero space.

But the dawn phase of gadgetry is now long over. It faded with the rise of bio-fiction. A triple force has driven science fiction ahead; the quality of writing has improved; the genre has attracted writers of high competence. The public that reads such fiction is adult (having gone through the child and adolescent phases). And, thirdly, science itself has shifted the accent of its main interest. The mechanistic picture is no longer satisfying. In the past people might have supposed that mechanism was the main bone of contention between scientific humanism and religious moralism. But as a matter of fact this has not been so. Religious moralism finds it far easier to get on with mechanism than anyone expected. For a kind of concordat was devised whereby the invisible and the realm of values and ends were left to religion while the tangible and the realm of means were handed over to science. Both sides assumed (and in this they were mistaken) that they were agreed about morality. Whether you were in a machine or a shrine, a factory or a church, such vague generalizations as the Golden Rule were supposed to run and to be able to control all the issues of means and ends, of private behavior and public business.

The interest in the sciences of life brought out, however, acute points of dispute. Nor was the source of the trouble that western man's religious tradition had a description (Genesis) that was at variance with geology. As Carl Jung pointed out many years ago, humane and humanistic man has no quarrel with the traditional religious findings in regard to four out of the five questions of the Sphinx: How may you use force? How use wealth? How regard your word? And how your thought? The more the social sciences have advanced, the more psychological insight and mental hygiene have advanced, the more it has seemed clear that the individual cannot be sane and healthy unless he can regard himself as a highly responsible unit in an organic society. About how that may be done in regard to the four questions given above, science and religion are ready to confer, convinced that their aims are the same—a responsible, highly-controlled person serving his community. But about the fifth question, as Jung has said, as knowledge has grown opinions have diverged. Today in our extraverted society for the first time the term "an immoral man" is ceasing to have the special sense "one who does not conform with the current sexual rules." And it is science which has done this. Nor is it the speculations of scientists that have caused this upset. It is their research results, their actual findings and answers to the prime question: "What is human nature and how is it natural for a man to behave?" The great hypothesis of evolution, which in the nineteenth century won against the elder hypothesis of special creation, disturbed, it is true, the fundamentalists. We see now it had little effect on the ordinary man. Whether he had climbed up from an ape or fallen out from the Garden of Eden, here he was, far and away the wisest of all beasts and able to change his environment to suit his needs and wishes. Darwin and Thomas Henry Huxley had far more in common with the bishops with whom they disputed than either party knew. Evolutionary biology made, then, very little difference to social mores.

It is physiology that has brought us to a revolution. Even the simplest physiological research began to upset our rigid notions of the normal and the right. Genetic research showed that animals carrying high-grade genes could sire thousands of descendents. A little research, and artificial insemination became a hard-working fact. But what about man then? Wasn't he, as far as his reproductive body went, a mammal? Already the process, everyone knows who chooses to enquire, is in full play. But the Law is unready, because it is frightened of the moralists who talk of the unnatural but fear to study nature. Already in Great Britain a self-appointed influential committee of clergy and clerically minded lawyers has met and fulminated. Whosoever so practices or countenances such practices shall be punished. The matter is not open. Further, knowledge is not sought. The question is closed and the penalties are chosen which shall put an end to such depravity. It is certain they will not. They would not do so even were artificial insemination the only new physiological knowledge that we now have.

Of course, it is but the least of the new revolutionary discoveries that physiology has made in the last thirty years and which today are altering completely our notion as to what is human nature and what therefore is natural. Names as little known as Bayliss and Starling were to make more practical difference to our lives than any of the famous evolutionists. These men, working in the first two decades of the century, had the real dynamite that would test our prejudices. For firstly their work with hormones gave rise to the slogan "man is only his glands." Certainly as the glandular secretions were employed an unprecedented scientific magic appeared. When cretins by being given thyroid changed from idiots into normal persons, that seemed "nice" and not at all "unnatural." When in rarer, but not uncommon cases, acromegaly came on and the patient's head turned into something terrifyingly like a horse's, this was considered a freak of nature. When we were told this was due to a slight change in the small pituitary ductless gland just behind the root of the nose, we took some time to realize what that might mean. And as the ductless glands were explored, we came inevitably closer to head-on trouble with the conventional.

What was human nature? What was natural? Moralists had always claimed that the rules they imposed were to prevent deviations from the natural. Early societies were consistent about this. Any birth that was odd was killed. In many societies even twins were looked on as so unnatural as to be exterminated. Our society gave up infanticide for all but the most monstrous deformities and even that had to be done clandestinely. We had gone to the moral extreme (beyond that of the savage) of accepting anything that happened to us reproductively. As we have seen right back to birth control, anything that interfered with the simplest forms of reproduction was condemned as unnatural. But to hold that position consistently the puritan had to be ignorant of physiology. For nature—very slight inspection showed—refused to conform to conventional man's notion of the natural. The ductless glands were fantastically but factually involved with sex. A small tumor on the small kidney hump, which is the suprarenal gland, can and does off and on turn a woman into a man. The whole of the ductless glands, any and every one of them, can play the most carnival tricks with what seems most basic and polar, an individual human being's sex. Indeed it is now recognized that if the ductless gland balance tends toward manifestation of one sex, say the female, but the actual sexual organs belong to another, i.e., the male, then the behavior of such a person will be dictated by the ductless glands and not by the ducted. What is morality going to do about such finds? At present there is a hush-hush attempt to use science to make nature conform to the simplicities which uninformed moralists thought was all that was natural. Quite a number of physicians and surgeons are performing what the ordinary person still regards as science fiction, the favorite magic of the Arabian Nights—transforming a man into a woman or vice versa. This is permitted by official approval still in the name of the natural. For (the present argument runs) if nature is going to change a citizen's sex then, as we cannot destroy such a monster (as would the earlier traditionalists), we must insist that the change is complete, back or on. We cannot let nature, as she very well might, stop halfway.

Now all these are live issues, the liveliest issues for they are what science has found out about life. As long as the public thought science was simply money-making-power-giving gadgetry science fiction wasn't mature. But now it must decide—will it remain the boys' fairy book with a space-suited Prince Charming as the arrested idea, or will science fiction take its new assignment? If ever a choice was a moral one this is. For science fiction when it does its job (and it has been doing it increasingly) does not merely extrapolate inventions. If it is worthy of the name of the true novel it makes real persons and makes them develop psychological maturity under the pressure of unsuspected portentous events. Will science fiction have the nerve to tell the contemporary truth to the growing-up in this unforeseen situation (wherein nearly everyone, politicians, soldiers, executives, spend their time getting ready for the last crisis or the last war)? Will informed authors dare say what the cards, now in hand and on the table, actually are, what are in the pool ready for the next pick-up, and what is the game when such cards are held? Take two examples, the first negative and therefore, of course, safer: What is going to be the actual power war if the contest of the ideologies goes on? The atom bombs, going on inevitably past the helium to the lithium, etc., have made soldier war futile. The aim of mechanized scientific war was to improve weapons by making them into what are called "scientific instruments of precision." This ideal, of hitting that and only that which, in Clausewitz' classic phrase, would alter the will of the opposing commander, has been destroyed by the imprecise violence of atomic explosion. Such violence is as inept in our complex society as attempting to correct a chronometer with a sledge hammer. But apt violence is already past its experimental stage. The progress in the barbiturates, the study with sodium pentothal in making the unconscious patient speak out all his most inhibited secrets, these advances are toward a complete revolution in the struggle for power. The battle will go on in a world-wide frontierless underground. It will be scientific because it will be doubly precise: (a) precise in its aim, because instead of slaughtering millions of cannon fodder (good simple highly suggestible types which submit easily to propaganda and so make excellent slaves) it will only attack those cross-grained types who make trouble; (b) precise in its method because, even with these negative types, the process would be reconstructive, the mind would be unmade and remade according to the will of the dictator. Of course with hard-set types this would probably entail a psychophysical modification by endocrine secretions. Indeed, as ridicule is the most powerful acid against heroism, it might be wise to transform the rugged rebel into a gay consenter—not degraded into a beast, that would be crude, but regraded and rejuvenated into an ephoebe, an Adonis elevated, apotheosized out of this dreary world by being made the latest "nova" in the heaven of the screen.

Such powers will be used if the struggle for political world dominance goes on. Science fiction in the hand of a character-draughtsman can create a new contemporary tension-of-choice, new moral decisions, and so indicate how they may be faced or flunked. These issues are not in a speculative tomorrow. Lobotomy is crude but already it is here and working. It is the new castration. The wild-beast paranoiac becomes the mild obedient animal. We can unbuild a rebel with a flick of a scalpel. The wizard's art is also offered us not merely to rebuild into fully human patterns of physique and behavior those who have given us trouble, but to make them into loyal supporters and truly thankful for our rejuvenating generosity.

The second example seems less sensational but in fact goes deeper and sets an even wider moral problem. Scientific research has from two directions converged on the problem: What will be the future society? And what its mores, its philosophy? We know from the history of the last seven thousand years that man has with increasing rapidity built up societies which in size and complexity are only equaled by the three great insect city-structures—the hive, the termitary and the ant hill. We know from the study of these three structures that though they are creations of three completely different insects they have certain striking characteristics in common. A social structure of such complexity (a complexity which goes beyond anything we have yet achieved though undoubtedly our process is directed to that goal), a civilization as perfectly integrated as is that of the bee, the termite and the ant, demands: (1) complete centralization (the individual finds its complete assumption in the society), and (2) such a completely organic society has successfully modified the original constituents —once simple male and female—into completely specialized parts of the whole. The force of the reproductive cycle, which, left to itself, will in the simple male and female relationship, be able to build up nothing larger than the family, is therefore canalized. No society, it is clear, can generate a loyalty as intense as that which the family generates. Hence in the communities that have been most successful in the social patterns of the three great insect groups, in order to make society come first, to make a unit of devoted loyalty larger than the family, a central reproductive unit provides a constant stream of embryonic life, and the servants of the state, the vast army of nurses and providers, rear these embryos. The facts are familiar; the implications extremely awkward and therefore repressed. Here is a sharp moral issue, as startling as, and indeed more unwelcome than, the apt violence of glandular operation and medication that can turn iron rebels into playboys or (if the statesman judges the joke would be more telling, the laugh more lasting) playgirls. The more complex the state is to be, the more it must have, between the simple extremes of male and female (that can only construct the family field loyalty), a series of stages. China more nearly and more long sustained a civilization able to embrace millions and transform in a generation barbarians into sophisticates. Every student of this amazing organism owns that its Achilles' heel was the fatal conflict between loyalty to the community and loyalty to the family. Conversely, it has been noted that every society (e.g., ancient Egypt and the medieval society of western Europe) when it becomes complex has to produce the clerk-priest type. In this administrative type two modifications are present: he is debarred from the usual male exercises such as war, and finally he is made celibate.

Today we demand ever higher specialization to give us the command of new elaborate violences in war, new techniques in surgery and drugs to prolong life and lessen discomfort, and new varieties of entertainment. These demands require a complex organic society. That society requires for its specialization of function that it be served by specialization of organism. Already, as Dr. William Sheldon (of *The Varieties of Human Temperament* and *The Varieties of Human Physique*) has pointed out, our society is sufficiently specialized that special physical types do tend to go toward and to fill special professions. It will be but one more step in "Scientific Management" when the psychophysical selectors of candidates and the trainers of the work teams give glandular treatments and/or operations to the members of each profession or "Shop" in order that, by psychophysical modification, they may become perfectly adjusted to their job. So the man and the machine would be brought into such symbiotic play as would fill Taylor (the father of scientific management) with ecstasy and Samuel Butler with "I told you so" despair.

Such themes, and there are many more, set character problems before the novelist beside which the old plots and play of temperament are rudimentary. It has been pointed out by E. M. Forster the novelist (and author of that lucid study of fiction's evolution, *Aspects of the Novel*) that Tolstoy is the first great novelist, and so established his psychological genius, because he can show his characters developing and changing—they are not static puppets. They are not mere stylized "humors" as for example are so many of Dickens' dramatis personae. Today we know that changes of character and indeed total modifications of the psycho-physique are possible. Further we know that the power to make such changes will increase in a way and to a degree that Tolstoy would have thought utterly fantastic, utterly beyond any realism and only to be relegated to the absurdities of the Arabian Nights entertainment.

It is here where science fiction will be tested as to whether it is prepared to become fully adult and responsible. Will it be prepared to take, for instance, a theme which, starting with the basic situation boy-meets-girl (the source of the family pattern), faces the fact that each may be "drafted" (and so streamlined by the forced draft that they may be alienated and finally transmuted). Here is the material for a completely new drama, a fresh development of tragedy and an original extension of what the Greek poets called irony. Till now we have had in the moral-making forms of drama only two situations, one of comedy and the other of tragedy. In the first, things turn out well and after some surprises and contretemps everything ends in Laughter and Fun. Nature in the end turns out to have been friendly after all to our main design and desire. The master force in us, the desire to make love, is backed up by the life force. "Journeys end in lovers' meetings" and only old spoilsport, crabbed age, gets fooled and beaten up.

In the second case nature does not co-operate; she does not care for man or his happiness even when he is a breeding animal seeking a mate. The universe is not friendly. It is hostile. But though it can and will smash man's body, it cannot bend his will or coerce his character. Here there is no possibility of a happy ending. But the audience gets its catharsis, its sense that you can let the cosmos do its damndest, because the individual protagonist "beneath the bludgeonings of Fate" has a head that is "bloody but unbowed."

Today however we have, in our morality and our drama, worked through stage two of tragedy and reached stage three. The character *is* altered by the crisis. And the "irony"—the onlooking "God's-eye view" of the audience—consists no longer in so simple a formula as being "purged of pity and of fear." We now face the fact that as the universe is in evolution so too is human character. The idea (basic to tragedy) that there is one thing unchangeable in the flux, and that it is man's "unconquerable soul" with its clutter of prejudices which it calls morality and its lack of humor which it calls dignity, goes overboard. So we come to the return of comedy—or rather meta-comedy. The first stage of drama (comedy) thought the universe was fun. The second (tragedy) thought man at least was dignified. The third sees man and the cosmos in play. If you can laugh at yourself and at the ever broader fun that the universe seems to be having at your expense, suddenly you will see the gigantic point of the joke. For the complete catharsis lies not in tears or in stoic repression but in laughter. The stoic tried to make himself invulnerable by his "apathy." But mind and body can't so be taken apart except by suicide—a course to which the stoic naturally resorted with increasing frequency. The only real freedom is by taking up a standpoint from which not only the body is seen as ridiculous but the personality also. The mind-body (not merely the body) is regarded with detachment and that detachment is not gravity (which is always full of self-focused concern) but laughter that is full of general amused insight. Comedy so seen is perceived as going far deeper than tragedy and so must be considered as the "real realism."

But where in this development of the human plot (whether in the novel, the stage or the screen) does science fiction come in? Right in the middle. For what is this blend of man and the universe (this the theme of meta-comedy) but the emergence into a complete art form of Taylor's dawn concept: that man and the machine must develop together as an integrated symbiot. Science fiction, in its attitude to morality, has today a double appositeness: (1) in its aim, and (2) in its method. In its aim it is bound, by its extrapolation of science and its use of dramatic plot, to view man and his machines and his environment as a threefold whole, the machine being the hyphen. It also views man's psyche, man's physique and the entire life process as also a threefold interacting unit. Science fiction is the prophetic (or to use a more exact special term) the apocalyptic literature of our particular and culminating epoch of crisis. It can shape our reactions to our destiny, it can show us how to react, how to adapt, how to endure. It can indicate by the convincingness of its stories how man's tensile strength of dynamic acceptance, his comprehending tolerance of new challenge can develop. So it will develop morality in the traditional sense—i.e., man's power to adjust to the demands of natural law. But further it can and must show how we can shape our destiny to our inherent demand, to our faith. For man is the one animal who profoundly modifies his environment. Science fiction must and can show man at last doing this intentionally and this is morality in the scientific sense. The aim of life, as far as man can see, is the increase of consciousness. A scientific morality (or a moralized science) is something more than the rather jejeune formula "the pursuit of truth." That aim begins to look fuzzy and merely emotional when we consider Niels Bohr's summation of modern physics "the end of objectivity." The aim of science today is then to discover that super self-control whereby man learns to master, shift and expand the focal length of consciousness and so apprehends further alternative universes, as in the nineteenth century the rise of alternative geometries opened the way to new cosmogonies. It has been long said, and it is true, that those who write a people's songs forecast that people's history. Social psychologists today realize that the most important people in any community or nation or civilization are those who create its "patterns of prestige." That is the huge task of science fiction today, now that it has come so rapidly to adulthood. That and nothing less must be and can be its aim.

Its method too is apposite. The old comedy "laughed things off." And when things became too obviously grim and man too grimly set, then such fun was bundled off scene: that is to say such old broad undignified pantomime was regarded as obscene— what must not be shown on the stage. There were things to which the reaction of laughter was outrageous. Tragedy with its pretentious solemnity and puritanism with its repressions and censorship took over. Now science has shown that truth cannot be regarded as obscene and what actually takes place can't be called and banned as the unnatural. The method of science fiction is so to narrate the facts science has discovered that we may be presented with a new play of character. So we can view this, the immensely enlarged picture of what nature and human nature are and what their interplay is, with a new interest, a new humor, a new fun. "Laughter is the sound made by an exploding tabu." "Solemnity is the sign of an oncoming psychosis." For first you must not laugh off pain: you must be stoically tragic toward it. (This is an attitude which scientific progress with its advances in analgesics is making increasingly anachronistic. The invalid who exploits his spasms is becoming rightfully a figure for satire.) And next you must not laugh with pleasure. You must be secretive, whispering, ashamed, guilty. But laughter is not merely frankness; it is a necessary force for insight. This aspect of essential extravagance (one of the main characteristics of vigorous science fiction when it keeps in touch as it should with fantasy) is given classical expression in the shout of delight, the *"Eureka!"* of Archimedes as he capered in the street so self-forgetfully delighted in his find. In Hobbes' famous definition of laughter, "it is the sudden glory." The profoundest insights arise from making associations and correlations which at first seem absurd and can only be sustained by regarding them as humorous extravagances. For as Dr. Synge (*Science, Sense and Nonsense* by Dr. John L. Synge) has pointed out in his stimulating book, advanced physics can no longer be called sensible. Only the mind made flexible to accept absurdity can grasp the non-sensory significance of our present cosmological notions.

But though the dramatic form, the psychological atmosphere in which science fiction (and indeed all really contemporary fiction that deals with real character) must work, is meta-comic, that has nothing to do with the farcical or the burlesque. Indeed it and it alone can produce the situation in which the meta-tragic emerges. A person is noble who surrenders ordinary domestic happiness because he is intellectually convinced that he can serve civilization best in that way. But he is still possibly very human and may become melodramatically ridiculous in his self-admiration of the sacrifice he is making. And so the realistic novelist can and does debunk him. But science fiction, with its new psychophysical challenges, with the endocrine choices now set human nature, can create decision-situations in which the central character, able to laugh at himself, can produce a super irony that leaves us unable to escape from the issue by mockery. Here then there is, in a sense even more penetrating than in Greek drama, the super irony which the Greek dramatist attempted as the acme of his art. His irony was the God's-eye view of the hero blinded by his own heroic *hubris,* the self-sufficient courage that will do everything but see itself as ridiculous. The super irony of science fiction can deal with the hero who does not bear off with a fine exit line "the pageant of his bleeding heart"—but who, undergoing endocrine change (because he thinks this is best for some cause he wishes to serve) watches his metamorphosis with increasing humor. He sees himself not merely altering in physique, not merely in a

Nessus shirt of self-imposed suffering. He sees his psyche changing too. He sees his romantic attachment to home and family, and
to the values which he considered to be eternal, fading away as
an adolescent sees his taste for toys and candy yielding to a taste
for girls.

Science fiction is therefore that creative myth-making which
Toynbee sees as one of the most important of man's social and
moral activities. But if it is to serve its distinctive purpose it must
be courageously contemporary. Science fiction, because of its
peculiar position, has a station as powerful and as influential as
that seized upon and held by Jonathan Swift two and a half
centuries ago. This terrific satirist saw how, with the new symbol-
ism of science, he could frame parables that, under the guise of
fairy tales, not only flayed the hypocrisies of his time but also (as
in the voyage to Laputa in *Gulliver's Travels*) put the science
of his day into an acid bath of contempt. There seems little doubt
that Swift so protected himself against ecclesiastical attack and
also lost the opportunity of founding a really creative science fiction.

That temptation again today is offered science-fiction writers.
They can play for safety by keeping their eye fixed on two patrons, by writing stories that meet the demands of childish minds
on the one hand and, on the other, minds that want to keep the
public childish. If, however, they realize their opportunity they can
take, one by one, all the rising issues wherein it is clear that within
a few years scientific research and applied science must demand
new interpretations of the traditional mores. This is certainly not
an easy assignment. And indeed the man who, with a facile gift for
exciting, picaresque narrative, takes to science fiction, may object to
finding that he is being turned into a prophet and lawgiver. The fact
remains that science fiction, partly because of the way in which
science has produced new problems for morality and partly because
of the many accurate forecasts science-fiction writers have made, has
now the opportunity to be taken seriously. It can work out in "model
form" what shape social behavior patterns will take. More than any

other form of literature it can educate people as to what are the
social situations in which they will soon find themselves. Further
its responsibility and opportunity are immensely increased in that
while it can make the public familiar with new conditions (which
without preparation would prove highly shocking) it can also create
the atmosphere, friendly or unfriendly, interested or indignantly dis-
gusted, with which these new finds and forces will be confronted.
It not only can show the new fact in an attractive guise. Even
more important it can show ourselves behaving in an attractive,
civilized, constructive, tolerant way toward the new knowledge
and event.

Science-fiction writers are not merely introducing us to new
scenes and new plots but to new characters. They can show us
as rigid, intolerant, savagely repellent to new knowledge. They
can play on old prejudices, making Martians monsters and any
human variety which is new, a ghastly misbirth. Or they can
show us of the next thirty years, surmounting each new wave of
knowledge and pushing out with a new tolerance and fresh curiosity on wider seas of comprehension. There is a truth behind
Oscar Wilde's absurdity, "Nature imitates Art," for it means
that man having observed nature more fully than he knows produces forms and styles which afterwards he consciously perceives
to be in nature and so to be natural. A more exact estimate of the
social power of fiction has been given by Aldous Huxley, when
he pointed out that character, ideals and patterns of prestige are
today largely created by the novelist. Shelley's somewhat pretentious phrase that the poets are the unacknowledged legislators of
mankind is given its share of truth when we recognize how the
great fiction characters have influenced men and women in choosing the parts they would play. Homer idealized Achilles and in
turn the actual Alexander played out the Achillean part in his
historically theatrical campaigns. Meanwhile at this moment
science fiction finds itself with two advantages. In the first place it
can indicate a dynamic morality. There is no reason why morals
should any longer be identified with reaction and conservatism. In

the second place, science fiction, because it is rightly identified with adventure, can make its appeal to the young who want to find meaning in the future rather than the past.

Of course this is a tough proposition. This program however is not an extravagance of "realism," a temptation to shock still further the frightened reactionaries. It is an obligation forced today on all popularizers of science. Here are the facts. How are you going to make ordinary conventional people face up to them? It is possible to break news so as to produce an "elastic reaction" and not a fracture. It is possible to add to the tensile strength of the cylinder so as to allow higher explosive power to be used. It is possible to build up the "tolerance" of the organism which permits the body not to reject or be toxicated by an injection but to react into a higher health by producing dynamic antibodies. No one else is going to give this essential service if science fiction flunks it. The ordinary science news service that boasts it keeps the public up-to-date certainly shows grave symptoms of serious failure. Dr. Abbott, once head of the Smithsonian Institution, and Dr. Sinnott, head of the Sheffield School of Science at Yale, have both stated in print their disappointment and concern at the obscurantist attitude taken by rank and file scientists and most science news editors toward the researches carried on in six great universities in extra-sensory perception. The attitude toward the mysterious upper-atmosphere craft (saucers, disks, giant tubes) that are now authentically sighted in some part of the world several times a week, has been as gravely disappointing. Until *Life* broke the official "silence of sceptical contempt," American people who used to be the most empirically and open-minded public in the world were afraid even to report finds which they themselves had personally witnessed—so much did they dread being laughed at, so pathetically had they become dependent on authority as to whether they might believe the evidence of their own senses.

With people reduced to such a medieval frame of mind, science fiction has certainly a stiff assignment. But it is all the more worth-

while. And in this vital diplomatic mission between the pure researcher, who too often denies any evidence outside his speciality
and who always researches in such detail that he cannot see the
social consequences, and the public that has to take the consequences, science fiction has an unexpected ally. Up to this point
only one part of this article's assignment has been dealt with—
morals. We have seen science creating so many new social developments that conventional morality will be hard put to accept such
changes and think out creative reactions. Indeed, do what the
most informed, courageous and tactful science fiction may, many
of the old-fashioned will not make a creative response. That is too
much to hope. But especially among the young to whom science
fiction fortunately most appeals, a decisive number of moderates
may be won over if science fiction keeps in mind one important
distinction: that though many moralists may be nothing more than
blind adherents of the past, this is not so of all. The real strength
of morality lies in those who, not afraid of new truth, do still demand that it should not take all worthy purpose out of life, all
meaning out of existence. They do not say that truth must be
made to yield to convenience or to goodness. What they urge is
that both the researcher and the applier should meet in constant
interpretive conference, wherein and whereby there may be
worked out jointly the creative reactions that human conduct
should and could make to and with the new information. Indeed
here lies a good theme for a science-fiction history forecast, showing a Supreme Court of the World which sits and rules for this
specific purpose. This bench would rule by deciding not whether
some social activity were "constitutional" but (a far more basic
finding) to what degree would a new discovery affect morals, and
how the new freedom and the accepted code, the new force of the
old frame of behavior, should be adjusted each to each. This shows
that there are two sides to man's problem: one we usually call
truth and the other goodness. And generally we have tried to hold
one rigid and make the other to yield. Today however we see this
is the grave mistake that leads to persecution and revolution. The

261

conflict between science and religion is because religion which should really be enlarged to be a fulfilment and interpreter of science has been reduced to an aspect and defender of morality. This sounds like fantasy. It is true though. For when we see that religion is the cause and morality the consequence then we can perceive religion's co-operative relationship with science. Religion is basically a cosmology, an all-over hypothesis (a binding all together as the word means) of all observations of our entire environment. And any workable ethic is a rule of behavior deduced from the general natural principles (the universal law) that has been perceived. On the other hand science is that empiric exploration and experiment, whereby, using an all-over hypothesis, a frame of reference, a *religio,* a belief that there is pattern and the universe can be understood, man increases his comprehensible knowledge. This, through the interaction of science (empiric research) and religion (the frame of meaning), leads to the discovery of principles of meaning and these principles of meaning are then applied to make efficient and free modes of action (morality).

So we perceive the real difference between morals and religion. Morals are the worthy arrangements whereby individuals, who are on one side physiological organisms and on the other social units, may manage to get along with one another. In brief, religion—as we have seen the word actually means—is the binding force that, when it is alive, makes the individual an integrated triple whole (1) with himself, (2) with his society, and (3) with nature. In this basic sense (that religion is the frame of meaning, the scheme of significance in which all findings are given purpose) there can be no dispute between science and religion. Science discovers and religion evaluates. Science produces facts; religion arranges them in a comprehensive frame and scale of meaning.

It is in this respect today that religion is coming alive, waking up again to its rightful place and vital importance. It is rousing itself after a long sleep during which it dreamed its duty was to defend the past and make the present conform with outgrown cosmogonies, inaccurate history and inapposite codes. The discovery of what Julian Huxley has called "the uniqueness of man"—that man is so richly various in the qualities of consciousness which he produces (the mathematician, the artist, the administrator, etc.), that he transcends any real comparison with animals in his mental power and indeed cannot rightly be called a species—has corrected the pessimism T. H. Huxley and many other moralists felt when they regarded the evolutionary picture. The discovery of the Brussels School, that open-ended systems (and living forms are such) are not subject to entropy, has made the vital process appear to be a far more formidable and initiatory power than nineteenth-century chemistry imagined. Von Frisch's astounding researches which now have convinced all zoologists that bees think, calculate, draw maps and by sign language talk to each other, have made us understand that instinct, instead of being automatism excluding intelligence, may rather be regarded as conscience advising understanding. President A. D. Adrian's work (see *Nature*, July 1951) in electroencephalogram study has (as Dr. Eccles has indicated) shown that whereas the brain is a three-dimensional detector, the mind shows evidence of being a four-dimensional field. Indeed today it appears that there is not a sector of the vast front of science wherein concepts are not appearing that (as Dr. Sinnott of Yale has pointed out) demote materialism as a basic hypothesis and make mechanism a notion convenient as a local generalization but inadequate as an all-over law. This, we must stress, will not mean the return of anthropomorphism. Many researchers still fear the public knowing how far materialism has vanished because they dread that might mean a return to superstition. It will mean an extension of meaning so vast that in this huge frame of reference man's adolescent anthropomorphism must go for good, must go with its companion piece of an out-lived science fiction—"mechanomorphism," the fantasy that the universe is a machine.

The return of meaning, the re-emergence of a contemporary religion is then what can give contemporary morality the courage to leave old tabus and construct an ethic deduced from a modern cosmology and producing rules of demonstrable psychiatric, hygienic and social value. This then is the second great task of science fiction today. No assignment could be of greater significance. It won't be an easier task than the first. What is called natural theology (i.e., the deduction that there is an all-over meaning from evidence obtained not from history but from science) is unpopular with the religious. The reason for that prejudice is however obvious: neither anthropomorphists nor mechanomorphists want to mention it. The anthropomorphists and mechanomorphists agree on one thing. And when they agree, it is so seldom and they are so strong that they are generally assumed to be right. They both assume in this case that any meaning that may be found in nature must be anthropomorphic—must support the old traditional picture as to meaning. Today it is clear there is a meaning and it is one so vast that to our geocentric religions it is even less welcome than mechanomorphism. It has no place for horizontal utopias which are seen to be no more than fanciful schemes for attempting to stabilize Homo sapiens in perpetual adaptation to that limited aspect of consciousness now apprehended as "the environment." So therefore neither has this new outlook much interest in our present notions of personality development or even of man's evolution. But it does point to an extension of conscious thought which indicates and will tend to explicate a vast directive, a concept that is more inspiring to the modern mind than any forecast of a concrete goal. Here, in fact, is the greatest revolution in man's thinking since he raised the first mastaba in protodynastic Egypt or the primal ziggurat after the Mesopotamian flood. Professional philosophy isn't going to help here nor is traditional religion. Science itself is too specialized. The job, thankless but immensely important, falls to the art which is as fresh and contemporary as the problem—the art of science fiction.

The Future of Science Fiction

by REGINALD BRETNOR

REGINALD BRETNOR'S *published fiction has appeared in a wide range of magazines:* Harper's, The Pacific Spectator, Esquire, Today's Woman, Galaxy, Magazine of Fantasy & Science Fiction, *etc. Most of his stories have been either science fiction or fantasy, and he has contributed to the anthologies* New Tales of Space and Time *and* Best Science Fiction Stories of 1951. *He has long been interested in the why of science fiction, in the influence which science fiction is exercising on our ways of thinking and in the cultural reasons behind its development and popularity. This book has resulted from that interest.*

During the war, and for some time thereafter, Mr. Bretnor worked for OWI and the Department of State, for the most part writing material concerned with, and directed to, Japan and the Far East. He is now free-lancing, and he and his wife live in Berkeley, California.

THE IMMEDIATE FUTURE of science fiction is beset with *ifs*, like the immediate future of mankind, from which, of course, we cannot separate it. This chapter, therefore, will be predicated upon two of the biggest and most frightening of these:

If the human race does not reduce itself to a new savagery with the weapons provided by the scientific method;

And *if* the free exercise of that method and a free discussion of its findings are not throttled in the western world as they have been in Russia.

In either instance, science fiction would have no immediate future, for it requires a certain cultural climate in which to flourish. It must have access to those factual and theoretical bases for its speculations which come from the free exercise of the scientific method, and it must have liberty to speculate beyond the limits of an official teleology. Today, despite security restrictions in certain fields, this climate still exists, and is still reasonably secure, in the United States, the British Empire, and a few free nations elsewhere. Let us assume—and pray—that it may continue to exist into tomorrow.

Science fiction itself is not prophecy. While it creates a multitude of futures for its readers, it does not claim that any one of these is the *real* future, predestined and inevitable. Out of the data of the past and present, the writer chooses such plausible hypotheses as he requires, extends them logically, and forms the rules by which events in his imaginary future must proceed. When his hypotheses are valid and adequate, when the logic by which they are extended is fairly accurate, there may be some degree of correspondence between the imagined future and the eventual actuality.

Consequently, instead of trying to prophesy *the* future of

266

science fiction, I shall attempt to apply the method of the science-fiction writer to the problem, in the hope, at least, that my basic hypotheses may be well chosen and logically developed—and that the resulting picture may assist the reader to form a perhaps better picture of his own.

In order to provide a basis for extrapolation, these fundamental questions must be answered:

What are the reasons for the emergence of science fiction as a genre, and for its rapidly increasing popularity?

And:

Is science fiction only another genre, comparable in signifi-cance and scope to the Gothic novel or the murder mystery?

Happily, the answer to the second derives from the answer to the first, and it is possible to consider the two together.

The emergence of modern science fiction *as a genre* is rooted in our failure to understand the scientific method and to define it adequately for the average individual and the average scientist. The method has existed, clearly formulated, for more than three hundred years. Its exercise has worked great changes in our world, our ways of life and death; and yet, for an overwhelming majority of men, these changes have been exterior, superficial. Our cultures have accepted the new tools which have been made available, only to misuse them for the same ancient ends. The method itself has been rejected, distorted, walled off in popular and academic and literary mythologies.

The exercise of the scientific method, the vast new worlds of knowledge and conjecture which it has opened to us, the number-less new problems which must in turn arise for it to solve—these constitute the great adventure of our age, the great adventure of which so few of us are consciously aware, in which so very few of us participate.

Why? The Renaissance exhibited the "universal man." His frames of reference comprehended the science of his time, the art, the statecraft, the philosophy. And this ideal of balance per-sisted through the eighteenth century; Goethe and Benjamin

Franklin are good examples. But, in the nineteenth century and in ours, it was destroyed. Each of the physical sciences became more complex theoretically; each piled up its own inverted pyramid of data, and evolved its own highly specialized technologies. It soon became apparent that no one man could master all of this. It gradually became apparent that the problem of fitting "modern science" into our Classical frames of general reference resembled that of squeezing Australia and the two Americas into a map of Europe. There were new logics, new mathematics, new concepts of structure and of process. They contradicted many of the primary postulates which the Greek synthesis had enunciated, and the Renaissance synthesis accepted, as true eternally—postulates as basic as that which states that two and two must always equal four.

Here, indeed, was a dilemma for educators. One of its horns demanded a denial of "modern science," an affirmation that the old map of things was wholly true. The other, equally sharp, insisted that the old map be discarded and a new one drawn. Our educators, and our philosophers of education, seized neither; instead, they reached for the dilemma's tail, where the horns could not reach them, and clung to it. They abandoned the Classical education, in which the old map was embodied, and which at least conveyed a cultural perspective in space and time. They introduced "practical" education, specialized education, retaining such narrow strips of the old map as might be necessary to show their students the way from A to B. They applied this principle in almost every field: the simplest of vocations, the pseudo-sciences, the semi-sciences, the arts. "New map" material was, of course, included in the specialized curricula of the exact sciences—but only to advance each specialty, and only when the student came to it along the narrow and outmoded strip prescribed for him. Certain other specialized curricula incorporated enough data derived from this material to satisfy the limited professional requirements of the technologist. Still others—and they were most important—either ignored it completely, or actually continued to assert that their strips of the old map were wholly and perpetually valid in their own spheres.

These statements, of course, imply no condemnation of educators. They do, however, constitute a fairly accurate generalized description of a process involving many millions of people over a period of many years—a process in which human emotions and social value-concepts were powerful operative factors. Their accuracy can be tested very easily by talking to almost any individual, by observing what goes on in almost any school, by reading the catalogue of almost any university. Invariably, the latest and most comprehensive knowledge comes *last*. The average college student gets almost none of it. Only in graduate schools—and only in the right departments—is he permitted to take a course in anything so recondite as, for example, "scientific method."

In short, education as we know it is *additive*. It tends to parallel the intellectual evolution of the race; and each new generation, instead of starting at the highest point attained by its predecessors, must retrace the entire path up which they climbed. Perhaps it is impossible, at present, to give pre-adolescent children a picture of the universe as seen by modern physicists. Perhaps we cannot show them that mathematics are languages which can describe that universe with accuracy, or acquaint them with logics which might enable them to avoid primitive pitfalls implicit in the tongues we speak. Perhaps we cannot yet present them with general frames of reference in terms of which their future specialties and all the world outside their specialties would alike make sense.

Perhaps not—but we should at least be able to convey some true conception of what the scientific method is, and what it does, and what it means to man.

In order to measure our neglect in this regard, it is necessary only to examine current *pseudodoxia epidemica* concerning "science." Our languages force us to speak (and think) of "science" as a thing, as though it had some independent being apart from man. "Science" says this and that; it proves or disproves this and that; it solves or fails to solve this, that, and the other. "Science" is praised or blamed, an oracle one minute, a whipping boy the next. Sometimes, by implication, we even credit "science" with a volition of its own, when we make such statements as: "If we don't find some way to control science, some day it'll control us," or, "Don't tell me that science doesn't know where it's going."

Not content with this projection of a pseudo-entity, we then endow it with certain attributes. We say that "it" is cold, and unemotional—which is true only of its verbal definition. We say this because we have been told that "science" is purely intellectual—and because we generally accept the old Aristotelian scheme, in which "the warm, spontaneous emotions" and "the cold, logical intellect" are assumed to function separately, like two frogs jumping in a basket.

These are the fundamental common errors, from which arise a multitude of others. Out of them all, four samples will suffice:

That "science" is opposed to "the emotions," and that somehow it is inimical to "human nature";

That "science" has failed to solve, and is incapable of solving, our great "human" problems;

That "science" *denies* all other ways of knowing: intuition and inspiration, for example;

That "science" is something only a "scientist" can understand.

Our failure to "bring education up to date" is responsible, in part, for the prevalence of these beliefs and attitudes; and they themselves, reflexively, help to perpetuate that failure. They widen the wide gulf between the popular and scientific pictures of the world. They are a barrier to the average man's participation in that greatest of humanity's adventures, the adventure of discovery in the world around us, in worlds beyond our world, and in the infinite unexplored territories within ourselves.

But *can* the average man participate in this adventure? He can if he desires to. The scientific method is no proprietary formula, and there still are countries where its comprehension and its exercise are not forbidden by the law.

"The chief characteristics of scientific method," according to Oliver L. Reiser, "are careful observation, classification of the facts observed, the formulation of laws of relationship between the facts observed, always testing these generalizations by reference back to the facts, and always excluding one's own prejudices in the processes." [1]

The scientific method, then, is a process composed of certain other processes. The important point is that it occurs *inside human beings, and*—unless, of course, there are other comparable or superior intelligences in the universe—*nowhere else*. In all probability, it has been occurring inside human beings since the beginning of the race; otherwise there would have been no progress. Therefore its formulation did not constitute a new invention, but was instead simply an awakening to the fact of its existence—the recognition of a perfectly normal human function built into every normal human being.

The scientific method is human, and purely human, and wholly human. To say that it is not, to say that it is somehow extra-human or anti-human, is to misrepresent reality. The fact that its products have so often been employed for the achievement of inhuman or subhuman purposes, does not prove otherwise. It proves only that we have not yet used the scientific method to change our understanding of ourselves, our motives, and our relationships. That the scientific method is intrinsically constructive, co-operative and sane has been demonstrated quite clearly. The vast body of knowledge and hypothesis which has resulted from its exercise by many men over the past few centuries may be offered in evidence. So may the reliable technologies already existing in many areas of its application. There is every reason to assume that its exercise will eventually produce comparable technologies in areas still scarcely touched—and that these

[1] *Humanistic Logic for the Mind in Action*, Crowell, N.Y. (1930).

technologies will be as constructive and as sane as the method which produced them. There is every reason to assume that, like that method, they will be fully human.

Some of us, today, are becoming increasingly aware of these potentialities inherent in the scientific method and in ourselves. At its best, this new awareness is partial; at its worst, it may be quite unconscious. Yet it is growing, despite educational restrictions which inhibit it, despite a literary convention which almost universally excludes it. It has grown most rapidly since the antibiotics and the sulfa-drugs showed that research in chemotherapy can accomplish more in a dozen years than all the medical fumbling of a millennium; since nuclear fission demonstrated to the world that theoretical physicists are among the most practical of men; since radar beams reached out and touched the moon. It has grown because all such events dramatize the contrast between the scientific method, which *works,* and pre-scientific, pseudo-scientific, and anti-scientific methods, which so frequently and tragically do not.

This new awareness, again, has given birth to a desire and a demand for participation in the great adventure. It has brought into being an imperative which cannot be completely satisfied even by exercising the scientific method within the limits of an active specialty. And, because the imagination will always make an effort to provide that which reality denies to us, modern science fiction has evolved as a response.

Today, science fiction appears as a genre because the main currents of our literature still adhere to sets of principles which are pre-scientific—principles whose validity can only be maintained by rigidly excluding the knowledge which would prove them false. It has developed as a genre because the scientific method has no more been allowed to change those principles than to revise the pattern of our general educations.

But is it just another genre? Can its significance be accurately compared to that of the *whodunit?* The answer is quite simple. A good murder mystery, while it has many merits as entertainment, must deal essentially with variations on a single theme, and that perhaps not quite the noblest of them all. Science fiction, however, can bring a new perspective to every theme already known, and can create innumerable fresh themes, unknown today but possible tomorrow.

It is not a genre. Its scope is universal. It holds the promise of an entire new literature.

This claim may seem immoderate at first glance. To those who accept conventional definitions of what "literature" should be, it will, indeed, appear quite absurd. However, in the contrast between modern science fiction and those contemporary forms which (because they exclude an awareness of the scientific method) can be lumped together as "non-science fiction," we can find much to justify it.

At this point, it will be necessary to do again that which has already been done several times in this book—define science fiction. The term, in my opinion, is legitimately descriptive of three major categories of works, listed here in a descending order of interest and importance:

Those which reveal the author's awareness of the importance of the scientific method as a human function and of the human potentialities inherent in its exercise, and do this not only in plot and circumstance, but also *through the thoughts and motivations of the characters*;

Those which reveal such an awareness, but only in circumstance and plot; and,

Those which reveal that the author is aware only of certain potential *products* of the scientific method. (The degree of awareness here corresponds roughly to that sometimes found in our non-science fiction—but with this difference: non-science fiction limits its awareness to those products of the scientific method already in existence. The difference is one of attitude, not of degree.)

Obviously, these categories are not discrete compartments, into one or another of which every work of science fiction must fit

exactly. Just as obviously, they bring into their periphery of definition much material which previously has not been labeled science fiction. Above all, in measuring the merit of a story or a
novel as science fiction, they alone do not decide its literary value.
It must be judged, too, by the criteria which we apply to fiction
generally—by the criteria of non-science fiction. What could be
fairer, therefore, than a reversal of the situation—an application
of the specialized criteria of science fiction to the main currents
of our literature?

In writing, as in the other arts, there have been a number of
responses to the problem posed by the new complexity of knowledge and the breakdown of the older synthesis. Characteristic of
almost all of these, especially in this century, is a peculiar process
which can quite accurately be called *the intellectual renunciation
of "the intellect."* Actually, this rebellion against "reason" is a revolt against the scientific method, reason's cold instrument in the
old scheme of things. It is a revolt prompted by the failure to
understand, and by a fear of the un-understandable. It has varied
in degree; it has been more or less conscious, more or less deliberate. It has included such seemingly diverse phenomena as the
complete Dadaist denial, the Existentialist dramatization of fashionable despair, and a highly verbalized insistence on restrictive
neo-Aristotelian frames of literary reference which themselves are
a retreat from the Aristotelian balance of the Renaissance. The
trend, in our most "serious" fiction, has been increasingly toward a focus of all emphasis on "the emotions," on "feeling"
rather than on "thought"—as though the two were mutually an-
tagonistic and mutually exclusive. In other words, although our
frogs still do their hopping separately, we now must concentrate
on one of them because the other has spawned a brood of scientific tadpoles too slippery, too frightening, and too numerous for
us to handle comfortably and with aplomb.

This sharply limited awareness, this formalized retention of
frames of reference now known to be inadequate, is reflected in
many recent small attacks on science fiction.

One critic[2] opens his preface to an anthology of "quality" short stories with this statement:

> The young writer of serious and honorable intentions must be struck (and either dismayed or allured) by two tendencies in current appraisals of contemporary fiction: the desire of the appraiser for novelty and his susceptibility to being impressed by phenomena—by *things*—rather than by people.

After elaborating this thesis in a longer paragraph, he goes on to say:

> A striking example, on a widely popular level, of the current interest in *things* rather than people is the mass success of science fiction, in which interest centers on the amazing event or the ingenious machine, and people are almost never more than a set of stereotyped responses to the marvelous.

The picture of science fiction which these passages convey is, of course, inaccurate and unfair. Science fiction is no homogeneous mass, uniform in its lack of quality, unvarying in its themes. It has been written and published on almost every literary level. Furthermore, science fiction has enjoyed no "mass success," if by that term we understand a sales volume comparable to those attained by Mickey Spillane, by that precocious amateur, the authoress of *Forever Amber*, or even by the learned Dr. Kinsey. The rapid increase of its popularity, so far at least, has been mainly among a readership of rather higher than average intelligence.

Errors of this sort are not too important. Of greater interest is the critic's apparent attitude to fiction generally, from which his view of science fiction may well derive. Having given us science fiction as one example of the current interest "in phenomena—

[2] Richard Scowcroft, in *Stanford Short Stories*, 1952.

in *things*—rather than people," he offers us some others "on various levels of literary excellence":

> . . . fiction that is more concerned with the trend, the tendency, the movement, than with the individual human beings who live the trends, tendencies, movements.

And we are told:

> This is not to suggest that man must be—or can be—viewed apart from the experience of his time, but it is to assert that the proper study of the writer is man himself—not political, social, moral upheavals. Not the machines that are to make monsters of us all.

There would seem to be a certain semantic confusion here. The application of rather elementary logic to everything which has so far been quoted reveals a singular implied equivalence of much that is intrinsically dissimilar: phenomena = things = amazing events = ingenious machines = trends, tendencies, movements = political, social, moral upheavals = the machines that are to make monsters of us all. We are informed that man can not be viewed apart from the experience of his time; then we are told that much of that experience is not the proper study of the writer.

There is one similarity between the various processes and objects listed as not the proper study of the writer—they fall within the province either of the scientific method or of elaborately specialized semi-scientific or pseudo-scientific methodologies. Some are themselves the product of "new maps" of structure and relationship. Others can now be understood in terms of such "new maps." For others still, "new maps" have not been drawn as yet, or have been drawn only partially, or may be drawn tomorrow. In any case, even the simplest "thing" no longer fits into the common understanding of all men; it is composed of mysteries.

"The intellect," unspecialized, employing "old map" ways of "reasoning," cannot penetrate them.

The over-all response of non-science fiction in this situation has been to avoid the area of new understandings, new semi-understandings, new possibilities of eventual understandings, and to retreat into the one remaining area where one can still pretend that parts of the old map "make sense." We are, indeed, assured that literature can only be *significant* if it restricts fictional experience to the "emotional" reactions and purely private meanings of characters who have to be themselves restricted. We are invited to believe that, in this area of restriction, we will find all value and all truth.

Consider the varieties of people who, often of a most beautifully contrived complexity, move in the mazes of our best non-science fiction. More and more often, we find them immature, if not in years then in some vital facet of development: children and simpletons, and psychopaths and period pieces, all certain to remain safely unaware of new problems and new comprehensions. And, on those rare occasions when they are none of these, when they seem neither mentally nor culturally inadequate, we almost always find awareness expressed only in blind frustration, flight, despair—in another mechanism for the restriction of fictional experience.

In a very limited, subjective, passive sense, non-science fiction does reflect the experience of certain sorts of people in our time; and there is nothing wrong with this intrinsically. What *is* wrong is the contention, outright or implied, that no literature can or should do more.

What is fiction? And what part do "people" play in it? The reading of fiction is a selfish process. It is a form of self-gratification. It is a way of experiencing, vicariously, that which the world denies one, wholly or in some measure. People are central to this process, *but they are not the entire focus of our interest; they are at once its focus and its instrument.* They—these people who live in fiction—do not exist. They must be evoked anew at every reading, uniquely recreated in the reader's mind out of *his* experiences and *his* emotional-intellectual skeins of meaning. So must those factors of action and environment which help to form them, and which they help to form—and which, with them, in a reciprocal relationship, make any fiction a complete and integrated and believable experience.

There is nothing wrong with emphasizing the importance of the people in fiction—for it is only through people, and because we ourselves are people, that we can share the experiences of fiction. What *is* wrong is emphasizing that importance at the expense of the entirety. Take Captain Ahab, for example. Lift him away from all those actual and symbolical phenomena of which he is at once the cause and the effect. Tuck him into a snug Old Sailors' Home. And where is *Moby Dick?*

Here the essential differences between the set attitudes of non-science fiction and the developing attitudes of science fiction become obvious enough for definition and discussion; and they deserve a close examination, for it is in the developing attitudes of science fiction that we can trace the outlines of what it may eventually become.

First, *science fiction is not self-restricted; nor is it restrictive of its readers.*

To science fiction, the "new map" areas—instead of being tabu —are territories to be explored, conquered, understood.

To science fiction, those "old map" areas to which non-science fiction restricts itself—instead of being accurately and thoroughly surveyed—still remain largely *terra incognita,* demanding re-evaluation in newer terms.

Secondly, *science fiction is not a literature of false dichotomies conventionalized.*

It does not split the world into the known and the eternally unknowable; into that which is a fit focus for literary interest and that which cannot be.

Nor does it so split man.

To science fiction, man is the proper study of the writer—man, *and* everything man does and thinks and dreams, and everything man builds, and everything of which he may become aware—his theories and his things, his quest into the universe, his search into himself, his music and his mathematices and his machines. All these have human value and validity, for they are all *of* man.

Indeed, to science fiction, a machine is an expression and a record of man's humanity as significant as a cathedral, *The Canterbury Tales*, the score of a Beethoven quartet, or—if we may be permitted such a heresy—the most artistic infant-strangling or corncob rape in our contemporary "serious" literature.

Science fiction, of course, *excludes* none of these. It may deal with human monsters or with man's machines. But it does not make the dreadful error of stating that even the most benighted monsterhood *must,* simply because it is "emotional," be more significant, more human, and more interesting than an intellectual-emotional creativeness. It does not state that we *must* bend our finest literary efforts toward the study, for its own sweet sake, of the torn, the twisted, or (at its very best) the thwarted mind.

Thirdly, then, *science fiction—because it is science fiction—is integrative.*

By re-emphasizing the rejected "intellect," by treating the scientific method as a completely natural function of the mind, by recognizing that "human problems" are any problems of which we are aware, science fiction can restore the wholeness of fictional experience—a wholeness which makes sense in terms of what we know today, and what we have good reason to suppose we may find out tomorrow.

In this, curiously, the developing attitude of science fiction is more closely in accord with actuality than is the attitude of many scientists, for it does not pretend that the exercise of the scientific method is "unemotional." It acknowledges, of course, that the scientific method, by definition, must seek either to preclude "emotionally-based" judgments and decisions, or—when such

279

judgments and decisions are announced—to test them. It does not, however, accept the popular idea that the method cancels or denies "emotionality"; indeed, it cannot—for the very existence of science fiction demonstrates the contrary. No experience can ever be purely "emotional" or purely "intellectual"; each, because of the way man is made, must be both. The exercise of the scientific method, the human problems and the human dreams arising from its attempts and failures and successes—each of these is an "emotional," and often a profoundly "emotional," experience. If it were not, no man would bother to become a scientist; no one would read a word of science fiction; and Keats, on looking into Chapman's Homer, would not have written:

Then felt I like some watcher of the skies
When a new planet swims into his ken . . .

(Or was this also only a "stereotyped reaction to the marvelous"?)

The qualifying term *developing* has been applied to the three fundamental science-fiction attitudes defined herein. It has been used because, quite clearly, many—perhaps a large majority—of science-fiction writers, and editors, and readers would not agree with the definitions. It has been used because, although there is much "science fiction" to which the definitions do not apply, the general current of development appears to be toward these attitudes.

There is a fourth difference between the attitudes of science fiction and non-science fiction. Because it underlies the other three, because it has already crystallized, it is perhaps the most important of them all.

Non-science fiction, giving a tiny twist to Hamlet's meaning, has resolved part of his quandary for us and for itself. It tells us, in effect, not only that it *is* better in the mind to suffer, but that to convey this suffering and to wallow in it are the sole purposes to which each writer's art and every reader's interest must be devoted.

Science fiction, on the other hand, has taken arms against our sea of troubles, for joy of battle, and to understand them— and because, if they are really troubles, we are responsible.

These differences of attitude are evidence to support the statement that science fiction holds within itself the seed of an entire new literature. They illustrate the magnitude of its departure from literary tradition. They show that this departure is a direct result of the transition, now in progress, from pre-scientific to scientific thinking.

Here, of course, two obvious objections may be raised: the first, that science fiction is too crude and too fantastic to be of any great significance; the second, that science fiction is not "scientific."

The charge of crudeness is not hard to answer. Most science fiction which appears so-labeled has been, and still is, printed on pulp paper—a circumstance which almost automatically removes it from the province of "serious" literary criticism. Those who are most unkind have seldom read much of it. Indeed, their acquaintance with it is apparently so slight that they cannot even identify it when it appears in the *Atlantic* or in some university review; on such occasions, they usually judge it as non-science fiction.

Let us, however, be charitable. Let us assume that every one of them, making a burnt offering of his sensibilities, has read each issue of every magazine in the entire field over a period of agonizing years. Even so, what are his criteria? Is he judging the literary merit of science fiction against the fiction in the *Yale Review*? Or against Steinbeck, or Hemingway, or Mr. Henry Green?

We are not informed. Science fiction, we are told, *is* this or that. That's all.

Actually, there is one way, and one way only, of measuring the literary merit of modern science fiction, and that is by comparing it, statistically, to the *entire* non-science fiction field—the love pulps, the confession magazines, whodunits, westerns, women's magazines, the general "slicks," the "quality" and "class" magazines, and all our novels of whatever sort. This criterion gives us a very different picture. It shows us that, compared to this vast flood, not a great deal of science fiction has been, or is being, published. It shows us, by comparison again, that science fiction already has produced much more than its *pro rata* share of work which, by any literary standard, is competent or more than competent—an achievement which appears the more remarkable when one considers that science fiction is dynamic and exploratory, while non-science fiction is essentially static and repetitive. Furthermore, in making this comparison, we even take the sting from that apparently most plausible of criticisms, the one which deals with character development.

We can conclude that, though there is quite a bit of crudely written science fiction, it no more justifies a charge of general crudeness than would the comparable material—so much more plentiful, and lacking even the saving grace of new perspectives —of non-science fiction.

The charge that science fiction is too fantastic to be significant derives, of course, from a confusion of ideas concerning the familiar and *believable,* and the unfamiliar and *therefore unbelievable.* Thus, Caliban and Ariel, and Banquo's ghost, and Mephistopheles, and Santa Claus are not fantastic—but space ships are. Similarly, it is not fantastic to exclude new understandings of reality from literature, but it is fantastic to attempt their exploration. Like "fantasy," "fantastic" is a handy term to use for quick dismissal. It is especially useful in connection with the charge that science fiction is "unscientific."

This charge—because "scientific" is a prestige term—is a most important one. If science fiction is "unscientific," if it is unrelated to the exercise of the scientific method, what possible significance can it have? Therefore the charge is often brought, directly or by implication.

Take, for example, a recent editorial in the usually more perspicacious *Saturday Review* (July 12, 1952). Its writer, discussing space travel and science fiction, says:

> Even before the German inventors created the first navigable rocket at Peenemund the writers of this somewhat crude form of entertainment had developed the rocket ships which cruised to the moon and the solar planets and then burst into outermost space and explored the galaxies of the Milky Way. Driven by atomic power, these apparently mad devices were as well known to the devotees of science fiction as the liners that cross our oceans. Nevertheless, it [space travel] remained unadulterated fantasy until scientists contemplated the experiments with rockets that have proceeded since the last war.

Of course, "outermost space" (at least from any geocentric point of view) is quite a bit beyond the Milky Way; and, as the Milky Way is itself a (one) galaxy, the exploration of *its* galaxies would be as neat a trick as the exploration of the continents of Europe. Such minor matters, though, need not concern us; we can put them down, together with that "first navigable rocket at Peenemund," to editorial license. We cannot do the same for the rest.

To say that space travel "remained unadulterated fantasy" until "scientists" could contemplate "the experiments with rockets that have proceeded since the last war" is to ignore the intimate connection between rocket research and modern science fiction, between rocket scientists and those science-fiction writers who have drawn upon—and sometimes even helped to stimulate—their work.[3] It is like saying that the potential development of atomic energy remained unadulterated fantasy until scientists began to contemplate atomic bombs going off. If we restate the thesis it

[3] The reader is referred to the chapter in this volume by Arthur C. Clarke, to others of his works, and to the files of *Astounding Science Fiction* over a period of many years.

implies, we can get something pretty much like this: people who think scientifically enough to extrapolate from atmosphere rockets to space ships without being hired expressly for the purpose are crackpots; people who do the same thing on a salary and at a later date, when rockets have already risen above the atmosphere, are not.

No, it does *not* make much sense. But it is an almost classic specimen of a misunderstanding of science fiction, the scientific method, and their relationship.

Science fiction is, and at the same time is not, scientific—depending on one's definition of the term. If it can be accurately applied only to the complete experimental sequence, then science fiction is unscientific—for science fiction, obviously enough, cannot go beyond observation, the abstraction of "laws" or "principles" from observation, and the extrapolative application of these to theoretical situations. If, however, the term is also taken to denote a fundamental outlook, a technique of approach to every problem of which we are aware—if it is understood to include a "speculative" phase, in which experiments are performed in the imagination—then science fiction can be considered "scientific," for it will be in full accord with the intention of the scientific method.

What, then, of the thematic material of so much modern science fiction; parapsychology in all its aspects, questions of metaphysics and religion, time travel, alternatives of choice available in parallel continua—the vast domain of the unproven and presently unprovable? Can any literary form dealing with such as these be scientific?

Here again, the answer must depend upon one's understanding of the scientific method and of the human intention implicit in its nature. In this regard, regrettably, we still are suffering a semantic hangover from our first big "scientific" binge—that high old time when "science" answered any and all questions absolutely, and "proved" or "disproved" any statements anyone cared to make, regardless of whether or not these made much sense in terms of the contemporary applicability of the experimental sequence.

This was due, primarily, to a misunderstanding and a misuse of the fragmentary "new maps" available. All maps, however "perfect," are limited. A map can answer questions *only about the territory it represents.* A map can answer only *certain* questions about this territory; it cannot answer any questions not stated in *its* own terms. And—except in the case of questions which accept its limitations—its negative answers are invariably not final.

Thus, while a general map of the United States can inform us regarding the location of Cleveland, the Columbia River, and the Catskill Mountains, it can tell us nothing whatsoever about Buenos Aires, or the Brahmaputra, or Mont Blanc—or Betelgeuse. We can learn nothing from it about the health of our Aunt Cynthia, who resides in Cleveland. And, if we find no other lands when we consult it, we are by no means justified in saying that the balance of the world does not exist.

This, of course, is a rough analogy. It is, however, applicable to the evaluation of those pronunciamentos which begin, "Science proves that . . ." It is especially applicable when they are negative. Examining them, we almost always find that they are stated in "off-map" terms. Examining the people who issue them, we find some scientists—for there are scientists who can't resist playing Junior Superman before the peasantry—but, much more often, we find columnists, dictators, university presidents with bad cases of administrativitis, and third-rate philosophers hitching free rides aboard the scientific gravy train.

A minor sample of this sort of thing appeared, not long ago, in *Look*. In its issue of June 17, 1952, *Look* printed an article by Dr. Donald H. Menzel, professor of astrophysics and associate director of solar research at Harvard University. Dr. Menzel had succeeded, by reflecting artificial light through liquids in jars and from liquids in kitchen sinks, in producing phenomena which (he said) resembled "flying saucers"; and he suggested that analogous processes in air were responsible for discs by day and moving lights by night.

This order of experiment, obviously, can provide just about any answer one happens to desire. It may have some relation to the phenomena it is designed to elucidate—or it may not. Thus, a large turtle permitted to perambulate the bottom of a fishbowl might very well produce phenomena startlingly similar to tides—thereby giving us material for some fascinating speculations about the sea.

At any rate, Dr. Menzel was properly careful to make no absolute claim. "These experiments," he wrote, "are suggestive rather than definitive. More work is necessary to prove the phenomena."

Not so the editors of Look. The article came out entitled, "The Truth About the Flying Saucers"; and this was followed by: *One of America's leading astronomers goes into his laboratory at Harvard and disposes of the flying saucer myth. He adds simple instructions for making flying saucers in your own kitchen.*

In other words, "Science has *proved* that flying saucers do not exist."

This statement is in the same general category as—to use the most familiar of absurd examples—those which flatly deny the existence of a God or gods, the possibility of survival after death, the actuality of ESP phenomena, the prevalence of witches, or life on other worlds, or poltergeists, or the meteorological effectiveness of a Hopi snake dance.

These are the areas for which we have no scientific maps. For most of them, we have as yet no mapping instruments. Nevertheless, much evidence has been accumulated—evidence of varying reliability, true—which indicates either that they exist or that some corresponding areas do. Therefore they are a proper study for the scientist and for the science-fiction writer, both of whom have as their function, not outright affirmation, not flat denial, but the exploring of every possibility—and of a great many apparent impossibilities as well.

According to this picture, we can divide science fiction into two types (which, incidentally, quite often are combined): that which extrapolates from verified "new maps," now best exemplified in the works of Heinlein and Clarke; and that which extrapolates from (or interpolates across) the areas for which no "new maps" have been drawn. This does *not* mean that the second type is only "fantasy" under another name, for fantasy accepts all its off-map phenomena uncritically, but science fiction must at least extrapolate a partial "new map" of its own to account for them.

Both types are equally legitimate—for neither the scientific method nor science fiction, which derives from it, can be self-restricting and self-consistent simultaneously. Neither of them can exclude any conceivable phenomenon or concept as unworthy of attention or as intrinsically outside its scope.

Furthermore, neither the scientific method nor science fiction can or does deny importance and validity to "the emotions." Neither of them can or does deny importance and validity to other ways of "knowing"—to "intuition" and to "inspiration," for example. For all of these play their own vital roles in the exercise of the scientific method, just as they do in the exercise of the writer's art. The scientific method simply gives us a way of checking the validity of "emotional," "intuitive," or "inspired" judgments *as bases for decision*. And science fiction, rather than rejecting these aspects of our being, presents us with a thousand new perspectives for their study and for their presentation.

Even if every work of science fiction were on the lowest literary level, even if the science in science fiction were invariably inaccurate and absurd, the form would still retain much of its significance—for that significance, like the significance of any living literature, lies more in its developing attitudes, in its intention, than in the perfection of its detail. No criticism employing less fundamental criteria can alter this; no fear of science nor dread of literary change can invalidate it.

To say that science fiction holds within itself the seed of an entire new literature does not mean that science fiction, as we know
it, *is* that literature. Nor does it mean that we can now foretell the
exact forms that literature will take when it evolves from science
fiction *and* non-science fiction. We can no more do that than we
can prophesy, in detail, the world which will emerge—in twenty,
fifty, or five hundred years—as a result of man's cumulative exercise of the scientific method, and of its impact on his pre-scientific heritage.

We can attempt, however, to project the lines of our analysis
—and this projection may give us some idea of what the future
holds in store for science fiction and for fiction generally.

Thus, we can say with some degree of certainty that, for the
time being, the gap between our older frames of general reference
and our new specialized understandings will widen. The impossibility of stretching the "old maps" to fit the new terrain, or of
preserving them by trying to exclude it, will become constantly
more obvious. The unperceptive reader will react to this as he is
now reacting, but even more intensely; he will demand and get,
on levels appropriate to his own complexity, stronger and
stronger "emotional shock" values in his non-science fiction—a
dangerous, dead-end process. The more perceptive reader, though,
will react differently. Non-science fiction will become even less
"valid" to him than it is today. With increasing clarity and force,
its lack of purpose will become apparent to him. He will sense
that, measured in newer terms of comprehension, the fictional
experience which it offers is incomplete, falsely restricted in vision and in scope—in short, *untrue*. More and more frequently, he
will turn to science fiction.

Simultaneously, the pressure on the "serious" writer of non-
science fiction will increase. With mounting frequency, he will
be forced to make a *definite* choice between an outright rejection
of reality (a course perhaps best symbolized by the present locus
of Mr. Ezra Pound), and some acceptance of it in "new map"
terms. Avenues of evasion now open to him—the false profun-

dity of human pettiness, the pseudo-realism of human degradation—will close as more and more "serious" readers find that they have no compelling reason to identify themselves with characters who are no more than symbols of restriction, of the refusal to attempt new understandings of the world and man. The "serious" writer of non-science fiction who is too honest with himself to mistake his own restrictions for the limits of the universe, or the restrictions verbalized by others for its "eternal truths," will move in the direction of those attitudes which science fiction is now developing.

Here it becomes necessary to take what seems to be—and yet is not—a detour. Our commonly accepted view today is that non-science fiction deals with "the present" and the past, while science fiction takes the future for its peculiar province. This view is superficial. It ignores the fact that fiction is invariably derivative, and that there is one source, and one only, for its materials—the world which has occurred, the world which has already been traversed by that enduring instant of awareness in which each one of us appears to have his being.

From this source, all the potential worlds of fiction are contrived. They may pretend to show the actual past; they may pretend to show that area, compounded of immediate past and vague awareness of immediate future, which we refer to as the actual "present"; they may pretend to show the future, immediate or remote. Whatever they pretend, none of these worlds can *be* the actuality. Each one of them, when it achieves existence in a reader's mind, will have its own dimensions, which *are not* those of actuality. Its span of time will be unique to it, regardless of any dates the author gives. Within that span, the past will be "imaginary"; so will the moving "present," realized in the act of reading; so will the future.

All fiction derives from the experience of reality. All fiction creates imaginary times, imaginary worlds, to be experienced only through acts of "the imagination." And the subjective reality of fiction depends, not on the spacio-temporal co-ordinates assigned to it, but on the author's direct or indirect experience of reality, on his frames of reference for the interpretation of reality, on his ability to abstract and synthesize fictional experiences, and on his selection of symbolic media capable of evoking these experiences completely for his readers.

Therefore, the "serious" writer of non-science fiction, once he begins to expand his general and literary frames of reference, will find himself confronted by no dichotomy between "real life now" and "fantasies about the unreal future." In discarding the illusion that "realism" is dependent on restriction, he will approach a scientific realism which seeks to explore rather than to delimit arbitrarily, to comprehend rather than to react dramatically to the incomprehensible, to develop rather than to die.

He will find that the expansion of his frames of reference will neither force him to write about the future nor forbid him to write about "the present" and the past. If he determines to write science fiction as we know it now, he will learn that a hypothetical future is merely an interesting and plausible device particularly well suited to the presentation of those human problems and experiences promised by the nature of the scientific method and by its continued exercise. He will see that it is possible to write science fiction set in "the present" or the past—possible, and sometimes necessary, and usually just a bit more difficult.

If, on the other hand, science fiction as we know it now does not appeal to him, if its means and methods seem too remote, then he will certainly apply his new perspectives to non-science fiction. Once he begins to do so, once he begins discarding older literary "maps" and using "new map" data as his guide, his work will cease to be non-science fiction. It will perforce become more "scientific"—a more complete and accurate picture of the realities of our existence as we now know them.

The "serious," honest writer of non-science fiction need fear no loss through a renunciation of restrictions. All the traditional themes and problems of fiction will remain—but they will now be new, demanding re-examination and restatement. All the artistic "values" and "ideals" of fiction, instead of being discarded or destroyed, will, when redefined, acquire fresh significance. The treasuries of the language and the literature will be as open to him as they ever were.

And he will gain, besides, the opportunity to join in the creation of a living literature; to pioneer new themes, as well as old themes suddenly turned new; to fashion classics in new ways for a new age; to achieve, in terms appropriate to his own time and place, the promise of his talent and his courage.

The problem of transition will be no easy one. The static or regressive attitudes characteristic of non-science fiction are part and parcel of the cultural lag which has resulted from our failure to provide adequate new frames of general reference.[4] They do, regrettably, to some extent reflect the attitudes of most non-science fiction readers. Therefore, those individual writers who start to break with them will, of necessity, move slowly against many handicaps and much opposition.

Nevertheless, the trend has started. There is much evidence to show that it is already well under way: the influence on fiction of such semi-sciences as Freudian and Jungian psychology; the increasing use in fiction of viewpoints and of data borrowed from sciences like cultural anthropology; a higher incidence of works which, though they appear as non-science fiction, come at least partially into the science-fiction sphere as defined herein; and, finally, the much more frequent use of science-fiction themes by writers who previously have written, and in periodicals which previously have published, no science fiction.

We can, of course, anticipate no really quick reforms. Most "serious" fiction dealing with "the present" and the past will continue to exclude any awareness of the scientific method. It will continue to enjoy prestige, and the absolute validity of its restrictions will be repeatedly and forcefully affirmed.

[4] In the opinion of this writer, the basis for these new frames of reference—for a new general synthesis—has already been laid by Count Alfred Korzybski in *Science & Sanity*.

Meanwhile, more and more "serious" readers will take up science fiction. More and more writers will concentrate on it. Though it will continue to deal mainly with the future, it will expand its scope, develop new techniques and new approaches to suit the varied tastes and backgrounds of its audiences, and crystallize those attitudes which it is now developing. Because, by definition, it is not self-restrictive, its progress will be much more rapid than the converging progress of the transitional forms which may develop from non-science fiction.

Eventually, we will again have an integrated literature. It will owe much, artistically, to non-science fiction. But its dominant attitudes and purposes, regardless of whether it happens to be dealing with the past, "the present," or the future—will have evolved from those of modern science fiction. That literature, however, lies far ahead of us. Before it can come into existence, our present cultural lag will have, very largely, to be eliminated.

For the immediate future, it seems probable that we will see a sharp increase of academic and critical interest in science fiction. This will be manifested in several ways. A greater number of serious, intelligent, and open-minded examinations of science fiction will appear in our less hidebound literary journals; and the editors of these, together with the commercial editors who tend to follow them, will print more science fiction than before. Correspondingly, there will be more blind attacks on science fiction by the unthinking and the uninformed, by those to whom non-science fiction is a symbol of status or security, and—of course—by persons of the extreme Left who, correctly, consider science fiction another threat to their totalitarianism.

A first result of this increasing interest and this controversy will be more bad-to-mediocre science fiction nicely written by non-science fiction writers—plus just a little with freshness and originality. (We have had many specimens of both already.) The increasing employment of science-fiction themes will probably be most marked in the field of the "serious" short story. Nowhere is the paradox of "serious" non-science fiction—the simultaneous appeal to "intellectual" readers and avoidance of anything appealing to the modern "intellect"—exhibited so clearly as it is here. Nowhere is the need for invigoration and release, for the restoration of wholeness to fictional experience, more apparent. Nowhere, outside the science-fiction field itself, are there such opportunities for experimentation and for the evolution of transitional forms.

The "serious" novel is another matter. It has much wider popular prestige. Unhandicapped by postal regulations, it can continue to satisfy its readership with the "emotional" shocks and irritants which, to such a sad extent, have become a substitute for wholeness of experience. We can expect some slight increase in the number of those off-trail works which either are, or come quite close to being, science fiction. But, for a long time to come, we need expect no change at all in the attitudes of the great majority of "serious" novels.

On other levels, the present wave of interest in science fiction very decidedly will *not* subside. The percentage of science fiction published in the more general magazines may fluctuate, but the number of these magazines which print science fiction will continue to increase. Similarly, while the annual tally of science-fiction novels and anthologies may vary, more and more general publishers will accept science fiction as standard output, and the over-all curve will be an upward one.

In the science-fiction field itself, we can anticipate both growth and change. An expanding market will force magazine publishers to raise their rates to writers, and an increased demand should enable them to raise their newsstand and subscription prices—something they have been much too timid about doing. Some of the cheap-john competition, in book as well as magazine production, may perish by the wayside, because of its inability to hold its own against publishers who do their best both for the reader and the writer. At a guess—and it may turn out to be as good a guess as any—the total number of science-fiction magazines will not rise notably during the next twelve months, but their circulation will; within the year, there will be at least one new magazine comparable to *Astounding, Galaxy,* or *Fantasy & Science Fiction* in quality; within two years, somebody will discover science fiction as a medium for technical, industrial, and "gadget" advertising— and, as a result, we will have at least one full science-fiction "slick."

This is guesswork—for, with regard to such specific happenings, we can only guess. However, we can do better with the future of science fiction in the more general sense.

Barring the two great *ifs* cited at the beginning of this chapter, that future is assured—immediately, by popular interest and popular demand; at longer range, by the developing attitudes of science fiction. For science fiction, unlike our other literary forms, accepts the scientific method, the exercise of which produces new understandings of reality. It uses these new understandings. From them, it derives material for speculation far beyond their frontiers. From them, it derives new pictures of old human problems, and pictures of new problems which the human race has not encountered, and an infinity of new approaches to all of these. Its potentialities appear as unlimited as those of the scientific method. And, because today's new understandings will seem primitive or incomplete tomorrow, its approach will be as fresh tomorrow as it is today.

What can we accomplish with it? That is a challenge to writers, readers, publishers—of science fiction *and* non-science fiction. The great adventure of our age has scarcely started; the greatness of its literature still lies ahead. We, today, can at least recognize it, and write of it and what it means to man, remembering that what we write is rooted in the past, and will extend into the future—and that we, as men, have our responsibilities to both.